'ROUND ABOUT MIDNIGHT

'ROUND ABOUT MIDNIGHT

A Portrait of

MILES DAVIS

Updated Edition

by Eric Nisenson

Da Capo Press / New York

Library of Congress Cataloging in Publication Data

Nisenson, Eric.
  'Round about midnight: a portrait of Miles Davis / by Eric Nisen-
son.—Updated ed.
     p.   cm.
  Includes index.
  Discography:
  ISBN 0-306-80684-3 (alk. paper)
  1. Davis, Miles. 2. Jazz musicians—United States—Biography. I. Title.
ML419.D39N6   1996
788.9′ 2165′ 092—dc20   95-52542
[B]   CIP
                                                                      MN

Photographs used throughout text with permission of the
following sources: The Frank Driggs Collection,
The Institute of Jazz Studies, The Elena Steinberg Collection,
David Chertok, and Michael Rankin.

First Da Capo Press edition 1996

This Da Capo Press paperback edition of 'Round About Midnight
is an unabridged republication of the edition published in New York
in 1982, updated with a new preface, two new chapters, and a new
discography. It is republished by arrangement with the author.

Published by Da Capo Press, Inc.
A Subsidiary of Plenum Publishing Corporation
233 Spring Street, New York, N.Y. 10013

Manufactured in the United States of America

For my parents

Contents

Hangin' Out with Daffy Davis
A Preface to the Da Capo Edition (1996)

I have idolized Miles Davis since I was about fifteen years old. I idolized him in the same way other kids worshipped Mickey Mantle or Elvis, or the Beatles a little later. I tried to get as many of his albums as I could afford back then, read everything I could get my hands on, and continually told Miles stories to my friends, most of whom couldn't have cared less. I do not think that even my imagination at its most febrile could then have conjured what would come years later: that when my phone would ring, especially late at night, I would groan, "Oh no, it's that damned Miles again. Why can't he leave me alone?" And I would pick up my phone to hear that famous whispered growl demand, "Bring your white ass down here, Eric. Now."

Back when I was a teenager, even the idea of meeting Miles Davis seemed preposterous. His reclusiveness was part of his legend, as was his supposed hostility to white people. Yet I always had the weird feeling that if we met we could be friends. Maybe it was because I felt as alienated as he did. And I understood why he did the things he was always being criticized for—not announcing tunes or introducing the members of his band, turning his back to the audience when he played, refusing to compromise no matter what. I found it wonderful that Miles refused to cooperate with *Time* magazine when they were planning to do a cover story on him. Who else would have the guts to turn his back (excuse the pun) to a cover on *Time*? Only Miles, who kicked their photographers out of the Village Vanguard when he was performing there (instead *Time* put Thelonious Monk on its cover). This was my kind of guy.

In the late seventies I moved into an apartment on New York's Upper West Side after having lived in San Francisco for several years. Although I had a day job working as a college textbook editor, I spent a lot of my time at the nearby home of my friend the great bassist Walter Booker. Bookie had converted part of his huge apartment into a recording studio, and when he wasn't touring with Sarah Vaughan or Nat Adderley, he recorded sessions with some of the finest musicians in jazz. Bookie looked at me as a kind of "historian" for his studio, someone who would record the unique musical events and the interplay of the musicians, many of them jazz legends, who constantly passed through. Needless to say, I was often enthralled and amazed by the music and musicians who went in and out of Bookie's home and studio. His place had become kind of a jazz salon where virtually every great jazz musician came by at one time or another. And one night Miles Davis dropped by.

I was actually scared of meeting him—afraid that he would make a nasty insult or simply be rude to me. But he was wonderful—talkative, funny, warm, and friendly. He walked up to me to shake my hand and acted as if he knew me. I had this strange sense—as if we had known each other in some previous life. He was much shorter here than he had seemed when I had seen him perform, and his intensely intelligent, probing, wary eyes pulled you in as if they were bright embers at the center of his pitch black face. The controlled muscularity of his movements were like those of the large wild cats, cheetahs and tigers, that he enjoyed watching fight on film. But there was no doubt—none—that he attracted attention whether or not you knew who he was: he was a walking definition of "charisma."

I knew enough not to say something like, "Gee, Miles, I really like that *Sketches of Spain* album." I knew Miles hated that sort of crap. I just shook his hand and said I was glad to meet him, wondering if he could tell how awed I was just to be in his presence.

But Miles and I hit it off immediately, which in some ways astonished me but in other ways seemed obvious and natural. We were both shy, basically loners. (Miles immediately picked this up—he had developed the perception of a fighter in that he was able to suss out somebody's character very quickly. Once I introduced him to a guy who wanted to be my agent. Miles shook his hand, the guy said a few words, and Miles turned to me and said, "He's a liar." He turned out to be—unfortunately—quite right.)

Miles knew how to use his voice—that famous whispered growl—to his advantage, as a way of pulling in those around him. He obviously knew that he was hard to understand unless one listened carefully, so he made everyone focus on what he was saying.

Miles invited me to see his home and a couple of days later I took him up on his offer. I called before I left and Miles repeated his invitation and asked if I could pick up a six-pack of Heineken when I came over. That seemed innocent enough, but I didn't know at the time that this was the beginning of a kind of indentured servitude. When I came to Miles's 77th Street house (it had been converted from a church) he was in the outer entranceway, a disgusted look on his face. "The Con Edison guy came here and asked me if he could talk to the owner of the house. He thought I was the janitor! I told him, 'You're looking at the owner, you white motherfucker.'" It was obvious that Miles had never become inured to such casual racism, that running into it was still shocking and profoundly upsetting. Later on, whenever Miles came to visit me, I had to go back to the street with him in order to hail a cab. Even Miles Davis could not get a New York City cabdriver to stop and pick up a black man, especially at night. I, of course, had no problem.

This took place during the late seventies, the period of Miles's so-called "retirement." In the early seventies Miles had been at a creative peak, breaking away from the post-bop which he had played for most of his career and creating perhaps his most revolutionary music. He valiantly toured and recorded, despite several overlapping physical ailments, often performing on crutches. But in 1975, Miles gave in to the toll on his body and entered into a period of supposed retirement. He was ostensibly healing mind and body, but he was really on a self-destructive roller coaster, staying up for days at a time on cocaine and then crashing with barbituates. "If I can't stay up for three days at a time, hell, I might as well forget about it," he used to say.

Miles's 77th Street house was a five-story building; Miles lived in the first three stories, and the top story was rented to a homosexual couple. The floor right above Miles's top floor was empty mainly because Miles was so sensitive to sound that just hearing footsteps or loud conversation bothered him. Later on in our friendship Miles offered me the apartment at a reasonable rate, but I was warned by someone who knew a previous tenant that living right above Miles was a very bad idea; I would have had to make all my guests take off their shoes before they entered, and if I watched TV or listened to my stereo I would have *had* to listen through earphones. Otherwise Miles would raise hell about the "disturbance."

The interior of the house itself seemed to be a reflection of Miles's state at that time. It was like a *Playboy* pad gone to seed. For instance, there was a large projection television—but a couple of the bulbs were burnt out and so it was like watching a 3-D movie without the glasses (interestingly, Miles usually had the channel set on a particular listings station that used jazz as background music; so jazz, not pop, was the music most constantly heard there). And in the bathroom was a tub big enough for two, but with a huge crack. There were boxes all around the house, almost as if Miles had just moved in (although he had been living there since the sixties). Even Miles's piano, on which he worked out ideas and composed new pieces, was in sorry shape—terribly out of tune with a few keys totally unplayable.

Of course, the house did not look so bad inside because Miles kept it dark all day long. He was a

dyed-in-the-wool "night person." This too was a reflection of his mood in the late seventies. He had stopped
playing because of a series of overlapping health problems, which he had fought against valiantly in the early
seventies, regularly touring and recording, but which
simply became too overwhelming in 1975.

Miles and I hit it off right away, perhaps because I
immediately caught on to the fact that what some
called "rude" or "insulting" was really his way of testing
people, playing with them to see if they were hip
enough to be trusted. With me that meant a continual
series of mock anti-Semitic jibes. It was obvious to me
that Miles was actually completely unprejudiced, and
he looked on racism, of any kind, as inherently ridiculous. His nickname for me was "Jewish bastard," and
he used to say things like "I'm having a party this
weekend and you're invited, Eric. Yassir Arafat is the
guest of honor." Of course, the funniest part of that
crack was the idea of Miles putting on any sort of
party during this reclusive period. Once Miles said to
me, "Okay you Jewish bastard, call me nigger, go
ahead. I've been called that a million times."

I replied, "Well, Miles, if you've been called that a
million times, I better call you 'wop.' That's it, you
little wop." Miles was stymied at his own game. This
kind of playful jousting was one of his favorite activi-
ties, and I was able to hold my own most of the time.
However, Miles often tried to get me to box with him,
throwing light punches which I refused to return
(Miles was, of course, a trained amateur boxer). I was
at least a foot taller than him and he continually
wanted to show how somebody his size could physically deal with someone like me. I conceded to him
that he undoubtedly could, but he kept on trying to
get me into a little back-and-forth anyway.

Almost from the beginning Miles confided things to me that few knew, particularly the extent of his physical problems. He was in intense pain frequently and was often emotionally discouraged. Our jousts seemed to cheer him up, and I felt glad to be of aid. Once we became friends it became hard for me to think of him as I once had, as a musical legend. He was my friend Miles now, amazingly enough.

I soon found myself in the position of being his errand boy. He would call me up (he seemed to know the moment I got home from work) and invite me— actually, command me—to come over and bring groceries or pick up a package at the pharmacy or cash a check, or any other errand that needed doing. And a few times he had me pick up little packages from one of his coke dealers who lived a block away from me.

I hated doing that, for a number of reasons. I had little interest in coke myself—it made me nervous and uncomfortable. I seem to be allergic to most intoxicants; I don't even drink coffee or alcohol in any form. I always turned Miles down when he offered me some coke (he made it a practice of insisting that if someone did some of his cocaine, that they do the same huge amount at one time as he did—I shuddered at the thought). My main concern was for Miles's health, not my own safety. But he would explain to me in great, and quite poignant, detail the reason for his use of coke. It distracted him from the pain better than anything else, he told me, and it elevated his spirit. Without it he sank deeply into depression over his physical state; without it, he told me quite earnestly, he had no reason to continue living. "I've done everything, been everywhere, done so much shit, there's nothing to look forward to." Except, he made clear, the coke.

I tried to get him to see psychiatrists, get some treatment for his depression. But he would hear nothing of it. He knew exactly what he wanted out of life. Yes, I should have been stronger, but I suppose I still looked at Miles, even in this state, as an idol, a god. And I did what this god wanted me to do. What can I say?—he got to me. I never made a nickel from delivering anything to him (if anything, I lost money for bus and late-night cab rides), including the coke, which I only had to deal with when he couldn't get his dealers to deliver.

Much of the time, however, Miles just wanted company—desperately. Although a lovely young girl was living with him at the time—whom I will call "Daisy"— she did not provide much intellectual fodder for a mind as brilliant as Miles's. He had also discovered that I was virtually a walking and breathing encyclopedia of his life and career. He was proud of the fact that he had forgotten so much—to him, that was the mark of a true artist and innovator, for if you cannot remember the past you are forced to continually create something new. But he did need to retrieve information from time to time that he had forgotten.

Soon, visiting Miles often became deeply depressing. He was so jaded, so world-weary and cynical, he almost seemed to be living at the heart of the void. A friend of mind begged me to bring him to meet Miles. But after we left Miles's home, my friend said, "I don't ever want to see him again. I'll just stick to listening to his music." I understood how he felt, but I also had deep compassion for Miles.

I don't remember how we first started talking about collaborating on Miles's autobiography. It seemed as much his idea as mine, although such a project had been a fantasy of mine long before I met him. At first

Miles was not too sure. "If we do this book," he told me, "I'll have to say in it that —— —— (a famous black entertainer) is a flaming faggot." (Incidentally, Miles was not at all homophobic—he was friendly with several homosexuals, including those who rented the top apartment in his building—and of course there have long been rumors that he was bisexual, although I never saw anything to bear them out.)

"No, Miles, you don't have to talk about him. Talk about those you respected like Charlie Parker."

"Charlie Parker," Miles declared, "was a hog." He then told me the story about the cornbread that is in this book.

"Well, okay, what about Coltrane?"

"Coltrane," Miles declared, "was a hog. You see, a genius like that, he has to be selfish. That's just the way geniuses are." As Miles said this, he was putting about half a gram of cocaine up his left nostril, deftly illustrating his point.

Finally, Miles agreed to do it, if the advance was sufficient. Thus began our "interviews," which were more like discussions, and, for me, like pulling teeth. Miles would start talking about Bird or the 52nd Street scene of the "Birth of the Cool" band ("Why," Miles asked rhetorically "am I called anti-white when my first band was almost all white?"), but then he would say, "That was so long ago, who cares what happened that long ago?" I tried to convince him as well as I could, telling him that lots of people did. He would not let me use a tape recorder for some reason. When someone asked him how I was supposed to remember all that he had said, Miles replied, "Eric will remember it. He doesn't need a tape recorder"—which was partially true. However, it certainly would have been easier with one. If I hid one in my briefcase or put a

small one in my pocket, Miles was always able to fer-
ret the damn thing out.

Miles had a very ambivalent attitude toward his past.
At times, he was proud of his accomplishments; at
other times his illustrious past almost seemed like a
weight around his neck. For example, I knew Jimmy
Cobb, Miles's former drummer (and, incidentally, a
greatly underrated player) pretty well. Jimmy had
found a tape of Miles's group with Coltrane from its
1960 world tour, the group's last. But when he tried
to give it to his old boss, whom he had not seen for
a while, Miles wouldn't even open his door, telling
Jimmy through the intercom just to slide it under.
Jimmy, who used to be close to Miles and is a very
sensitive person, simply left. He did give it to me,
however. The music, particularly Coltrane's, was really
extraordinary, so I invited Miles over, telling him I had
something I wanted him to listen to. Several days later,
returning from a trip to Connecticut, Miles dropped
over. I asked him if he wanted to hear the tape; at
first he said no. I told him who it was and he said
he still did not want to hear it. Then a little later, in
the middle of a conversation that had nothing to do
with music, Miles said, "Put it on, Eric."

The first tune was "So What." Miles groaned. At the
beginning of the trumpet solo, Miles acted as if he
were on the bandstand, grumbling to the bassist Paul
Chambers, "Play the right fucking notes, Paul." He
turned to Daisy and said, "Hey that's some pretty good
trumpet playing, don't you think, Daisy? I wonder who
that is." I doubt if even Daisy was unaware who was
playing the trumpet.

But when Coltrane came on, Miles really got sucked
into the music, exclaiming when Trane played a brilliant series of ideas or a particularly roiling arpeggio.

Miles moved his body to Coltrane's solo, more caught up in this music than I had ever seen him. When it was over, Miles stood up to go, indicating to Daisy that it was time to leave. I said, "Wait, Miles, there's a lot more on the tape."

Miles looked at me with more sadness in his eyes than I had ever seen and said, "How could you do that to me, Eric? I thought we were friends." Needless to say, I was devastated.

From experiences such as his ability always to know when and where I had secreted a tape recorder, I often wondered just how powerful Miles's mental powers were. Believe this or not, but on more than one occasion when I called him on the phone he answered by saying, "Hey, Eric, what's up?" And on more than one occasion he heard, or sensed, Daisy a block away walking toward the house (the drapes were drawn and he had been talking to me, sitting on his huge curved couch, his back to the window, so there was no way he could have seen her). "Go downstairs and open the door. By the time you get down there and undo the locks, she will be at the doorway." Needless to say, he was correct. Real *Twilight Zone* stuff.

Miles now had great leverage with me. If he wanted me to do something, and I was hesitant, all he had to do was threaten to pull out of the book. Eventually I began to ease the amount of control he had over me. If he said, "I want you to pick up a six-pack of Heineken and get over here now," and I told him "absolutely not," he would usually reply, "Well, that's it Eric. Just forget about the book. It's all over." But I knew that he would call back an hour later, a day later, or sometimes two days later, and once more make a demand, as if nothing had happened.

Sometimes Miles's imagination worked overtime in figuring out a ploy to get me to run him an errand or just to come over and keep him company. Here is a particularly bizarre example. It was late—after one in the morning—and I was at my girlfriend's place. We were just going to bed when the phone rang— somehow, Miles had obtained my girlfriend's phone number—and he wanted me to pick up some coke for him, because none of his dealers would deliver. I hated that particular errand, especially late at night. I was dog tired to boot and had the beginnings of a flu. Miles went through his usual threats, but I would not budge. "All right," he muttered, "this is the end, Eric," and hung up.

A few minutes later the phone rang. It was Daisy this time wanting to talk to me. "Eric," she said in a virtual monotone, "Miles says that unless you get over here now he's going to kick your white Jewish ass." I could clearly hear Miles's whisper in the background telling Daisy exactly what to say. "Well, Daisy," I replied, "you tell Miles that I'll see him tomorrow so he can kick my white ass then. It's cold outside and there is no way I'm going to run around, especially for Miles's poison. And tell him that I'm coming down with the flu, Daisy." I got the feeling that, as was often the case, Miles did not need coke as much as company. How deeply saddening—one of the great geniuses of this century truly desperate just for a little company at one-thirty in the morning. "Okay," said Daisy, obviously embarrassed.

A few minutes later Miles called again. This time he talked to my girlfriend. He told her he knew exactly how to give me a treatment for my flu that would get me well in a matter of hours. But of course

I had to come down there for the treatment (which had something to do with soaking in a bathtub with some special salts). I told my girlfriend to tell Miles, "No dice."

Finally I crawled into bed, thinking—foolishly—that Miles had certainly given up for the night. But a few minutes later the phone rang yet again. I told my girlfriend not to bother answering it, but she did anyway. What a surprise—it was Daisy with a terrible emergency—Miles had fallen down his stairway! I have to come over right away!

"Oh my God, Daisy, that's terrible. Listen, call 911 immediately. Do you want me to? I'll call them for you." I heard that whisper in the background. "No, uh, Miles wants you to pick up something for him and to come right away." Another whisper. "This is an emergency."

"Sounds pretty bad, Daisy. But you have to call 911 right now, I can't help him. Understand? Miles has to get treated as soon as possible."

Hesitation. "Uh, okay." And she hung up.

And yes, a few minutes later the phone rang yet again. I answered it this time. "Eric," said Daisy—I could hear Miles's whisper in the background—"Miles wants you to know that he did not really fall down his stairway."

"Oh, really?"

"No, Miles says that he just doesn't like bullshit."

"Tell him, neither do I, Daisy, neither do I."

If all this seems like a game, of course it was, at least to a degree. On a number of occasions Miles would have me come over, supposedly just to discuss the book, and then after five minutes or so say, "Okay, Eric, I want to be alone. Get the fuck out of here." His house was about ten blocks from mine, not just around the corner, so I did not find this particular ploy very amusing.

I cannot say that Miles did not return my favors. One time I went to his house right after a horrific haircut. Miles insisted on recutting my hair, telling me that I was the first white guy whose hair he had cut. And when he had the straight razor against my necks he cracked, "Now I've got you where I want you, white boy." Real funny stuff, Miles.

Another night Miles and I had a lengthy argument about the book. I wanted his old friend Bobby, his long-time boxing trainer, to help with the book, since he had known Miles for so long. But Miles was adamant, furious that I would even broach the idea. "He's just a boxing trainer. He doesn't know about any other shit." I thought that was very unfair to Bobby, who was not only highly intelligent but who had been close to Miles over a period of many years. He had even toured with him on several occasions, so I thought he would be helpful in jarring Miles's stubborn memory. But Miles insisted that if Bobby was part of the project, he would pull out.

As I was leaving that night, Miles told me to wait for a minute. He went into his bedroom and came back with a pair of his boxing gloves and an old jockstrap. I knew it was his way of saying, "Okay, I'll allow you in the same ring with me." I was being accepted on existential terms by Miles.

Miles constantly surprised me. For instance, he was a superb chef. One night he invited me over for what he claimed was "the best fried chicken you will ever eat." He was right. And he was knowledgeable on a wealth of subjects. He discussed literature with me, comparing the great writers to the great jazz masters. Although I had never seen Miles read, he knew who the important American writers were—he mentioned as "the masters" Hemingway, Steinbeck, Fitzgerald, and Faulkner. He told me that there was one writer he simply could not stand—Herman Hesse. He once had a girl living with him who loved Hesse and had all his books. Miles gave her an ultimatum—get rid of the Hesse books or leave. I was not sure whether Miles hated Hesse because of his pretentious style or just because he was German (although he never mentioned Thomas Mann or any other German writer). But he had the same low regard for Hesse as a writer that he did for such musicians as Stanley Turrentine and Oscar Peterson ("Oscar had to be taught how to play the blues" was his dead-on comment).

Sometimes Miles's generosity took strange twists. Somehow he heard that I had had a big fight with my girlfriend and he invited me over to talk about it. As soon as I walked in he told poor Daisy to give me a blow job "to cheer Eric up." Daisy—who until recently had been living a relatively sheltered life in the Midwest—was horribly embarrassed by this sort of thing. "Not tonight," I told Miles, "we've got a headache." I was pretty sure that if I had been unhinged enough to take Miles up on his offer, he would have caused me great bodily harm.

By the way, I have heard many rumors about Miles's supposed bisexuality. I never witnessed anything that made me think he was anything other than heterosexual—he certainly never hit on me—but he thought of himself as being beyond sex. He told me a story about a brief affair that he had with a woman in Chicago. According to Miles, right in the middle of lovemaking, he realized that sex completely bored him—so, as Miles told me, he withdrew from the situation, explaining to this poor woman that he simply had no more interest in this sort of thing. I wonder if she ever recovered.

I am not so humble that I am not able to repeat what Miles said about me to my girlfriend. Early one afternoon he came over to visit, which he rarely did. He was having problems with Daisy, he told me, and he wanted my advice. While I was out of the room he said to my girlfriend, "I love your old man. He reminds me of Gil Evans, a white guy with no prejudice." Being compared to Gil Evans by Miles Davis—I could have died with a smile on my face when my girlfriend reported it. (He would never, of course, say something like that directly to my face.)

Miles seemed facetious about most matters, and he could be very funny. His sense of humor could be downright silly. One time I started a sentence, "Miles, I . . ." and he interrupted me, saying, "Eric, I'm really sick of being called Miles. Call me Daffy from now on. Daffy Davis."

But there were dark moments too. His jaded outlook on life often made me depressed, and many times he sank into deep blue funks. And the darkest moments concerned his treatment of Daisy. One night he called me up and asked me to come over. I had not heard from him in a few days and I could tell from Miles's voice that there was a problem. When I got there, he was by himself. He had broken Daisy's jaw, he explained, and she was hospitalized. "So, what do you think, Eric. Am I an asshole?"

I was furious; Daisy was one of the sweetest, most innocent creatures on earth; she cared deeply about Miles although she was about thirty years his junior and did not really know who he was. "Yes," I said, "you're a damned asshole, Miles. How could you do such a thing?"

"I meant to pull my punch. I know how to pull my punch."

This was Daisy's crime: a few nights previously, one of Miles's dope dealers came to the house with his girlfriend. Miles gave the girlfriend a red hat of his. After they left Daisy said to Miles that he had never given *her* a red hat. And that's what did it.

Miles had had a private telephone line put in her hospital room. Although it was after midnight, he decided to call her, despite my protest. When she answered, Miles asked what she was doing. Well, she was trying to sleep, of course, despite the pain in her jaw.

It was obvious that Miles felt bad about this incident, just as he probably felt bad all the times he had beaten and abused women throughout his life. Miles is, of course, one of the great jazz heroes, but few jazz writers have mentioned this aspect of his personality. The jazz world is notoriously male-dominated, a place where few women are truly respected. And most jazz writers are male, too. So the fact that this musical genius has brutally abused women—and this was very well known throughout the jazz community—has apparently not been thought worthy of mention.

Can you imagine if, say, Stan Getz had routinely brutalized blacks, how he would have been portrayed by the jazz press? I doubt if such a "little idiosyncrasy" would have been avoided. And yes, I am as guilty as anybody else. There is little in the original edition of *Round About Midnight* about this aspect of Miles's life. But now, after the O.J. Simpson affair, I really think it is time to view such activity for what it is—sick and evil. I guess when I wrote this book I still thought of Miles as a friend, but there is really no excuse. It amazes me how people like Miles can scream about the evils of racism—rightly so—and then continually abuse women. What utter hypocrisy.

This incident deeply troubled me, and in many ways our relationship was never the same. Daisy moved right back in with Miles when she was released, which I could not understand. One day I said to Daisy that she seemed a bit depressed. "What's she got to be depressed about?" growled Miles. "She's in her early twenties and I'm fifty-two." I thought, she's got plenty to be depressed about, Miles.

Eventually I put together enough materials from our "interviews" to create a proposal. I talked with several publishers, but they all wanted to know the same thing—would Miles participate in publicizing the book? Miles had been very explicit about this, so I had to tell the truth: he was so reclusive during this point of his life that he could not even come to the publisher's office to sign a contract. Most publishers had no interest without Miles's participation in the publicity. I was offered a relatively small advance, but Miles refused—he knew that he deserved at least six figures since, in his words, "I've got a million dollars worth of information." So the publisher offered me a deal to write an unauthorized biography. I told Miles about this and he expressed no problem with my doing such a book. He even let me continue, from time to time, to ask him questions about his career.

My editor for the original edition of 'Round About Midnight was Joyce Johnson who, besides being a superb editor, was also a fine writer herself (some of her most fascinating work concerned her long relationship with Jack Kerouac). Joyce despised Miles simply from what I told her, and pretty soon it became obvious that she did not like me much either. From my current perspective, I think I know why: I obviously greatly admired Miles despite his despicable treatment of women. It is a great human dilemma—can we love parts of a person and simply ignore that which is repugnant? Now I believe that Miles's brutality toward women simply cannot be denied or avoided. (By the way, it was Joyce's idea to call the book *'Round About Midnight*. I was not crazy about the idea since it is the name of a well-known composition by Thelonious Monk. I wanted to just call it *Miles*—which was, of course, the eventual name of Miles's autobiography.)

Several years later when Miles did get a large advance to do his autobiography, he was well out of the reclusive mode of his supposed "retirement" and he agreed to publicize the book; he even did that incredible *Sixty Minutes* interview with Harry Reasoner, something I cannot imagine him even considering during his "retirement."

I stopped seeing Miles, for the most part, when Cicely Tyson came back into his life. I was a little surprised about that—Miles used to do nothing but complain about her. I was equally surprised to see him hanging out with Bill Cosby when I had seen him get livid at Cicely for giving Cosby his phone number. But I believe that the part of Miles that still wanted to survive saw in Cicely a strong woman who could push him to actively turn things around in his life—which is exactly what she did. However, she insisted that Miles drop his old friends, completely change his environment. Naturally, there were those such as myself who felt that we had been good friends, that we had tried to discourage Miles's self-destructiveness. But maybe she was right, as painful as it is to admit it. Maybe Miles had to be cut off from everyone who "enabled" him to get high, no matter how unwillingly.

And she did save his life, inarguably. Later, Miles would explain that she wanted complete control over him and did not want him to have his own friends. I do not know whether or not that was true. But even if it was, Miles owed her a tremendous debt.

Miles cut me off very sharply and I, like a number of other friends, was hurt. I had been very careful when I wrote *'Round About Midnight*—really, far too careful—about intruding on his privacy. So there was virtually nothing about his treatment of women or his voluminous drug use (although he had few compunctions about describing these things to interviewers and in his autobiography). However, I was told by many who had long been on the jazz scene that Miles did this all the time, often for not much reason at all—Jimmy Cobb is an excellent example. One person told me that sooner or later Miles did this to almost everybody close to him; for some reason I thought that I was an exception.

But the bottom line is that I owe Miles an enormous debt. He went out of his way to try to teach me how to think at the highest level of creativity. Miles was trying to show me the *way* of the artist—his attitude was definitely that of master and student. He was not teaching me any specific technical points about the work of an artist, but rather the existential terms—the stance and consciousness of the artist (although many of his lessons I had to suss out for myself—such as the gift of the boxing gloves and jock strap).

Despite his inexcusable treatment of women, despite the way he treated me at the end, despite even those final years of his life when he seemed to turn his back on most of the things he had once believed in, Miles changed my life for the better, and changed the lives of all who were moved by his music. A number of musicians told me that it was listening to Miles that made them dedicate their lives to music.

In the following book, you will read his story as close as I could get it to the way he told it to me. It was my first book, and therefore a great learning experience. Some sections I had to get completely through secondary sources, but I tried to bring in Miles's own point of view, at least as it was filtered though my own, as much as possible—except when my own voice can be clearly heard, mainly in the discussion of the music itself, which is fairly perfunctory anyway.

Knowing Miles Davis was without doubt one of the highlights of my life and I have no doubt it will remain so until my dying day. I hope that the reader of this book will glean at least some of the profound lessons I learned from him and his wonderful music.

Foreword

The first time I heard Miles Davis's music, it made little impression on me. I was fourteen and my older brother, a classical cellist newly won over to modern jazz, had brought *Kind of Blue* into the house. The music on the record seemed calm and ethereal, almost background music, especially in comparison with the raucous Dixieland that up to then I had thought to be the true sound of jazz. After several weeks of listening in, however, the record began to insinuate itself into my life, especially when I discovered something wonderful and mysterious about this music: every time I listened to it I heard something different and new; there seemed no limits to its depths. My curiosity was piqued— What sort of genius could make music so nearly perfect using such apparently casual methods?

When I finally met Miles, my years of curiosity were well rewarded. He was every bit as brilliant, profound, constantly surprising, and mercurial as his music. When I brought up my early perceptions of his genius to him, he laughed and said, "Everybody calls me a genius, but I don't even know what that is." I learned a great deal from Miles, and not just about his life and music. Although my background was quite different from his—I am white and Jewish—nevertheless I became obsessed with the idea of writing a book about this complex man whose genius I perceived as being as universal as that of Stravinsky, Joyce, or Picasso. Although Miles had shifting feelings about such a book, he was nevertheless more than generous in talking to me about his life, his music, and most importantly, his world view. To him I owe my utmost gratitude.

Of course, there were many others without whom this book would have been impossible. The patience, understanding, and assistance of my editors, Joyce Johnson and Doug Stumpf, were beyond anything I had a right to expect of them. To Elena Steinberg I owe a special thanks for introducing Miles to me as well as for her encouragement and photographs. And to Cya and Walter Booker I am grateful for so many different things that I do not have room here to enumerate them. Special thanks also to the Rutgers University Institute of Jazz Studies.

It should be clear in reading this book that I talked to many different musicians in the course of its preparation, but among those who were especially helpful were Jimmy Cobb, Dexter Gordon, Nat Adderley, and Larry Willis. I also want especially to thank Bobby McQuillen, Miles's boxing trainer, for his generosity, stories, and insights. Among many others I wish to thank are David Chertok and Frank Driggs for their films and photographs; my agent, Jim Witker, and my lawyer, Joe Barnes; James Crawford for his useful advice; Alice Schell for teaching me how to think about art and feelings; Debby Morgan; Joan Ariessohn; Fred Olmstead; Peter Merner; Dennis Dalrymple; Peter Occhiogrosso; Denzil Norwood; Charlotte Crossley; Sharon McCoy; Buddy Williams; Bruce Ricker; and last but certainly not least, my older brother Peter for introducing me to the world of modern jazz.

Foreword

There were a number of secondary sources that were extremely helpful for the background of this book. I should immediately mention *down beat, Metronome,* and the *Jazz Review* as being key periodicals that have covered the career of Miles with intelligence and insight. Marc Crawford's excellent article about Miles in *Ebony,* Leonard Feather's in-depth interview in *From Satchmo to Miles,* and Julie Coryell's and Elena Steinberg's provocative interview in *Jazz-Rock Fusion* were rich in illuminating anecdote. Ross Russell's excellent biography of Charlie Parker, *Bird Lives,* was especially useful for the chapters about Bird. I must also mention Bill Cole's *Miles Davis: A Musical Biography,* for its musical analysis, bibliography, and discography.

'ROUND ABOUT MIDNIGHT

Early/Late Miles

It didn't really matter that it was one thirty in the morning, because Miles's duplex apartment, which was perpetually kept in womblike darkness, always had an ambience of the wee small hours of the morning. Indeed, before one's eyes could adjust to the dim light, Miles's features could, like those of the Cheshire cat's, seemingly fade and reappear in the dark of his living room. But now his eyes were flashing as he animatedly spoke on the phone in his hoarse whisper of a voice, which fit so well in the atmosphere of his home. "Listen, motherfucker, I'll play when I feel like it. Nobody can tell me when I should play again." He listened for a few moments, his eyes rolling in exasperation. "Hey, fuck you, man. You can't tell me what I'm doing. Nobody can but me." He angrily slammed the phone down and *muttered something which nobody could hear. Then he turned to his guest and said, "Why don't people mind their own damned business?" The way he phrased it, the statement was an actual question, not rhetorical.*

He walked into his bedroom with its small flickering gas fireplace and changed his shirt. Occasionally when the mood in his home palpably shifted, Miles would go to his enormous wardrobe and put on different clothes to reflect the change, as he was doing now. When he returned from the bedroom, he was smiling, obviously recovered from the latest attack on his private intentions. "Hey, man, stand up," he said to his guest, who sighed and replied, "Come on, Miles, I don't feel like fighting." Miles squinted his eyes in mock seriousness: "You're in the house of a superstar, you white motherfucker, a king trying to hold on to his throne. Now, stand up, I want to show you a few moves." As in his greatest solos, much of what Miles said seemed to have levels of mysterious meaning. The guest stood up, hearing in Miles's words more of a plea than a command.

"Try and hit me," Miles demanded.

"I don't want to hit you."

"You're not going to. Just throw a right jab."

Reluctantly, the guest complied. Lightning fast, Miles slapped the fist away.

"Now try your left."

Once again, Miles slapped the attacking hand away, this time countering with a hard left to the guest's midsection.

"Damn it, Miles," the guest groaned, "you knocked the wind out of me. Why did you do that?"

Miles chuckled and replied, "Because we're friends, motherfucker."

The guest, still gasping, sat back down on Miles's semicircular couch. "You're crazy as hell, Miles."

Early / Late Miles

Miles made a face. "What else can you be in this world? You know, my mother always used to call me crazy. She was some strong bitch. I've been in a lot of pain these days, but nothing like my mother when she was dying of cancer. But she never made a sound. If it had been me, you would have heard me all the way to New Jersey."

Ever the generous host, Miles offered his guest a Heineken beer and a piece of his own excellent fried chicken. "This is the way chicken should be cooked," he declared. "Spicy. Not like you white people eat it." The guest asked if he had been to East St. Louis recently. "Nah," Miles replied. "I used to like to go there and hang out on my father's farm. But I haven't been back there in a while. You know, I had my own band there when I was just a kid. There were some of the best trumpet players in the world in St. Louis when I was growing up, and they were the guys that I first learned from, and jammed with. Those were some of my very best times, you know, when I was coming up in Saint Louis."

Indeed, St. Louis would have the reputation in jazz circles as being a "trumpet man's town," but that would be a few years after Miles was born. Actually, Miles Dewey Davis was born in Alton, Illinois, twenty-two miles up the river from East St. Louis. A year after Miles's birthday (May 25, 1926) his father, Miles Sr., a successful oral surgeon and dentist, moved his family—which included his wife (the former Cleota Robinson) and his daughter, Dorothy—to East St. Louis, Illinois, just across the river from St. Louis, Missouri. Dr. Davis's practice became even more prosperous in East St. Louis, and two years later a second son, Vernon, was born. Soon after Vernon's birth the Davis family moved into an all-white section of the city. This was a brave move for a black family in the early thirties, even in the mostly black city of East St. Louis. However, the Davis family had long had a history of pride along with a stubborn determination to overcome the barriers of American racism.

Once, when talking about his son's musical accomplishments, Dr. Davis said, "By genetics and breeding Miles is always going to be ahead of his time. Historically, way back into slavery days, the Davises have been musicians and performed classical works in the homes of the plantation owners. My father was born six years after the emancipation and forbade me to play music, because the only place a Negro could play then was in barrelhouses." Miles's grandfather had been a bookkeeper in Arkansas, respected by white landowners who would come to his house at night in order to have him fix their books. Although he made a good deal of money and obtained a considerable amount of land, he was eventually driven from most of his holdings by jealous whites. He did manage to retain a thousand acres, which would pay for the schooling of his children. Dr. Davis went on to acquire three degrees.

Soon after the move to the white neighborhood Dr. Davis bought some country land of his own, a hog farm not too far from East St. Louis. In all, the Davis family was as solidly bourgeois as a black family could be in the early thirties. However, they were still unable to avoid racial prejudice, which dominates some of Miles's earliest memories. As he stood on a corner in his new neighborhood, a white man came running toward him yelling "Nigger, nigger." Shortly afterward, Miles was stopped by another white man, who said, "What are you doing here? This ain't no nigger street." Miles's enraged father got his shotgun and went looking for the man. Fortunately, he never found him.

The phone rang. Miles picked it up and said, "What the fuck do you want?"—his special telephone greeting. After listening for a minute or two, he croaked, "Listen, man, I can't talk right now. I'm resting. All that stuff you heard is bullshit, I'm just taking it easy," and abruptly hung up. "I'm going to have to get my number changed again," he muttered as he walked over to the piano. He began playing eerie chords that, to the casual listener, seemed only tenuously connected to each other. "Isn't this pretty?" he asked softly.

"Miles," asked Dixie, the current girl friend, "can I change the channel to Starsky and Hutch?"

Miles hardly ever turned off the Advent television with its giant screen (although he usually paid only the slightest attention to what was on it).

"Listen to this bitch," Miles snorted. "I'm playing this beautiful music and she wants to watch Starsky and Hutch. *You know, my mother could play some good blues on the piano, but I didn't find out about it until I was grown up. It's funny, because she always looked like she was going to hit me every time I picked up my horn when I was a kid."*

The middle-class attitudes of Miles's parents were reflected in their feelings about music. Although Miles's mother had a small collection of Duke Ellington and Art Tatum records, which provided young Miles his first taste of jazz, she encouraged her children to pursue classical music. Miles would always peek through the door when his older sister was with her piano teacher. His own musical inclinations were apparent even when he was a small child. Miles insists that when he was only a few years old he had the ability to tell whether music on the radio was being performed by white or black musicians.

Young Miles had other interests. He enjoyed the outdoors and loved riding horses on his father's land. He also still remembers with fondness, especially now that he has become such an urban figure, fishing, hunting, and taking long walks in the Illinois countryside. In addition, he was a superb, constantly curious student, especially in mathematics, in which he gained enough skill to tutor his older sister. To this day he retains his childhood ability to instantly add up long columns of figures.

It was this and other factors which led Dr. Davis, a loving and protective father, to look for a means to give his son's restless intellect a new outlet.

When Miles was about to turn thirteen, his father asked one of his patients how best to encourage his son's incipient interest in music. The patient, a trumpeter and music teacher named Elwood Buchanan, replied, "Send Miles around. I go to the grade school every Wednesday to teach music; buy him a trumpet for his birthday."

Miles's mother objected strenuously to the idea of having to listen to a beginning trumpet player practice every day. In addition, she associated the trumpet with jazz, a music she privately enjoyed but which she considered slightly déclassé. Certainly a violin, she insisted, an instrument associated with "classical" music, would be a more fitting instrument. But Dr. Davis overruled her objections and bought his son a trumpet for his birthday—"Because he loved my mother so much," Miles would say sardonically years later.

Miles's teacher, Elwood Buchanan, had been a professional trumpeter with the great Andy Kirk band. His favorite players were the lyrical Bobby Hackett and Harold Baker (who played with Duke Ellington). Buchanan had definite ideas about how to play the trumpet. "Fast, light, and no vibrato" is how Miles describes his own style, and these elements were essentially derived from Buchanan's approach. "Never play with vibrato," Buchanan would tell his students. "You're gonna get old and start shaking anyway."

In those days the St. Louis trumpet players included bandleaders Dewey Johnson and Charlie Creath as well as such highly individual stylists as Ed Allen, Joe Thomas, Harold Baker, Mouse Randolph, and Clark Terry.

Buchanan's teaching approach was strict and traditional, encouraging competition among his students. As Miles remembers, "Everybody would fight to play best. Lucky for me that I learned the chromatic scale right away." A key to Buchanan's teaching was making his students hold notes in order to achieve a full, round, brilliant sound. Sound itself, he would teach, was the key to playing the trumpet. Years later Miles would say, "If you don't get sound on the horn, then you don't get nothing. Musical ideas are easy, but it's the sound that you need."

Because Miles was so small, he acquired the nickname "Little Davis" in his music class. But Buchanan liked Miles, recognizing the great potential of the youngster. In an interview, Miles recalled, "Buchanan used to say, 'Little Davis, come here.' I'd say, 'What you want?' He'd whisper that Ellington song 'Do nothing till you hear from me, pay no attention to what's said . . .' Every time he'd get drunk, that's what he'd sing."

The boy became obsessed with learning his horn. His friends often noticed him spitting rice or peas on his way to school—a mouth exercise he had learned from Buchanan. He also began to carry his trumpet with him at all times, and whenever he had a free moment, he would practice his latest exercises. Within a year the horn had become an extension of Miles's being.

Miles always lost the music contests at his high school to white boys with a fraction of his ability. These experiences became a catalyst in his drive to become a great musician. In 1962 he told an interviewer, "It made me so mad I made up my mind to outdo anybody white on my horn. If I hadn't met that prejudice, I probably wouldn't have had as much drive in my work. I've thought about that a lot. Prejudice and curiosity have been responsible for what I've done in music."

Miles got up from the piano, sat down on the couch, and poured the rest of his Heineken into a glass. The guest started to ask him a question: "Hey, Miles, uh . . ."

"Don't call me Miles, man. I get tired of hearing that. Call me Daffy. Daffy Davis."

"Okay, Daffy, whatever you say."

"Hey, Dixie," Miles said to the lady of the house, "bring me some cream to put on my face."

"She seems depressed tonight."

"What's she got to be depressed about? She's in her early twenties and I'm fifty-three."

"I was going to ask when you last had your horns fixed. I'll get them fixed for you."

This stratagem didn't fool Miles for a moment.

"Hey, man, when I'm ready to play, I'll fix the horns myself. I don't need anybody else to fix my horns." He picked up a beautiful black trumpet sitting behind the couch and played one perfect round note. "See? It sounds okay. I learned how to fix my horn from my teacher—he showed me. I also learned shit about my horn from a lot of other guys in St. Louis, like Clark. He showed me all kinds of things."

"Clark. . . . Clark Terry?"

"We were good friends back in St. Louis. I haven't

*seen him in years. I don't know why. I don't know why
the motherfucker never comes up here."*

By the time he was fifteen, Miles was working regularly with a little group on weekends. He was also part
of a high school band that rehearsed and played music
styled after that of Count Basie's band, which was then
peaking in its popularity. He also began to go to jam
sessions, which were ubiquitous in the St. Louis area.
The town had long been a popular stopover point for
steamboats coming up the Mississippi. In addition to
other cargo, the boats carried the latest evolution in
black music, from early ragtime to New Orleans jazz.

At one of these jam sessions Miles heard the young
trumpeter Clark Terry. Terry's style was a revelation to
Miles, who up to that point had patterned his own style
after Buchanan's favorite, Bobby Hackett, and after
Harry James, whom Miles emulated because, as he
would say later, "I liked to break out all my teeth"—
referring to James's unique embouchure. Terry's style
was faster and lighter than either Hackett's or James's,
and Miles was immediately taken with it. But the initial
meeting of the two trumpeters was hardly dramatic.
Terry was playing in a small band led by the one-legged
piano player Benny Reed. One day the band played a
picnic grounds where there was a sports meet between
various Illinois high schools. An old friend of Terry's
brought Miles over to meet him. As Terry remembers,
"The kid started right in asking questions—how did I
do this or that? We talked, but my mind was really on
some girls dancing around a maypole and I kind of
fluffed the kid off." Miles was hurt, but he remained
impressed with Terry's distinct, light, and soaring trumpet style.

Elwood Buchanan remained Miles's mentor. When he heard of a little club in nearby Springfield, Illinois, that needed a trumpet player, he recommended his young student to the owner. Miles was hired there for his first professional gig, a job which paid him a hundred dollars for the week's work. The place was a small-time burlesque joint, and the band primarily played for the strippers.

At sixteen he joined the musicians' union and was soon regularly playing gigs around St. Louis. Dr. Davis permitted his son to use the family car to drive to the clubs. At this same time Miles began his lifelong love of clothes—he spent hours shopping for clothes at pawnshops.

Miles increasingly found himself involved in the jazz world. Together with two friends, trumpeter "Bruz" and piano player Duke Brooks, he formed a small band. Miles had been told by the union that he was "too modern"; he hoped that with his own band he could get more gigs, but it wound up getting little work.

One night Miles was jamming in a St. Louis club when a young saxophonist named Sonny Stitt came in. After the set, Stitt walked up to Miles and introduced himself, saying, "You look like a man named Charlie Parker, and you play like him, too." Miles had never heard of Parker, but he was very impressed when he heard Stitt play. Stitt, like Miles and his friends, was obviously interested in broadening the harmonic and rhythmic horizons of jazz. What Miles didn't know was how much Stitt's playing sounded like the man he'd been told he resembled—Charlie "Yardbird" Parker, who along with trumpeter Dizzy Gillespie was on the verge of causing a major revolution in American music.

Stitt asked Miles to join him in the Tiny Bradshaw band, which needed a trumpet player in order to complete its tour. Miles was excited about the offer, but when he asked his parents' permission to go on the road, his mother insisted that Miles finish high school before even considering a tour. Miles was furious—he slapped his mother and then immediately apologized. But he didn't talk to her for two weeks. Around the same time, he received other offers to tour—from tenor saxophonist Illinois Jacquet and A. J. Suliman, the trumpet-playing manager of McKinney's Cotton Pickers—but his mother was adamant, and he turned them down.

Miles joined Eddie Randall's Blue Devils, probably the hottest band in Saint Louis. The Blue Devils played a style of jazz and blues that sometimes sounded like early Count Basie, Kansas City–style jazz, and at other times like something close to rhythm and blues. One night when the band was playing the St. Louis Elks Club, Clark Terry came to hear it. Climbing the stairs to the club, Terry heard a unique style of trumpet that bore some resemblance to his own. Terry was quite familiar with the Blue Devils, but not the teen-aged trumpet player, although he knew he had met him somewhere. Terry remembers, "As I said 'Aren't you—?' he broke in with 'Yeah, I'm the kid you fluffed off in Carbondale.' We've often laughed about it since. He was a nice quiet little kid then."

The two of them became close companions, and Terry enjoyed playing the role of mentor to his younger friend. When boats with musicians would stop in St. Louis, Terry would call Miles and invite him to a jam session. Much to his embarrassment, Miles would have to ask his father if he could go, but his father almost always agreed. Miles and Terry would jam with musicians from New Orleans, or Kansas City, or Oklahoma City until five or six in the morning, learning and trading the latest musical ideas. "I used to watch the way different

Miles (back row, fourth from left), age sixteen, playing at Club Rhumboogie, St. Louis, 1943 (Frank Driggs Collection).

guys carried their horns," Miles remembers, "and the way they'd lip their horns. I could tell what they were trying to play and what embouchure fit." The two young men played "fast and light with no vibrato," and they always impressed other musicians. "Clark used to play so fast 'cause he played out of a clarinet book," Miles recalls, "and I used to play out of a piano book and a French book on clarinet. I'd play a whole page in one breath. He'd play everything down the scale. Sometimes, just to tease him, I'd play just what he'd play. We had a ball."

Miles sat slumped on the couch, looked at the elaborate mural that a friend had painted on his wall. "You know," he said slowly, "I always thought that if you looked at that picture on the wall when you were play-

ing you could play almost any musical idea that there was." He turned abruptly to his guest and said sharply, "It's time for you to go, man."

"You were just telling me how you met Charlie Parker."

Miles sat upright with an angry look and made a sweeping gesture with his hand. "Oh, man, that was so long ago. I don't want to talk about that. But I'll tell you one thing about Charlie Parker—he was the biggest hog I ever met. I remember one time back of the Three Deuces somebody brought us a whole homemade corn bread. Bird gave me one thin slice and then stood there and ate all the rest by himself in about three minutes. That was Charlie Parker for you."

Miles saw his friend downstairs to the door, and as he opened it he said, "Those were my best times, you know, with Bird on Fifty-second Street. Now get the fuck out of my house." But playfully he slapped his guest's back as he closed the thick wooden door.

When Miles graduated from high school in 1944, he knew that music was the only profession of any real interest to him. His mother hoped that her son would outgrow his obsession with his trumpet and would, like his father, become a doctor. Dr. Davis, however, was more supportive of his son's musical ambitions, always encouraging him to find his own way.

That summer Miles got a job playing with Adam Lambert's Six Brown Cats, a swing band that was fairly modern for that time. By then Roy Eldridge, the brilliant post-Louis Armstrong swing trumpeter, had, along with Terry and Hackett, become Miles's principal influence. But Miles was beginning to discover that he could not play with the tremendous range of Eldridge, and especially that he could not reach the amazing high notes of the older trumpeter.

After a brief tour with the Lambert group, Miles returned to East St. Louis, where he heard exciting news: the Billy Eckstine band was coming to the Club Riviera. Eckstine was becoming an increasingly popular vocalist, but it was his band that most interested Miles and the other young musicians. Its personnel included Dizzy Gillespie and Charlie Parker. Miles had never heard either of them in person.

Gillespie and Parker had become the talk of jazz; they were the vanguard. They were already looked upon as pariahs by the more conservative members of the jazz community, and their pioneering musical explorations often took on the trappings of a crusade. Their first experimentation had been done in small Harlem clubs such as Minton's or Monroe's Uptown House. The new modern jazz had by this time been dubbed bebop, and it was flowering in the Eckstine band. Eckstine was using his popularity as a singer to promote the new jazz, and among the modernists in the band, besides Parker and Gillespie, were drummer Art Blakey, tenor man Budd Johnson, and a young singer named Sarah Vaughan.

Miles considered himself a fellow modernist and had a fantasy that he might get to sit in with Eckstine's band. When Eckstine arrived in East St. Louis in July 1944, Miles showed up at the Riviera with his horn under his arm. As he remembers it, "As soon as I walked in, this guy runs up to me and says, 'Do you have a union card?' It was Dizzy. I didn't even know him. I said, 'Yeah, I have a union card.' 'We need a trumpet player. Come on!' So I got on the bandstand and started playing. I was third trumpet. I couldn't even read the music at first from listening to Dizzy and Bird, but I knew the book because I loved the music so much. I played with the Eckstine band around St. Louis for about three weeks. After that I knew I had to go to New York."

Miles might not have been so euphoric if he had known what Eckstine actually thought of his playing: "When I first heard Miles, I let him sit in so as not to hurt his feelings, but he sounded terrible; he couldn't play at all."

Miles realized that these brilliant musicians from New York were way ahead of him. He had been playing in something of a vacuum in St. Louis. In the late fifties, when Miles was among the most famous trumpet players in the world, Eckstine told him, "You know, Miles, when you first played with my band, you couldn't even blow your *nose.*"

Gillespie and Parker immediately recognized in the teen-ager a fellow spirit, and they took Miles under their wing. Despite his technical limitations, they could hear that he was harmonically precocious, and Miles's comprehension of their theories and practices was a tonic, especially coming from someone so young. A few days before the band returned to New York, Parker took Miles aside: "Look, Miles, I think that you can play. But you should get out of East St. Louis and come to New York. You can look me up there. I play the clubs on Fifty-second Street all the time, particularly the Three Deuces. Come to New York and maybe we can play together."

Miles was excited by the invitation: it was already clear to him that Parker was a genius, pouring out an apparently endless stream of brilliant new ideas every time he soloed. From the other musicians in the band he had learned that Parker lived hard, but even that did not sway Miles. A genuine musical master was giving

Charlie Parker (Institute of Jazz Studies).

him a chance, despite the wide disparity between their technical abilities on their respective horns.

This was the final bit of encouragement that he needed. He already knew about the New York jazz scene from other musicians who had been there and from the *Esquire Jazz Book,* which had pictures of the many clubs on Fifty-second Street.

But there was a new complication in Miles's life—a girl named Irene. Like many musicians, Miles had been sexually active since his midteens, and many women were attracted to him—due to his burgeoning good looks, his impressive wardrobe, and his life as a musician. Although Irene was only sixteen, she wanted Miles to marry her. Miles agreed because, as he would say later, "I didn't want to hurt her feelings."

Reluctantly, Miles's parents consented to the marriage and permitted the couple to stay in the Davis house. However, they insisted that Miles complete his education, even though he was now a married man. Miles's mother wanted her son to go to Fisk, a major black university in Nashville, famous for the Fisk Jubilee Singers. Miles had another idea. He told his father he wanted to go to the Juilliard School of Music, certainly a school with an excellent reputation. But its academic excellence was not nearly as important to Miles as its location: New York City. Dr. Davis, once again overruling his wife, acceded to his son's wishes and agreed to send him to Juilliard for the winter term of 1945. But by this time Miles had a very good idea where his real schooling would be—Fifty-second Street, with Dizzy and Bird as his teachers. He knew he had to be where the new jazz was.

New York Bebop

Leaving Irene in East St. Louis, Miles came to New York with only a vague plan. Yes, he had to register at Juilliard and at least make a pretense of attending classes. He had promised his parents he would study at the school. He was also voraciously curious about music. If Juilliard had something to teach him, he definitely wanted to learn.

The day he arrived, he found a tiny apartment—a single, small room—close to Fifty-second Street. The next day he traveled by subway up to Juilliard to register and attend orientation sessions. He'd already figured that the school was primarily for rich white kids whose only interest was in classical music. There was little to change his opinions on that first day: the catalog contained descriptions of courses in harmony, composition, and music theory that he knew were far too elementary to be relevant for him at that point. As he had suspected, black music was almost unknown at Juilliard. The teaching staff considered jazz, blues, and the work of Duke Ellington, Louis Armstrong, and Lester Young to be vulgar, "popular" music. Nevertheless, Miles felt an obligation to his parents and registered for classes.

That night, for the first time, he ventured down to Fifty-second Street, "Swing Street," as it had been nicknamed by the musicians. Bird's invitation in St. Louis may have been a whim—a kind, offhand gesture of the moment—but it was an offer no young musician could refuse.

The fact that in 1944 Miles recognized Charlie Parker as one of the greatest American musicians was rather remarkable. Many musicians and critics disparaged the new jazz of Gillespie and Parker. They shrugged off its practitioners as virtuosic but confused and even obnoxious musicians who were destroying the melodicism and swing of jazz. Even Louis Armstrong dubbed bop "Chinese music." But Miles knew that ideas which had been brewing since the late thirties were coalescing in the music of Dizzy Gillespie and Charlie Parker in the great jazz cauldron of Fifty-second Street.

"On Fifty-second Street," recalled pianist Marian McPartland, "you could walk through the history of jazz. In several hours you could travel musically from New Orleans up to Harlem and bop." During the late twenties and early thirties Harlem had been the source of jazz and black entertainment; in the late thirties and midforties Fifty-second Street offered, for the first time, a variety of undiluted black talent to the white downtown audience of a major city. Places like Club 18 fea-

"Swing Street," Fifty-second Street, New York City, 1949 (Frank Driggs Collection).

---

tured Don Rickles–type insult comedians; there were strip joints with "cabaret entertainers"; but jazz was the most prevalent attraction.

Important jazz performers were playing in one tiny club after another, all crammed onto a single block. Imagine strolling down it in January 1945: at the Onyx, Coleman Hawkins was playing with his sextet, with Thelonious Monk on piano, second-billed to Billie Holiday singing "Lover Man" and "What a Little Moonlight Can Do"; Art Tatum was playing solo piano at the Front Door between sets of jazz violinist Stuff Smith's famous group; Roy "Little Jazz" Eldridge was at Kelly's Stable along with a young blues singer named Dinah Washington; Joe Marsala's New Orleans group played traditional jazz, spelled by Marian McPartland's trio; Sidney

Inside Club Downbeat on Fifty-second Street (Frank Driggs Collection).

Bechet, who along with Louis Armstrong was one of the first great jazz soloists, played soprano sax at Jimmy Ryan's. But this list of musicians and clubs does not even begin to convey the intensity of the musical ferment; between sets, musicians would often visit the club next door or across the street and sit in with the group playing there in order to exchange ideas.

Swing Street exerted a profound influence on the entire American musical scene. Frank Sinatra and Frankie Laine frequented the back of the Onyx club, listening with reverence to Billie Holiday. Duke Ellington, whose band never played The Street, could be seen listening at the Front Door to Art Tatum, or concentrating on the bebop sounds filling the Three Deuces, and from time to time even sitting in himself with a band.

Actually, that first night Miles probably regarded The Street as more a distraction than anything else. He had one goal in mind, and that was to find Charlie Parker.

By 1945 four clubs on Fifty-second Street were featuring bop on a regular basis—the Spotlight, the Three Deuces, Kelly's Stable, and the Onyx. In East St. Louis Parker had mentioned the Three Deuces specifically, and Miles headed there first. He was both excited and disconcerted when he walked in. The tables were so jammed together in the tiny space that there was virtually no room to move about. The bandstand, if one could call it that, seemed hardly large enough to hold a combo, and the piano seemed to take up two thirds of the entire place. Don Byas, the great tenor saxophonist who had played with Dizzy Gillespie and Oscar Pettiford in the first bop group to perform on Fifty-second Street (in early 1944), was on the tiny stage with his group. Miles immediately sensed the palpable atmosphere of musical vitality. He stood at the doorway, looking around in the dim light of the club for any musicians he might recognize from their travels through St. Louis. But he saw no familiar faces. The owner of the Deuces spotted the innocent-looking young man and asked him what he was doing there.

"I'm looking for Charlie Parker," Miles told him.

"He's not here tonight, son. And you got to be eighteen to come in."

"I just want to find Charlie Parker."

Struggling to talk above the din of the music, the clubowner tried to set Miles straight. "Listen, kid, you're looking for the wrong bird, and that's no joke. That guy lives like a bum, and he's got a lot of bad habits you don't even want to know about. Where you from, son?"

Miles didn't like being called "son." "I'm from East St. Louis."

"Maybe you oughta go back home. You don't want to get mixed up with Charlie Parker."

Miles turned and walked out. He already knew that Charlie Parker had a bad heroin habit and drank heavily. He knew that Parker lived like a bum and cared only about music and getting high. But none of that bothered him. Bird's musical genius was all that mattered.

The Onyx was further east. Walking to it, Miles felt bewildered by the turbulence of Fifty-second Street itself. He had heard that blacks and whites intermingled freely here, but he wasn't ready for drunken sailors, southern army men glaring at him, dope pushers and panhandling bums, or loud businessmen parading their showgirl mistresses.

That night at the Onyx, Coleman Hawkins, the first great jazz saxophonist, was playing with his sextet. Hawkins had begun his career with Fletcher Henderson in the twenties, and throughout the thirties he had been among the most harmonically advanced of all jazz musicians. He was also one of the first older players to sympathize with the new sounds of bebop. Unlike many of his contemporaries, who felt threatened by the virtuosity of the bop players, Hawkins possessed a musical curiosity that bridged the gap. He actually led the first genuine bebop recording sessions, with bop pioneers Dizzy Gillespie, Don Byas, Oscar Pettiford, and Max Roach.

The Onyx was packed, as Hawkins was one of the more popular musicians who regularly played there. After his experience at the Three Deuces, Miles felt self-conscious about his youthful appearance. Again he lingered in the doorway searching for a familiar face—perhaps someone from Billy Eckstine's band—who might know the whereabouts of Charlie Parker. While Hawkins was taking a break between sets, he noticed Miles peering at the musicians and walked over and said hello.

"You're Coleman Hawkins, right?"

"Yes, who are you?"

"My name's Miles Davis. I've played trumpet with Billy Eckstine's band in St. Louis. You know Charlie Parker?"

"Miles, everybody on The Street knows Bird. What do you want with him?"

"Well, when I played with him in St. Louis he told me to look him up on Fifty-second Street." Miles felt at ease with Hawkins. "I want to play with him. I could learn from him."

Hawkins chuckled and shook his head. "Listen, Miles, maybe you should just go back to St. Louis. Now, don't get me wrong, I love Bird, but you're just a kid. How old are you anyway, sixteen, seventeen? Believe me, you don't want to get mixed up with Bird."

Miles insisted. "Look, I want to find him. I'm going to Juilliard, but my reason for being in New York is to learn from Bird. Do you know where he is or not?"

Hawkins shook his head again. "You're a persistent little bastard, aren't you? Look, nobody ever knows where Bird is, or where he'll turn up, unless he's got a gig. And even then, nobody's ever really sure that he'll show. But you may want to go uptown to Minton's or Small's Paradise—Bird loves to jam at those places." Hawkins turned and started to walk back to the stand. He glanced back over his shoulder at Miles. "But my best advice to you is, just do your studying at Juilliard."

Miles had tremendous respect for Hawkins as a musician, but these words of warning meant nothing to him. He had already made up his mind to find Charlie Parker, and as Miles still says, "When I make up my mind to do something, I do it. Period."

Dr. Davis had given his son enough money to last a

month, but Miles went through the entire amount that first week, looking for Charlie Parker. Following Coleman Hawkins's tip, he went to Harlem hoping that Parker might be hanging out at Small's Paradise or Minton's, the club known as the birthplace of bop. No luck. However, a bass player at Small's told Miles that Bird had friends in the Village—artists, writers, drug dealers, the new generation of hipster bohemians. But Miles's subsequent trip downtown was also to no avail—no one at the coffee houses on Bleecker Street knew for certain where Bird was. Everyone, however, was up on the latest rumors about him, and Miles found himself chasing all over town.

During his search he made a valiant attempt to attend classes at Juilliard, although they had already begun to bore and irritate him. As Miles recalls, "They showed me things that I already knew when I was fourteen, about theory and all that shit. They stretched everything out at Juilliard—but I did improvisation and I had imagination."

During that week he became an increasingly familiar face on Fifty-second Street. To the regulars he was, in the words of drummer Jimmy Cobb, "Good people, just a timid little guy looking for Bird, not getting into any trouble, minding his own business." Dexter Gordon, considered to be the first important bop tenor saxophonist, remembers, "Back then we used to call him Sweetcakes. He was drinking malted milks and eating jelly beans. But of course that didn't last too long." Musicians noticed this new young kid at the back of the Front Door, listening to the astonishing Art Tatum, or hanging out at the Onyx and becoming friends with Coleman Hawkins. He was constantly alert for rumors about Parker's whereabouts, but no one really seemed to know where he was.

Miles finally got the break he was waiting for. In a musicians' trade paper he noticed that Parker was scheduled to play a jam session at a funky little club in Harlem called the Heatwave. Miles asked Coleman Hawkins if Bird was really going to be at the session. Hawkins just shrugged and smiled. "I'll bet *Bird* doesn't even know if he'll be there."

The Heatwave was a dingy club in an even dingier neighborhood, but Miles remembers it with reverence. "Sure, the Heatwave was a shithole in a crummy part of Harlem—where else? But the only thing that was important to me was that Charlie Parker was playing there. I couldn't wait to walk through the door of that fuckin' dive."

The jam sessions that took place at clubs like the Heatwave, Minton's, or Monroe's Uptown were meant mainly for the ears of fellow musicians. Jam sessions had long played an important role in the development of jazz, but in the forties they took on a special significance: the musicians used them to test their ability to handle bop's labyrinthine chord progressions, unpredictable rhythms, and melodic complexity. Many musicians who had mastered the music of the swing era had second thoughts about continuing as jazz players when they played in sessions with Thelonious Monk, Kenny Clarke, Dizzy Gillespie, or, of course, Charlie Parker. According to legend, when Ben Webster—the great tenor saxophonist who played with Duke Ellington, among others—first heard Charlie Parker wailing on a tenor sax, he went up and grabbed the horn out of Bird's mouth. "This horn is not meant to be played like that," he asserted adamantly. But later that night he went all over New York telling fellow musicians that the new messiah of the saxophone was in town.

Miles had played in numerous jam sessions in St.

Louis, and he was anxious to find out how he would fare with some of New York's more advanced musicians. Coleman Hawkins had once said, "No matter how good a musician is at home, he sounds different in New York City." Miles was aware that New York was the real test, and he hoped to prove himself that night at the Heatwave with Charlie Parker.

Among the players Miles met at the club were tenor player Allen Eager, one of the few white musicians respected by the great black players; Tommy Potter, the bassist who would eventually play with Miles and Bird in the classic Parker quintet; and Joe Guy, one of the early bop pioneers who played with Monk and Kenny Clarke at Minton's. Miles's attitude toward them was "Who cares? Charlie Parker is coming."

Not surprisingly Bird wasn't there for most of the evening, and Miles began to worry that he wouldn't show up after all. He kept an eye on the entrance, and finally, late in the evening, walked outside the club for a breather. He was standing on the street for only a few moments when he heard a voice behind him say "Hello, Miles. I hear you've been looking for me."

Miles turned and saw Bird. Wearing old, baggy clothes, his face haggard and his eyes drooping, Charlie Parker seemed far older than his twenty-four years. He had an aura of experience and street wisdom, and Miles knew enough to keep his cool in the presence of this consummate hipster.

"Yeah," Miles answered. "I've been looking for you. You remember me from St. Louis?"

Bird smiled his sunniest junkie smile. "Sure I remember, Miles. You play trumpet, and you knew my music."

"Well, you told me to look you up if I came to New York. But you're not the easiest motherfucker to find."

"Well, I move around," said Bird, chuckling. "But I heard you in there. You've improved some since I heard you in St. Louis." He put his arm around Miles's shoulder and walked him back into the Heatwave. "Let me lead you into the kingdom, my boy." He spoke with a thick British accent learned from many of the films that he loved.

That night at the Heatwave, Miles witnessed a transformation he was to see many times again. Charlie Parker approached the bandstand a nodding junkie, but when he put his horn to his mouth, he played a continuous flow of inspired melodic ideas, with such a sense of authority that he aroused gasps and joyous laughter from even the most jaded musicians. This contrast between Bird's seedy appearance and the brilliance of his playing was a large part of his legend.

Beginning with that night at the Heatwave, Charlie Parker would be at the core of Miles's life for three and a half years. When Parker learned that Miles had a midtown room, he easily convinced Miles to let him move in. At night Miles would listen to Bird play, and he would notate the chords on matchbook covers. The next day he would go to Juilliard and instead of attending classes would go to a piano practice room and play the chords. He was really creating his own curriculum, based on what he heard on The Street.

Bird was not Miles's only teacher. Dizzy Gillespie also took an immediate and genuine interest in him, and soon became his primary influence. Miles and Freddie Webster, another young trumpet player, would go together to Fifty-second Street and listen with amazement to Gillespie's soaring virtuosity. At fantastically fast tempos Gillespie could play in seemingly any range, pouring out a stream of musical ideas almost as star-tlingly original as those of Charlie Parker. Gillespie was also the consummate showman, joking with his audi-ence, always alert to making his complex new music di-gestible to the average listener.

Gillespie encouraged Miles to study piano in order to expand his knowledge of harmony. Parker took him to the West Side home of the iconoclastic pianist Thelon-ious Monk, who was one of the chief architects of the bop movement. Monk was also one of the most eccen-tric men in music. He would rarely speak to any musi-cians who played with him; rather, he would demonstrate his musical intents by playing elliptical chords on the piano. Years later he even showed Col-trane how to play two notes on the saxophone at once, although he had never played the horn himself. When he soloed, he would dangle his feet in a macabre dance and grunt for rhythmic emphasis. He was also stub-born. He played his uniquely idiosyncratic music in the forties, when his unorthodox tunes and approach to the piano sounded totally bizarre and foreign, a private musical world. Twenty years later, when he was ac-cepted as a jazz original and had enthusiastic fans throughout the world, Monk's music remained un-changed.

Miles was intrigued by Monk's masterful and idiosyn-cratic manipulation of mysterious-sounding chord pro-gressions, but he was especially fascinated by Monk's use of space in his solos. Most young bop musicians seemed intent on squeezing in every possible note while soloing, but Monk had a very definite sense of when to play, when to hold back, and when to introduce a mu-sical idea subtly through variants and fragments rather than overtly stating it. This use of space had a tremen-dous impact on Miles; transformed by his own personal

Coleman Hawkins (far left) and his band playing at the Spotlite Club, 1944, with Thelonious Monk on piano (Frank Driggs Collection).

touch, it eventually became one of the keystones of his style. Thanks largely to Monk, he realized that although he couldn't play trumpet as fast or as high as Dizzy ("I couldn't even hear him up there," Miles would later say), he could use his fine musical mind to forge a style based on subtlety and musical restraint.

Miles looks back on these times as "the most exciting—the best times of my life." But he quickly discovered that living with Charlie Parker was often a nightmare. He was surprised to see how casual Bird was about his heroin habit and was also amazed at Parker's other voracious appetites. Bird was an incredibly heavy drinker, which is unusual for a junkie; also unlike most junkies, he had an enormous appetite for food, as well as for sex. His casual attitude toward sex surprised even the most sophisticated hipsters.

In order to support his drug habit, Parker conned everyone around him out of money. As his roommate, Miles found himself a frequent victim of these cons, particularly since he was receiving support money from his father. Bird would approach him with a line like "Miles, I had to hock my horn. I can't play the gig tonight unless I get my sax out of hock. If you could lend me twenty dollars, I'll be able to make the gig. Don't let me down, Miles. I got to play tonight." Who could turn down a great artist in need of his tools? Certainly not his apprentice. More often than not, Miles would "loan" Parker the money. Bird would then go out and score some junk, then hit up another friend with the same story. He always seemed utterly sincere; he was as great an actor as he was a musician.

He was even less scrupulous when he was in desperate need of a fix. Once, Miles came home to find his suitcase missing. Bird was sitting on the floor, nodding out. He had pawned the suitcase. Dexter Gordon remembers another story that demonstrates the lengths to which Parker would go:

> One night Bird was working at the Three Deuces and he came on the stand wearing a suit with the sleeves ending about four inches above his wrists. And the bottom of the pant legs ended at the middle of his calf. I mean, you could see that this ain't this guy's suit! He was wearing Miles's suit because his own suit was in the pawnshop and he had to make the gig. So Miles had to stay in the pad because he didn't have another suit. Bird was five feet nine, and that suit was for a man Miles's size, five feet four; but when the motherfucker

came up and played he sounded just like he was wearing a tailor-made. The next day he got his own suit out of the pawnshop so that Miles could have his suit back and finally come out of the room.

Although Miles was often irritated by Parker's con games and bawdy life-style, he still looked up to the saxophonist in a very special way. And Bird, in turn, often referred to Miles as his "son." Miles often reflected on how totally different Parker was from his real father: Dr. Davis constantly worried about his social status, while Parker didn't give a damn what anybody thought about him. Miles's father took great pride in his appearance, a trait which he passed on to his son, while Bird dressed like a hobo. Miles's father believed in the Puritan work ethic; to Parker, work was a way to have kicks and earn enough money to stay high. And yet he did become a sort of father figure to Miles, although he was only six years his senior. At times when Miles felt he was not yet ready to sit in with Coleman Hawkins or Benny Carter, Bird would literally push him toward the stage, whispering in his ear, "Go on up there, now. Don't be afraid." Since Miles still was hampered by a limited trumpet technique, he often heard musicians mutter "I'm walking off if that motherfucker comes on the stand." Parker reassured him by telling him how he had gone through the same thing as a young and inexperienced saxophonist in Kansas City. Without this constant reassurance, Miles, sensitive and vulnerable, might easily have done what many others did—gone home and forgotten about a career in jazz.

Charlie Parker's sponsorship of Miles piqued the interest of a number of musicians, among them Herbie Fields, a saxophone player in Lionel Hampton's band, who hired Miles to play his first record date. Miles was nervous and on edge at the session, and this was readily apparent to the seasoned Fields. So Miles played only in the ensembles, not taking any solos. But the experience boosted his ego considerably and made him feel like a professional.

Gradually he gained acceptance among the musicians of Fifty-second Street. He kept so busy playing, listening, and learning that he had no time for the omnipresent distractions of liquor, drugs, or even sex. As Miles remembers, "There were lots of bitches who threw themselves at the musicians, but I wasn't interested in fucking or getting high, or any of that shit. I just wanted to play." Music was his entire life.

Among the friendships that Miles formed during this period was one with the trumpet player Freddie Webster. Although Webster didn't play with the flash or fire of Dizzy Gillespie or Fats Navarro, he had a full, gorgeous tone which he used to maximum effect in fashioning lovely ballad and blues solos. His legato style would have great influence on Miles's own developing ballad approach. The two trumpeters would spend hours practicing with each other, trading ideas leading toward a more refined form of bop. They would then go to the Three Deuces or the Onyx to hear Dizzy play his superhumanly fast solos, which both men found overwhelming but stimulating to their own artistic growth. Unfortunately, Webster died a very young man, but his influence was almost as important as that of Gillespie on the young Miles.

Miles especially enjoyed playing with Coleman Hawkins's band at the Three Deuces. Billie Holiday was the star attraction at the club, and she had recently married Joe Guy, the trumpet player in the band. Both of them used drugs heavily. Joe, who was even more erratic than Billie, often didn't show up at all at the

Deuces, and when this happened, Hawkins let Miles sit in. Within a short time he knew the entire repertoire of the group.

When Joe did show up, Miles would walk two doors down to the Spotlite Club to sit in with tenor man Eddie "Lockjaw" Davis. Lockjaw was, and still is, an exuberant player; his style lay somewhere between bebop and the swing-style tenor of Chu Berry. Davis eventually hired Miles for his first professional New York gig—one month at the Spotlite—although Miles was not sure whether it was due to his persistence or his musical ability.

In mid-autumn of 1945 Miles joined Charlie Parker's band for a two-week engagement at the Three Deuces. Bird had Al Haig on piano and Stan Levey on drums, two of the select company of white musicians who were respected by the bop elite. Curly Russell, who played intermittently in Parker's band, was on bass. Immediately upon joining the group Miles realized that the sound of Parker's alto made him play differently from the way he did with other saxophone players. Bird's tone was fuller than his records suggest. After Parker's death Miles told a writer, "They should have recorded Charlie Parker with a good big band. Then you would have heard how big his sound was." Although the trumpet has traditionally been the lead instrument in jazz, Miles knew that his own tone was not large enough to dominate the ensemble playing of the quintet. Therefore, in order to complement Bird's sound, he played "under" the saxophonist on the melody and, in Miles's words, "let Parker lead and swing the note."

Although Miles was steadily improving as a musician, he was unfailingly overwhelmed by Bird's virtuosity and musical brilliance. Every night he would ask Parker "What do you need me for?" and often he would quit, or at least make a pretense of quitting. However, Parker's superb ear recognized Miles's original approach to jazz trumpet, and he would insist that Miles stay with the band.

Miles's personal style was already apparent. Dexter Gordon recalls, "We were all like brothers. It was like one big family. As far as Miles's style . . . why, Miles sounded like Miles. He had that same sound that you still associate with him. . . . He already had that special musical conception for trumpet."

In November 1945 Charlie Parker held his first recording session as a leader for Savoy Records, a small independent label. To Miles's surprise, Bird brought him in to play trumpet on the date; Miles genuinely didn't believe that he was ready. The session became legendary, not only because of the exciting and important music that was produced, but also because of the bizarre circumstances of the date itself.

The musicians originally scheduled for the session were Bud Powell on piano, Curly Russell on bass, and Max Roach on drums. Powell, the great bop pianist, was extremely erratic and did not get along well with Parker. Bird once said, "I taught him everything, including how to be crazy." Not surprisingly, Powell never showed up for the session. The first order of business, then, was to find a piano player, and fast, since the recording facilities had been rented by the hour.

But it was difficult to sort anything out. There was a constant flow of curious musicians, hipsters, girlfriends, dope dealers (looking for Bird, of course), and other fringe characters of the Fifty-second Street bebop scene. Parker himself was late, and when he finally did show up, he seemed to have little concern for getting the session underway. By this time Miles was so exasperated that he went into the control room and took a nap.

Parker disappeared into the bathroom with a dope

dealer and emerged an hour later, announcing that he was ready to begin. By that time the harried producer had found a replacement for Bud Powell, a Monk-influenced pianist named Argonne Thornton. Dizzy Gillespie also appeared, anxious to help out in any way he could.

Dizzy actually wound up playing piano, as an accompanist, for more than half the session. He might also have been tempted to play trumpet, because Miles was having difficulty with much of the new material. Dizzy did wind up playing on "Ko-Ko," because Miles was simply unable to play the fast tune. Parker's playing was not only one of the highlights of his career but a milestone in jazz, particularly on the magnificent "Ko-Ko." Miles's technical limitations are evident on these records, but his solo on "Now's the Time" showed that he had a unique blues approach, and that his musical ideas were both lyrical and original. However, when "Now's the Time" was released on a Savoy 78, the reviewer for *down beat* overlooked Miles's potential and attacked his playing: "The trumpet man, whoever the misled kid is, plays Gillespie in the same manner as a majority of the kids who copy their idol do—with most of the faults, lack of order and meaning, the complete adherence to technical acrobatics. This is the sort of stuff that has thrown innumerable impressionable young musicians out of stride, that has harmed many of them irreparably. This can be as harmful to jazz as Sammy Kaye." This first review of his playing undoubtedly laid the foundation for Miles's contemptuous attitude toward critics.

As exciting as Miles's musical experiences continued to be with Charlie Parker, he became increasingly exasperated living with him. Irene lived with them for a while, but she found Parker impossible to deal with, particularly as a roommate. He was constantly bringing people into the apartment: girlfriends, dope dealers, other musicians. Irene found Bird's addiction distasteful, and the dope dealers who came by to collect from Miles seemed dangerous (and probably were). She eventually went back to East St. Louis, with Miles's consent, although once she was there he urged her to return to New York.

Miles continued to go to Juilliard, but he spent almost all his time in the practice rooms, where he could concentrate on music without being bothered by Bird and his friends. He told his parents that he was working hard as a student, though he knew they would be upset if they found out the real nature of his studies.

When Parker announced that he was going on the road in an all-star bebop group with Dizzy, Miles decided to return to East St. Louis, at least for a while. He had to straighten things out with his family and his wife, to let them know that, like it or not, he was committed to being a bebop musician. In addition, he needed to get away from the frenzy of the Fifty-second Street scene in order to catch his breath.

But he knew that he would be back, that Swing Street held an unrelenting grip on his future.

Chasin' the Bird

Miles's stay in East St. Louis turned out to be short. His parents were confused by his return. They had hoped he would start leading a "normal" life and could not understand why he had stopped going to classes at Juilliard or why he was not going to settle down with his wife. Miles told them, "There are these two musicians named Yardbird Parker and Dizzy Gillespie, and they're playing a new kind of jazz called bebop." Yardbird? Dizzy? Bebop? Miles's mother couldn't understand what he was talking about. Surely, these crazy jazz musicians were affecting her son. But Dr. Davis was impressed by Miles's dedication.

In December 1945 Benny Carter's band came to East St. Louis to play the Riviera. Miles went backstage to see Benny, whom he knew from Fifty-second Street. En route to Illinois one of Carter's trumpet players had quit, and Benny asked Miles to join the band as lead trumpet. Miles was surprised, since he had never thought of himself as a lead man. When Carter told him that the band was heading for the West Coast, Miles agreed to join, because Parker and Gillespie were in Los Angeles and he was anxious to hook up again with Bird. But he firmly declined to play lead trumpet.

Miles's parents and wife were understandably distressed upon hearing his decision to tour with Carter. He explained to them as best he could that touring was part of a musician's life and that his mentors were now on the West Coast.

He joined the tour and quickly became bored. As great as Benny Carter was, Miles still had no interest in playing charts or being a big-band trumpet player. He could never stop thinking about the music Bird was playing; big-band swing was dull by comparison.

Meanwhile Parker and Gillespie were not finding California hospitable. They had arrived on the West Coast as missionaries, bringing the word of bebop and believing they would be treated like the new princes of jazz during their eight-week engagement at Billy Berg's nightclub in Hollywood. But though the opening was a huge success, within a week the band was playing to half-filled houses consisting essentially of nondrinkers, a small clique of jazz enthusiasts and musicians. Billy Berg suggested to the band, "You're gonna have to sing or something."

Struggling to establish a musical foothold in California, Parker and Gillespie made some novelty recordings with Slim Gaillard and participated in an Armed Forces Radio Services broadcast. But they were still unable to generate much enthusiasm for the new music.

The Parker-Gillespie sextet closed at Billy Berg's the

first week of February 1946. A young jazz enthusiast named Ross Russell arranged for the group to record on his new label, Dial, with a special guest appearance by Lester Young, one of Parker's idols. Lester, however, led a life almost as disorganized as Bird's, and neither showed up for the session. This is unfortunate, because the ideas of Parker and Gillespie derived from many of Young's musical innovations of the thirties.

The band's appearances on the West Coast were not entirely inconsequential. Their music excited and encouraged many of the more progressive West Coast musicians as well as the hipper members of the jazz community, who up until that time had heard the new jazz only on the few bop records that had been released. But Dizzy decided that it was imperative for business reasons to return to New York, where he and the other members of the band were becoming genuine stars. He bought airline tickets for each member of the band, all of whom were glad to return home. At the last minute, however, and in typical fashion, Charlie Parker decided to sell his ticket for heroin.

Parker quickly found a job in the Finale Club, located in an old office building, in L.A.'s Little Tokyo. The long room, once a meeting place for a Japanese cultural society, had a small stage at one end and a low tin ceiling that provided excellent acoustics. Bird was the main attraction at what soon became a West Coast Minton's, drawing such up-and-coming West Coast musicians as Stan Getz, Zoot Sims, Gerry Mulligan, Shorty Rogers, and Charlie Ventura. The sessions at the Finale Club in 1946 were considered by many musicians to be among the best in the country.

In late February Parker signed an exclusive, one-year contract with Dial Records. He told Ross Russell that he was turning over a new leaf and that he wanted to record with people who would bring a new sound to his music. He wanted a trumpet player who played differently from Dizzy. According to Russell, Bird was interested in playing with "a different sort of musician, someone who played a relaxed legato style, with a warm tone in the lower and middle registers, someone like Miles Davis."

As soon as Miles arrived in Los Angeles, he heard that Bird was playing at the Finale. He went to see him that night.

A poster in the lobby proclaimed "Charlie Parker— New Star, Alto Saxophone, 1945 Esquire Jazz Poll—and His Orchestra." Miles walked past darkened offices until he came to the club. Although only five feet four, he could almost touch the low metal sheeting overhead. On stage Bird glanced up but continued playing.

After the set ended, Parker walked off the stand and, smiling, joined Miles at one of the small tables. "I had a feeling you were going to show up," he said.

"I just got into town. I'm playing with Benny Carter's band."

Bird seemed embarrassed. "Diz and the rest went back to New York. Dizzy got out while the getting was good, and now I'm catching everything. People here just aren't ready for our music, Miles." Bird's eyes were red and his pupils were pin-sized. Miles detected something; he had heard a difference in Bird's playing, and now he could see a difference in his face, too. Bird was very sensitive, and the emotional strain he was suffering in California was taking its toll.

They went outside for a smoke. Bird was silent for a few minutes. Finally he looked up and asked, "Miles, why don't you play with my band?"

Miles knew even before this invitation that he had to play with Parker again, but he didn't want to give up the regular pay he was getting from Benny Carter. So he decided to stay with Carter, who was performing at an L.A. hotel, and play with Bird after he finished his last set with the big band. This worked for a while—until the union learned he was "doubling" and fined him. This made him angry enough to quit Carter's band and play exclusively with Parker.

In March 1946 Ross Russell held his first recording session for Dial Records, not counting the aborted Charlie Parker–Lester Young affair. This time he made sure that Parker was sober enough to conduct a session, and had him assemble the best modern jazz musicians available on the West Coast. They included Miles, tenor saxophonist Lucky Thompson, pianist Dodo Marmarosa, guitarist Arv Garrison, Vic McMillan on bass, and Roy Porter on drums.

Miles was nervous and stiff, and his solos reflect his mental condition. He had trouble learning some of the tunes Bird wanted to use, in particular Dizzy's classic "A Night in Tunisia." If anything, he seemed to have stepped backward from the original approach he'd displayed the year before on "Now's the Time." Parker was magnificent, however, particularly on "Tunisia," where he took a break which left the other musicians gasping. Unfortunately, the ensemble was too clumsy, mainly due to Miles, and the tune had to be redone. Among the other tunes recorded were Parker's lyrical "Yardbird Suite," "Ornithology," and "Moose the Mooch," named after Bird's L.A. drug connection, who collected half the royalties in exchange for heroin. Despite Miles's technical clumsiness the session was so successful that upon release of the records Dial was established as an important new label on the jazz scene.

Shortly after this session was completed, the Los Angeles area suffered a severe drug drought. In addition, the vice squad started to crack down on the shadier nightclubs, and the Finale Club was closed down. One night when Miles showed up for work, he was told that not only was the Finale Club having its finale, but that Bird had disappeared.

Parker was not found until a few days later, going through heroin withdrawal in a converted garage and subsisting on a diet of port wine. He had been staying with Dorothy and Howard McGhee (a fine modern jazz trumpeter). They were a racially mixed couple who, despite constant harassment by the Los Angeles Police Department, took over and reopened the Finale Club. Bird resumed playing there and now had a place to live with loyal friends. But, forced to give up heroin because the drug was simply not available, he was drinking heavily, sometimes more than a quart of whiskey a day. In addition, he was taking pills, particularly benzedrine. The combination was wreaking havoc with his nervous system.

Once more Miles hooked up with him, but Parker was obviously out of control. Some nights Miles would arrive at the club and find him backstage, fast asleep. He would wake him up and push him onstage. Once the rhythm section started up, Parker would blow, but the sound wasn't nearly as pretty as it had been. His body would often twitch; sometimes he would play while sitting on a chair facing the rear of the bandstand, his leg kicking up or his head jerking to one side. Miles knew that the young musicians playing with the band were confused, but they worshiped Bird—up to a point. One night, in the middle of a set, Parker stopped and sang to Joe Albany, the piano player, in order to show him how he wanted to be accompanied. This totally confused Joe, and in the middle of a tune he turned to Bird and said, "Fuck you." Bird fired him right on the bandstand.

As it became increasingly frustrating to work with the self-destructive Parker, Miles began to look for other work in Los Angeles. Lucky Thompson offered him a job playing with his small band at the Elks Ballroom. There was a young bass player in the band who was very anxious to meet him, Lucky explained, because he idolized Bird and wanted to know anybody who played with him. The bass player's name was Charlie Mingus. Mingus was a very ambitious musician who had already played with Louis Armstrong and Lionel Hampton and who wanted desperately to play with Charlie Parker. That Bird was a god to Mingus annoyed Miles, who knew firsthand about Bird's mortality. He told the young bassist how Bird was declining rapidly, barely able to lead a group. Mingus was disgusted: he had expected Miles to be totally loyal to Parker, the man who had given so much to the world. Miles could only shake his head.

Charlie Parker's relationship with Dial Records became understandably strained. He was demanding advances against future earnings, and he kept insisting that he was ready to hold another recording session, using Miles and the rest of the Finale band. Ross Russell had serious doubts, but finally agreed to another session. He rented a studio for several hours, ample time for a recording, and brought along a psychiatrist. At the last minute Bird arrived with a different band, substituting Howard McGhee for Miles. Bird was obviously in very bad shape, and when he finally started playing, he sounded mechanical and uneven. The psychiatrist talked to him for a while and decided—although he was not really sure—that Bird was probably suffering from acute alcoholism and malnutrition. He gave him six phenobarbital tablets, not really knowing how they would affect the musician's nervous system. The band recorded one tune right after another—"Lover Man," "The Gypsy," and "Be Bop"—without wasting time for playbacks and rerecording. The barbiturates took their effect, and by the time "Be Bop" was finished, so was Bird. He collapsed in a chair and had to be taken to a room at the Civic Hotel.

Later, still groggy from the phenobarbital, he wandered downstairs into the lobby to make a phone call, oblivious to the fact that he was naked. The hotel manager persuaded him to return to his room. Shortly after this the fire department was summoned. Bird's room was on fire.

Ten days afterward, Ross Russell found him, straitjacketed, in the psychopathic ward of the county jail. From there Bird was eventually transferred to Camarillo State Hospital.

When Miles found out that Bird was in a state hospital, he felt a sense of relief, knowing that at this point hospitalization was necessary. He hoped that Bird would kick his addictions and come back on the musical scene.

Work was scarce in Los Angeles for a modern-jazz musician, and most of the time Miles was unemployed. But Mingus had saved some money, and while waiting for Bird to be released from Camarillo, he decided to record on his own with a small band including Miles, Lucky Thompson, and a young reed man named Buddy Collette. This recording was never released. In August, Lucky Thompson put together a band consisting of many of the same musicians. He leased the Elks Ballroom and billed as a key member of the band "the brilliant young trumpet player Miles Davis, last heard here with Benny Carter." This did not come to much either, and Thompson, discouraged by the lack of interest in modern jazz in L.A., soon joined the popular Boyd Raeburn band.

Miles found work here and there at some of the small clubs around town, but he was quickly tiring of the West Coast. Since no one knew when Bird would be released, it seemed pointless to remain in California. In September, Billy Eckstine's band showed up to play engagements as part of a cross-country tour. Eckstine's trumpet player was the brilliant Fats Navarro, but Fats had problems tragically similar to Bird's and midway through the tour he had to quit. Eckstine offered the seat to Miles, who immediately accepted. Not only would he have steady work, but Eckstine's band was still the most musically advanced around. It was also heading, eventually, for New York, and Miles longed to go back east.

Mingus, having heard that Miles was returning to New York with the Eckstine band, cornered him one night between sets. "Tell me how you can go to New York and leave Bird behind," he angrily demanded.

Miles was silent.

"He needs you, and you're abandoning him!"

"I can't do nothing for Charlie Parker, Mingus, much as I love him," Miles told Mingus. "Listen. He's in a mental hospital, and no one knows when he'll get out. He's all fucked up."

"You're an asshole, Miles. That man made you."

"And I've got to get back to New York."

"Bird's your papa."

"He'll understand, Mingus. Bird will understand."

Mingus gave up. Miles was adamant about returning east. They would work together in the future, but they would never be on close terms. When Mingus died in 1979, all Miles would say about his death was, "He was too fat."

Miles went east with Eckstine in the fall of 1946. By this time the band included tenor men Gene Ammons and Sonny Stitt, drummer Art Blakey, and Tommy Potter on bass, the cream of the bebop crop. Miles recorded with them when they returned to New York and played a few engagements, enjoying the work. But by 1947 big-band work was scarce, and keeping a band together was economically difficult. Even with his popularity as a singer, Eckstine found it impossible to find enough work to cover the payroll, and he finally gave up and disbanded. Miles formed a group with Sonny Stitt and Gene Ammons that briefly managed to find a little work, playing Chicago's Jumptown. By March 1947 he was once again playing in a Fifty-second Street club, the Spotlite, with tenor man Illinois Jacquet. Miles welcomed the opportunity to play once again with small groups. He loved the Eckstine band, but it didn't give him enough opportunity to stretch out as a soloist.

Around this time he began hearing rumors that Bird had been released from Camarillo in good health, that he was recording in Los Angeles and was due back in New York soon. Miles hoped this was true. His hopes were realized one April evening when Bird walked into the Spotlite, looking ten years younger. For the first times Miles could remember, Parker's eyes were clear and he seemed free of drugs.

Parker was glad to see Miles, too. "I'm fine," he said, "I'm clean. I have so many ideas. I just want to play and write music, and I want you to play with me again." His plan was to put together a band that would play regularly. He included first Miles and Max Roach, then he hired Tommy Potter and Duke Jordan, a young pianist and composer. Despite the nightmarish experiences of the past, Miles was extremely happy to be playing again with his mentor. Not only did he play better with Parker's encouragement, he simply loved to listen to Bird's seemingly endless supply of beautiful musical ideas, night after night.

Bird rented the Nola studios, a favorite among jazz musicians for rehearsing their bands. This would be the first time he had taken the time to carefully rehearse his band, and the musicians were excited about the prospects of the group. But on the first day of rehearsal, everybody showed up except Parker. After waiting almost two hours, Miles finally said, "Okay, we're supposed to open at the Three Deuces in a couple of days, and we have to rehearse with or without that motherfucker, so I'll just try and keep the shit together."

Opening night at the Deuces, Parker showed—the first time anyone in the band had seen him in days. Incredibly, he knew every tune, in the key the band played it in. And his playing was better than ever, more lucid, with an even prettier sound and as exciting as it ever had been. Miles continued to rehearse the band for as long as it existed, because the leader never came to rehearsals.

Because of Miles's efforts, this was the tightest band Bird ever had, and probably the most coherent bop unit around. The Deuces extended their engagement indefinitely. Parker seemed happier than he had ever been. For the first time he let audiences glimpse his warm sense of humor. He would announce, in a fake British accent, "Ladies and gentlemen, the management of the Three Deuces has gone to *enormous expense* to bring you the Charlie Parker quintet, who will now perform for you a composition that I hope you will enjoy." His exaggerated dignity was a hilarious parody of square announcers.

Max Roach remembers how Parker liked to warm up the band: "He would begin the first set with the fastest, most difficult tune in our book. I would be scuffling with the drums, Miles would be spitting, neither of us warmed up enough to play such a tune. But then the rest of the night he would play 'Slow Boat to China' or anything that was slower and easier than that first tune. Playing that fast first one was just how he liked to warm up his own horn. But it drove Miles and me crazy."

Bird was off heroin, but he was drinking heavily. He would often line up eight double shots of bourbon, drink them all in rapid succession, and then get up on the stand and play brilliantly. In typical style, he was spending enormous amounts of money, and often had some ridiculous excuse to explain why he couldn't pay the band, but they still stuck with him.

Fortunately Bird was no longer staying with Miles, who wanted to concentrate totally on music. Irene was again living with him in New York. He also scupulously stayed away from drugs and alcohol, unlike the many young musicians who were convinced that they could play like Bird if they indulged in the same vices. But Parker always told Miles that he played best when he was straight. He also confessed to Miles that he realized that many young musicians were turning to heroin be-cause of his influence. This worried him. "Miles," he would say, "if I ever catch you using junk, I'll kill you. And I mean that. I'll kill your ass if you mess with that shit." While Miles was in Bird's band he didn't even smoke pot—in fact, he hated the stuff.

Women were a bit more difficult for him to avoid. Every night after a gig there were women—the group-ies of their time—waiting for the musicians. But Miles put so much energy into his music that generally he had neither the time nor the energy to get involved with them. He didn't even pay much attention to Irene.

Bird's attitude toward women was, of course, far different. Women were mad about him, and if there was a woman in the audience with whom he was having an affair, he would look at her and play a musical quote from "You Go to My Head"—an easy enough code for the band members to decipher. Bird's sexual prowess never diminished—even after he went back on heroin, late in 1947.

Throughout 1947 Bird recorded regularly with his quintet, both for Savoy and Dial. The material was usually the blues or such standards as "I Got Rhythm" and "Indiana," although he used the common bop device of outfitting the harmonic structures of these tunes with new melodic lines. This technique had economic as well as artistic benefits, in that any royalties for use of the tune would be paid to the musicians rather than the composer of the original tune.

Listening carefully to the recordings, it is not difficult to recognize Miles's musical thinking and trace its maturation. Of course, Parker could play brilliantly at any speed and loved the faster tempos that gave Miles difficulty. Much as Miles wanted to emulate Fats Navarro or Dizzy Gillespie—trumpeters who had no trouble keeping pace with Parker—his chops would not respond. The more he played with Parker, the more he realized that he had to be selective with his notes, since he could not play every note in any range. In such ballads as "Embraceable You," which the band recorded for Dial, we can clearly see Miles's special musical intellect at work. As British critic Michael James wrote, "In such leisurely conditions [Miles] obviously found it much easier to think clearly. The line he creates is full of inventive twists and turns and his tone has a beauty that is all its own, admirably suited to the clear-cut phrases."

When these records were originally issued, many fans and critics thought that Miles, with his limited technique, was scarcely a foil for Parker. Indeed, many called his style "cold" and "lifeless." Thirty-five years later, however, it is evident why Parker used Miles rather than Navarro or Gillespie. Particularly in such ballad performances as "Embraceable You" or "My Old Flame," Miles is the perfect *complement* to Parker. His lovely, seemingly simple legato solos contrast wonderfully with Bird's ofttimes baroque solos. It was perhaps here that Miles began to conceive of the jazz performance as an entity unto itself, not simply a string of solos. This idea—that a jazz performance must have an overall coherence— was the musical direction that led years later to *Birth of the Cool,* the quintet recordings with John Coltrane, and even *Bitches Brew.*

In 1948 when Miles won the Esquire New Star Award for trumpet, he felt he had won because of his association with Bird, an association he was finding more and more difficult to maintain. Bird was slipping back into his old ways, accelerated by his return to heroin addiction.

Miles and Bird at the Spotlite Club, 1947 (Frank Driggs Collection).

An early publicity still of Miles (Institute of Jazz Studies).

One night backstage at the Three Deuces, as Bird sat at a table eating an enormous platter of fried chicken, Miles demanded furiously, "Bird, when the fuck are you going to pay me? I haven't been paid in weeks!"

Bird looked up, grinning his broad Buddha-like smile, not saying a word.

"Listen, Bird, you cocksucker, I want my pay and I want it right now."

Bird simply lifted a chicken breast to his mouth.

Miles grabbed Parker by his thick throat and shouted, "Pay me, motherfucker, or I'll kill you!"

Bird put the chicken down on the platter and said softly, "See, now you're mad." His manner was so matter-of-fact that Miles could do nothing but turn and walk away.

About a week after this incident, both Miles and Max Roach decided they were fed up. As much as Miles loved Bird's music, he could no longer put up with Bird's unpredictable behavior. Besides, he knew it was time to find his own musical way.

Miles walked off the bandstand and muttered to a friend, "Bird makes you feel one foot tall." Max and Miles left the club and went down to the Spotlite to see if they could get their own gig.

Birth of the Cool

Any authoritative list of essential jazz records is certain to include Miles's 1949–50 recording, *Birth of the Cool.* The "cool" or "West Coast" jazz movement is now merely an interesting footnote to jazz history, but Miles's recordings are still considered vitally important. Though cool jazz eventually became associated with the West Coast, its basic tenets were developed by such men as Miles, John Lewis, Gil Evans, Lee Konitz, Lennie Tristano, J. J. Johnson, and Gerry Mulligan. Most of these men were New York habitués associated with the Fifty-second Street modern-jazz scene. Even Max Roach and Kenny Clarke—the essential behop drummers—played with this seminal group.

If there was a birthplace of the cool-jazz movement— as Minton's and Monroe's Playhouse were the birthplace of bop—then it certainly was arranger Gil Evans's basement apartment on West Fifty-fifth Street, near Fifth Avenue. Located behind a Chinese laundry, it was an incredibly cramped one-room space, containing the pipes for the entire building, a piano, a small bed, a sink, and its one and only real appliance, a single hot plate. There was no heat other than whatever warmth radiated from the pipes.

Despite its distinct lack of comforts, Gil's tiny apartment attracted an astonishing flow of talented people: Gerry Mulligan, John Lewis, the composer John Benson Brooks, singer Blossom Dearie, Max Roach, arranger-composer George Russell—the list is very long. All of them had been excited by the new music on Fifty-second Street, and especially by Charlie Parker. Perhaps their central concern was the development of a somewhat more formal approach to the new jazz.

Miles first met Gil Evans when Evans approached him about adapting one of his compositions, "Donna Lee." Gil had been arranging for the Claude Thornhill band since the early forties and had been instrumental in establishing its subtle style. Miles had tremendous respect for Thornhill, and once told a reporter that Thornhill had "the greatest band of these modern times, with the exception of Billy Eckstine's band with Bird." He therefore immediately agreed to Evans's request, asking in return that Evans teach him his intricate harmonic style and let him study some of the Thornhill scores. Thus their friendship was born, as well as a musical collaboration that continues today.

This was, on the face of it, a peculiar collaboration. Gil Evans was a tall WASP, whose parents were Australian. Thirteen years older than Miles, he had spent most of the thirties arranging for white "sweet bands," until he started working for Claude Thornhill. With Thornhill, he began experimenting with instrumentation and advanced harmonic ideas. He was excited by the bebop revolution, immediately fascinated by the new music on Fifty-second Street. Despite the apparent differences between them, Gil and Miles immediately recognized that they were kindred spirits. Later Gil would say about Miles, "We think alike. We are complementary in that we are opposites. My inclination is just less extroverted than his. We both like the same kind of music." And about Gil, Miles would say, "You know, my ambition has always been to write like Gil. I'd give my right arm to do it—no, my left one, because I'd have to write the notes down."

Of course Miles had mixed feelings about leaving Bird's band. As difficult as it was working with Parker, it would be nearly impossible to find a musical group as challenging. And of course Bird had been the main impetus behind Miles's enormous musical development in the midforties. Nevertheless, Miles and Max Roach were convinced that they had to form their own band, even if it meant playing third on the bill at the Spotlite or the Onyx. Although their band was superb—it included brilliant Dexter Gordon on tenor sax—they soon found the going rough. Neither Max nor Miles had a big enough name to find steady work.

In addition the jazz scene was going through a difficult time. At the end of 1947 James Petrillo, head of the musicians' union, ordered a ban on recording. He was demanding that a percentage of the royalties on records go into the union's pension fund, claiming that due to the growing popularity of recorded music, jobs for professional musicians were becoming ever more scarce. Also, the Fifty-second Street musical scene was dying. In early 1948, Leonard Feather wrote an article for *Metronome* magazine called "The Street Is Dead: An Obit." Feather claimed that The Street was "headed for oblivion" due to "lack of talent with sufficient drawing power; exorbitant demands of talent with a following; rotten liquor and clip-joint attitude toward customers; and the low-life reputation The Street had acquired through its fringe of dope addicts and peddlers, pimps, prostitutes and assorted characters." Club owners were finding strippers far more lucrative than jazz, so much so that The Street acquired the new nickname of "Stripty-second Street."

However, Miles did manage to get the band a gig that lasted several weeks at a new club called the Royal Roost. Located on Broadway near Fifty-fourth Street, the Roost was a symbol of the changing times of jazz in New York. Unlike the clubs on Fifty-second Street, it had a cover in addition to a minimum. The owners of the Roost were serious businessmen and had a far less casual attitude than the club owners on Fifty-second Street. They did not encourage sitting in, which had made the Fifty-second Street scene so exciting and which helped to constantly revitalize the music. The Roost was to become the model for Birdland and almost every jazz club that followed. While gigs for jazz musicians at such establishments might be more lucrative, the demise of Fifty-second Street and its multitude of jazz clubs diminished the opportunities for professional musicians.

During this period Miles spent more and more time at Gil's little basement apartment. The group that assembled there often made a volatile mixture. Parker frequently dropped in, as did baritone saxophonist Gerry Mulligan and trumpet player and arranger John Carisi, who were both very hotheaded. Sometimes musical arguments nearly erupted into violence. But the general enthusiasm overrode personal differences. While Miles enjoyed this musical theorizing, he found himself becoming impatient: "Don't talk about it, do it." This is a philosophy by which he still leads his life.

The ideas that were being discussed had to be put to use in a larger, more formal band, rather than the usual bebop quintet of two horns and a rhythm section. Miles was anxious to put together a band with this unusual kind of instrumentation. The others were interested in Miles's ambition but doubted his ability to find work for them.

For the most part the big-band era was over. Many of the most popular bands of the thirties and early forties were broken up when their musicians were drafted during World War Two. And by the time the war had ended, such vocalists as Frank Sinatra, Billy Eckstine, and Peggy Lee were the popular favorites, none of whom needed the economic burden of retaining a big band in order to successfully tour. Dizzy had tried to keep a bebop big band together and found it economically impossible. Even such established leaders of the swing era as Count Basie and Duke Ellington had severe difficulties. For a while Basie even led a more economically viable septet.

Nevertheless, Miles was determined to go ahead. At this point Gil Evans, John Lewis, and Gerry Mulligan were his chief supporters. It was decided that a group consisting of six horns and three rhythm instruments was the smallest that could successfully convey their ambitious musical ideas. Groups of this size were not unknown to jazz at this time, but the particular instrumental configuration was unique. Miles insisted that they use both French horn and tuba. French horn had been used by Gil Evans in the Thornhill band, and Miles loved the effect. The tuba, which had been used in early jazz as a bass instrument, had long since gone out of style, and had never before been used in jazz as a melodic instrument. The other instruments were Miles's trumpet, alto sax (Lee Konitz), baritone sax (Gerry Mulligan), and trombone (various players, though usually bop innovator J. J. Johnson or Kai Winding). Gil Evans stated that this ensemble indicated "what voicing can do, how it can give intensity and relaxation. Consider the six horns Miles had in a nine-piece band. When they played together, they could be a single voice playing a single line. One-part writing in a way. But that sound could be altered and modified in many ways by the various juxtapositions of instruments."

Although Evans was clearly the leader of the burgeoning cool movement, he contributed only a few arrangements to Miles's nonet. "Gil had been ill and lost his feeling for arranging, temporarily; just as I lost my feeling for my horn after I was hospitalized," Miles recently recalled. So Gerry Mulligan and John Lewis did the bulk of the arranging, although Gil contributed at least two classic arrangements, including "Boplicity" (a tune written by Miles and Evans) and the old standard "Moon Dreams." Although Miles arranged only one piece, "Deception" (a vehicle he would record again with a small group), the sound of the band was, according to Gerry Mulligan, "the conception of the leader [Miles], mostly. Miles dominated that band completely; the whole nature of the interpretation was his. He took the initiative and put the theories to work. He called the rehearsals, hired the halls, called the players, and generally cracked the whip."

Since work was scarce, it was difficult for Miles to keep together a stable group of musicians who could play the difficult arrangements. A special problem he anticipated was finding French-horn players who had a feeling for jazz. Fortunately, there were a few who shared the enthusiasm of Miles, Mulligan, and Evans. One was Gunther Schuller, who became an important American composer and conductor, and who, along with John Lewis, was one of the leaders of the Third Stream movement, which combined jazz with classical music.

"It's funny," Miles said in a recent conversation, "everybody thinks that I'm a racist, that I hate all whites, or some bullshit. The band on my first record was almost all white! How could anybody think that I hate white people?" Actually, the members of the nonet changed, but the fact that the band was usually predominantly white was significant. The cool movement was associated, for the most part, with such white musicians as Lennie Tristano, Mulligan, Stan Getz, Dave Brubeck, and Chet Baker. However, the chief musical inspirations for the movement were Charlie Parker's ballads and medium-tempo blues, Lester Young's lyrical tenor saxophone, and Miles's restrained approach to bebop trumpet. White musicians, in particular, seemed attracted to this more introverted approach to modern jazz. There was a school of tenor sax playing that was actually called "white tenor." It included Brew Moore, Allen Eager, Al Cohn, Zoot Sims, Stan Getz, Warne Marsh, and Bill Perkins. Their styles were fashioned closely after that of Lester Young, and late in his life Young bitterly commented on the number of tenor men playing Birdland who never would have had a job in music had it not been for their ability to ape his style. In a *down beat* Blindfold Test, Miles commented that "all those white tenor players sound alike to me."

During his gig with Max Roach and Dexter Gordon at the Royal Roost in the summer of 1948, Miles had come to be on relatively good terms with the owners of

Miles and Stan Getz, 1949 (Frank Driggs Collection).

the club. And now again, through the impresario Monte Kay, he approached them about getting a gig for his new group. Count Basie was due to appear, and the owners agreed to use the nonet to spell the Basie band. Miles requested a special stipulation for the engagement—that the club put a sign out front that read "Miles Davis Band, Arrangements by Gerry Mulligan, Gil Evans, and John Lewis." This was the first time that the names of the arrangers were given such prominence in the billing of a band. Until the Roost gig the band had performed only at the Nola rehearsal hall, and then only when the musicians had some free time between performing or recording engagements. The Roost would be the acid test for the ideas they had hashed out at Gil's apartment.

Playing as a relief unit for Count Basie, the Miles

Davis Band provided a sharp contrast for jazz listeners
at the Royal Roost by its radical departure from the traditional big-band sound personified by Basie. Perhaps
one of the most interesting aspects of the engagement
was Basie's enthusiasm for the nonet. "Those slow
things sounded strange and good," Basie told a writer.
"I didn't know what they were doing, but I listened and
I liked it." Critics were for the most part enthusiastic,
but the nonet hardly scored a sensation. Miles, Evans,
and Mulligan were not surprised—they had expected
that any audience that came to hear Count Basie would
have difficulty sympathizing with their new sounds.

Despite the lukewarm response, Miles was determined to find the nonet more gigs and a recording contract. He had little else to distract him, unlike the other
musicians involved. His wife had again returned to East
St. Louis and he had virtually no interests outside of
music.

After the Roost owners decided to drop the nonet,
Miles convinced them to let him continue playing there
with a smaller group—Lee Konitz, John Lewis, Al
McKibbon, and Max Roach. In general, however, he
suddenly found himself with a lot of free time, which
he spent with aspiring musicians and the many han-
gers-on that have always afflicted the jazz scene. "I was
hanging out with the wrong types of motherfuckers,"
he recalls. "The main thing they wanted to do was get
high. But that's the way I was feeling. Things were
slow." Much of his enthusiasm for the jazz life had been
dampened by the disappointing reception to the nonet.
He had ingenuously assumed that the enthusiasm and
musical brilliance that had gone into the group would
be somehow rewarded. But the few gigs he got did little
to match the excitement of playing with the incompa-
rable Parker quintet.

One bright spot was his discovery that Capitol Records was interested in recording modern jazz. On December 15, 1948, the recording ban ended and when he approached Capitol with the idea of recording the nonet, his name was well enough known for them to sign him to his first contract. It called for the group to produce twelve sides.

Shortly before the first session, Miles played the Audubon, a small uptown jazz club, with Art Blakey and a nineteen-year-old tenor man named Sonny Rollins. Rollins was one of the second-generation bebop musicians, and Miles was tremendously impressed by him. Rollins had been a protégé of Charlie Parker and had learned from Thelonious Monk to solo using space and to incorporate the melody of a tune (rather than just the chord changes) into a solo. During the gig at the Audubon, Miles discovered that he and Rollins were working in similar directions, and they agreed to work together in the future. Rollins recalled, "Miles was a giant already to young guys like me and Jackie McLean [a young alto player]. We all looked up to him then. Of course, he turned out to be a star maker." But that would not happen for a few years, at least not for Sonny.

Also around this time Miles began playing with Tadd Dameron, one of the first and most important modern jazz arrangers, both in Dameron's rehearsal band and occasionally at the Royal Roost, where Dameron led the house band. Like Gil Evans, Dameron was one of the bop movement's chief theoreticians. He had a distinctly lyrical approach to the new jazz, and this had a strong influence on Miles. Dexter Gordon said, "I think Tadd really is the romanticist of the whole period—he's a poet." Also playing with Tadd was Fats Navarro, the trumpet player whom Miles, and many other musicians, consider to be the greatest of them all. Miles spent

Recording Birth of the Cool, *1949, with Lee Konitz (Frank Driggs Collection).*

a lot of time rehearsing with Navarro, learning his approach to fast tempos and teaching him, in return, his personal ballad style.

In January 1949 Miles went into the studio with the nonet. They recorded four tunes—"Jeru," "Move," "Godchild," and "Budo." These sides, in addition to offering marvelously ingenious arrangements, contained the most assured solos Miles had recorded until that time, completely unlike his hesitant playing on the recordings with Bird. He had found his style, a style he felt comfortable with. There was even a joyous quality, especially in the solos of "Godchild" and "Jeru."

Soon after this session the nonet played the small uptown Clique Club. This short engagement would be their last public performance. Attendance was small, and most of the customers were confused by the band's intentions. The music seemed too, well, *cool* for bop fans, who were used to the often feverish music of Bird or Dizzy or Bud Powell. "As for that 'Birth of the Cool' shit," Miles recalls, "I don't understand how they came to call it that. Someone just dropped that label on me. I think what they really mean is a soft sound—not penetrating too much. To play soft, you have to relax—you don't delay the beat, but you might play a quarter triplet against four beats, and that *sounds* delayed. If you do it right, it won't bother the rhythm section." Nevertheless, the cool label stuck to Miles for much of his career in the late forties and early fifties.

Although the nonet failed to gain public acceptance, Miles's spirits were somewhat buoyed by Capitol's release of two of its sides, "Move" and "Budo," a few weeks after they were recorded. Although the 78 sold poorly, the record company honored its contract and recorded the band again in April. Four more sides were completed, including "Boplicity" and "Israel," arranged by

Gil Evans and John Carisi respectively. These sides are regarded by many, along with Evans's arrangement of "Moon Dreams" (recorded at a later session), as the masterpieces of the series. In 1953, André Hodeir wrote, in *Jazz: Its Evolution and Essence,* " 'Boplicity' is enough to make Gil Evans qualify as one of jazz's greatest arranger-composers." Hodeir also observed in his now-classic book that "Miles Davis seems to be a kind of leader. After collaborating with Charlie Parker, this young colored trumpeter, the most gifted of his generation, took the initiative and produced straight off the most representative of the new school's works [the recordings of the nonet]. More than any other, his art attests the accomplishments and the promise of today's jazz."

Shortly after the April recording sessions Miles got some good news: he was booked to play the first Paris International Festival of Jazz, as coleader with Tadd Dameron of a group that, along with Charlie Parker's quintet, would represent modern jazz. The purpose of the Paris Festival was to present, within the space of eight days, the entire panorama of jazz, from Sidney Bechet to Charlie Parker and Miles Davis. In Europe, and especially France, jazz had a wide and serious audience. Miles discovered that he was a widely respected figure in France due to his recordings with Parker, and Bird himself was considered something close to a god. Miles appreciated this respect and admiration, as well as the Parisians' apparent lack of racial prejudice.

Two of the musicians playing in the Davis-Dameron quintet were black American musicians who had settled in Paris: James Moody, a brilliant saxophonist and former Dizzy Gillespie sideman, and Kenny Clarke, the father of bebop drumming. Moody would eventually return to America, but Clarke, after many years of shuttling back and forth, would become a permanent resident of Paris, only occasionally visiting his native land. He became a well-known, even revered, figure in France—something he probably never could have achieved in America.

The Paris Festival was a tremendous success, and Miles was particularly well received. Henri Renaud, a French pianist, remembers:

> Miles on that night—the first night of the festival—took his audience completely by surprise. On medium and fast tempos, people expected him to play *mezzo forte* and he played *forte*. Everybody thought he only felt at home in the medium register of his horn, only to discover that he could brilliantly court the high notes.

Indeed, Miles's playing at the festival was extraordinarily different from that on the nonet sides, recorded only weeks before. Here he was the virtuosic bopster; quite obviously the spirit of Fats Navarro had rubbed off on him during their recent association. The Davis-Dameron quintet played almost every concert during the eight-day festival, and Miles continued to play with extroverted confidence.

Through Clarke, Moody, and a coterie of Parisian jazz fans, most of whom were obsessed by the new music, Miles found himself meeting many of the most renowned figures in France. He recalls spending many hours on the Left Bank with Jean-Paul Sartre, Albert Camus, and Simone de Beauvoir. The improvisational nature of jazz, and the life-style of the jazz musician, had a special fascination for the French intellectuals. And Miles felt a kinship toward Sartre, saying recently, "I knew that Sartre was a lot like me. I knew that the

Nobel prize was just a lot of bullshit to him, just like all the awards I've won are to me. I told everybody that he would turn it down—I knew that he would." Of course, Miles himself has yet to turn down an award. His various placques—from *down beat, Playboy,* and *Esquire,* among others—hang on the wall behind his piano. "I like nice wood," is Miles's explanation for their prominent display.

He also met the French chanteuse Juliette Gréco. She, like Miles, was an up-and-coming musical star, and they were immediately drawn to each other. They began an intense affair, Miles's first real affair since his marriage. Juliette was fascinated by black music, and Miles was engaged by her lack of prejudice and her European manner. When Juliette asked Miles to travel with her— at her expense—to Mexico for a singing engagement, he seriously entertained the idea. However, his music was still his top priority: "I want to go with you," he told her, "but I have to go back to New York and finish a record—I don't have any other choice." He was referring to the third recording session planned for the nonet. Miles was still convinced that his brilliant music would eventually find its audience in America.

But bad news greeted him on his return to New York in the early summer of 1949. The nonet's first 78 had sold so poorly that Capitol had postponed the next recording session. Monte Kay, who had been managing the group, gave up trying to get the band any more gigs; clubowners were uninterested in anything larger than a quintet, and they viewed the nonet as a bizarre offshoot of bop, hardly a crowd pleaser. Even jobs for small modern groups had become more difficult to come by, except for the top names in bop—Parker and Gillespie.

Miles felt that he had reached some sort of dead end. The cohesive, familylike atmosphere of Fifty-second Street seemed to be dying. His colleagues in the nonet were all involved in regular gigs wherever they could find them—often in theater orchestras or society bands. Others were simply wasting away from heroin, the plague that seemed to touch everyone Miles knew. It should be no surprise that he finally turned to junk himself. As Dexter Gordon stated, it was simply an "essential part of the young musicians' social scene at the time." This was partially due to Parker's widespread influence over so many of the younger players. But Parker hardly deserves all the blame. Drugs had long been part of the jazz subculture, and musicians found heroin the ideal way to relax from both the tensions of improvising and the unstable jazz life.

His career at loose ends, many of his dreams apparently dashed, Miles entered the world of drug addiction as completely as he had music. Never one to do things in a small way, he began a very expensive habit in the summer of 1949, one which would take almost five years to kick.

Blue Haze

"The strain of looking for junk twenty-four hours a day can make a man snap," said Dexter Gordon, who acquired his habit about the same time that Miles did. Miles didn't snap, but the constant appetitite for drugs almost wrecked his life and career during the early fifties. And it is no small miracle that he survived.

He wouldn't, couldn't, compromise and play more commercial music in order to find work—he was dedicated to the music he had been playing with Charlie Parker, Gil Evans, and Max Roach. By 1949, at the age of twenty-three, he felt a bit like a has-been. Heroin made this easier to accept, and it seemed just part of the musician's life-style, "part of the social scene at the time," according to Dexter Gordon. But according to Miles, the main reason that he drifted into addiction was simple boredom.

Blue Haze

By the beginning of 1950 bebop had peaked in the imagination of the jazz public, and a number of bop leaders were looking for new directions. Charlie Parker had recorded an album with strings, his own favorite album, and was touring with a small string group. Dizzy Gillespie had become interested in Latin music and was also recording vocal novelties. A number of musicians, such as Gerry Mulligan and Dexter Gordon, moved back to California, where the West Coast jazz movement was burgeoning. Still others found their careers, and their lives, destroyed by drugs or alcohol or both. Among these were Tadd Dameron, who was jailed for drug possession, Allen Eager, who left jazz in order to stay away from narcotics, and Fats Navarro, who died in July 1950 at the age of twenty-seven.

Jazz fans began to look for an alternative to the complexities of bebop. For many, the most exciting new developments were taking place in California. Stan Kenton's orchestra and its "progressive" jazz captured much attention in the jazz press. In the early fifties much of the jazz spotlight was on white performers such as Kenton, Stan Getz, Gerry Mulligan, Dave Brubeck, and Chet Baker. Most of these musicians had been influenced by Miles's nonet recordings as well as by the pioneering work of Lennie Tristano. The music, notwithstanding the blaring sound of Kenton's big band, was lighter and more melodic than bop. Although it incorporated many of the rhythmic and harmonic characteristics of bebop, it was smoother and more accessible to the casual listener. In addition, record companies found it easy to market the All-American good looks of white musicians Getz, Mulligan, and Baker in trying to reach the broadest market.

By the end of 1949 Miles's life had begun to center totally around drugs. The money that his father continued to send him could only go so far in maintaining his habit. He did occasionally get work, playing anywhere, often out of town with local, and usually inferior, rhythm sections. Like many musicians who became deeply involved with drugs, he became more and more erratic as a performer. He would show up late for work and cut sets short if he was not well. Onstage, it would be readily apparent that he was high. Word of his behavior got around to most club owners, who had tolerated Charlie Parker only because of his musical reputation, something that Miles, at that time, could not match.

In order to support himself and his habit, he transcribed music from records for lead sheets, for which he was paid thirty dollars a transcription by music publishers. "I'd take the thirty dollars for the transcription, go uptown and get high," he remembers. But this was barely enough to keep him going. Recently he sardonically noted, "During those years I put one million dollars up my left arm and two million dollars up the right one." An exaggeration, of course, but an indication of how financially draining his habit was.

Increasingly he began to resemble his mentor Charlie Parker, using the same cheap street cons and low-rent hustles—and betrayals. "I remember one day on Broadway," recalls Clark Terry:

> I found Miles sitting in front of one of those ham-and-eggs places. He was just wasted, actually sitting in the gutter. I asked him what was wrong and he said, "I don't feel well." After buying him some ham and eggs, I took him around to my hotel, the America on West Forty-seventh Street. I was getting ready to leave on the bus with Basie's band, and I told him, "You just stay here, get some rest, and when you leave just close the door."
>
> The bus waited longer than I'd expected, so I

went back to the room. Miles had disappeared, the door was open, and all my things were missing. I called home, St. Louis, and told my wife to call Doc Davis to see if he could get Miles, because he was obviously in bad shape and had become the victim of those cats who were twisting him the wrong way. And you know what? Doc Davis was very indignant. He told her, "The only thing that's wrong with Miles now is because of those damn musicians like your husband that he's hanging around with." He was the type of guy who believed his son could do no wrong. So he didn't come to get him.

Not only did Miles's father refuse to believe that his son was in deep trouble, he unwittingly supported Miles's habit by continuing to send him money.

The only bright spot during this period was the third and final Capitol recording session of the nonet. The company finally relented and agreed to the last four sides stipulated in the original contract. Miles was able to reassemble virtually the same group of musicians that he had used for the second session, and the band produced four superb sides. One, "Darn That Dream," included a vocal by Kenny Hagood—it was the hope of Miles, as well as Capitol, that a vocal might make the nonet more popular. But the stand-out of the session was undoubtedly Gil Evans's arrangement of "Moon Dreams." The sheer lushness of sound and sensuously slow-changing textures presage *Sketches of Spain* and *Quiet Nights,* collaborations between Miles and Evans recorded a decade later.

To most listeners, however, the sound of the nonet was still too strange. It was up to such West Coast musicians as Shorty Rogers and Dave Brubeck to simplify and popularize the concepts of Miles and Gil—which they had been doing since hearing the initial nonet side. Miles loved the new recordings, and for a short while he regained some hope for the commercial viability of the nonet. But even with the vocal the records did not sell, and no new bookings for the group were forthcoming. However, a growing number of influential critics, such as André Hodeir, recognized both the importance of the nonet recordings and the maturity and profundity of Miles's musical conception.

Unfortunately none of the critics were record producers or club owners, so Miles had to continue struggling to find work. Early in 1950 he was interviewed in *down beat*. The article described him as being mild, modest, quiet, and cheerful, even though he was quoted as saying, "I've worked so little, I could probably tell you where I was playing any night in the last three years." Miles's wife and his three-year-old son, Gregory, stayed with him occasionally, but Irene found living with a junkie was a nightmare. "I didn't have a twenty- or thirty- or forty-dollar-a-day habit. It cost me whatever I had in my pocket," Miles recalls. He could not tolerate Irene's pleading that he change in order to be a better father and husband; when her nagging became intolerable, he would send her back to East St. Louis.

When he heard that Billy Eckstine was putting together a new band, he immediately approached his former employer for a job. Miles didn't like playing charts, but Eckstine worked steadily and the band would be touring, heading west to California. Miles liked the idea of getting out of his rut in New York, and the steady pay would keep him and his habit going. Since a number of other musicians in the band were addicts, Miles knew that he could, with their help, score dope in any city that they went through.

It turned out that the drudgery of touring with the

Eckstine band was alleviated only by the haze provided by drugs. Miles wasn't thinking of the future; he had no real plans. In Los Angeles the inevitable happened. Miles and Art Blakey were stopped by some police who were suspicious of their behavior. Finding needle marks in their arms, the police arrested them for drug possession, even though neither one actually had heroin on his person.

Miles immediately called his father in East St. Louis, who quickly found an L.A. lawyer for his son. Since there was no evidence except for the needle marks, the case was dropped. But the attendant publicity was harmful to Miles's career.

Rather than return east with Eckstine, he stayed in Los Angeles, moving in temporarily with Dexter Gordon, who was living with his mother. Miles somehow landed a job for Dexter and himself in Oakland at a little club called Wolf's. Dexter put a band together, but Miles pulled a Bird on him. Dexter remembers:

> At this particular time, I was somehow not solvent. I didn't have a draw every night. So at the end of the week I wanted to get paid. I think the owner gave me about $16.17. I said, "What the hell is this?" The club owner said, "Well, man, you've been drawing every night." The owner was a nice guy. He said, "You and Miles . . ." I said, "Me and Miles?" I knew that Miles was drawing every night, but I didn't know that he was drawing my pay, too. He was drawing for the both of us, and somehow there was $16.17 left. But I used to do the same thing myself when I was using junk.

Shortly after this gig Miles's father sent him money to return east, since work in California proved to be nonexistent after the gig at Wolf's. When he returned to New York, Miles moved in with drummer Stan Levey, with whom he had lived for a short while in 1945. Work was scarce, but Miles's friend Sonny Stitt hired him to play in a band at the Onyx with Bud Powell and tenor man Wardell Gray. Modern jazz was rarely heard now on Fifty-second Street, and for the Onyx this was something like a final attempt to present bebop on The Street. Clubs like the Three Deuces and the Spotlite were featuring strippers and novelty acts, leaving jazz to clubs like Jimmy Ryan's, which booked only traditional or Dixieland groups. This two-week gig at the Onyx was the last major presentation of modern jazz at a Fifty-second Street club.

Toward the end of 1950, Miles received some good news: he had been elected to *Metronome*'s All Star Band by the magazine's readers. A number of jazz fans still thought highly of him due to his association with Charlie Parker and the release of the nonet recordings. In those days the all-star band was actually assembled for a one-time recording session. Strangely, the entire band was white except for Miles and Max Roach. In addition, many of the players, including Kai Winding, Lee Konitz, John LaPorta, and Stan Getz, were associated with the nonet and cool jazz—a fact that made the nonet's lack of commercial potential even more mystifying to Miles.

The same month that he recorded with the Metronome All Stars he participated in a recording session with Charlie Parker for the first time in two and a half years. Bird was now recording for Verve, a major record company that was trying to popularize his music by presenting it in a variety of musical settings, such as with strings, or with Latin percussion, or perhaps oddest of all, with a vocal group using arrangements by

Miles playing on Fifty-second Street, 1948 (Institute of Jazz Studies).

Gil Evans. In addition, the label was also recording Bird in more characteristic settings, reuniting him with Gillespie and Monk, and with Miles and Max Roach. The session with Miles was an artistic success, resulting in brilliant playing by Parker, and the most assured and fluent trumpet playing that Miles had ever recorded with Bird.

The same day of this session, January 17, 1951, Miles played in another recording session of even more significance. Bob Weinstock, an ardent jazz fan who had long wanted to record the music he had been hearing on Fifty-second Street, founded Prestige Records, specifically to record some of the young boppers who were being overlooked by the larger record companies. Miles was one of the first musicians he had in mind, and on that day in January, Miles recorded his first sides on Prestige, with John Lewis, Percy Heath, trombonist Benny Green, and Sonny Rollins, the young tenor saxophonist who had impressed him at the gig in the Audubon Ballroom. Rollins, only twenty-one at the time, used a rope attached to his sax for a strap, and he seemed at first to Weinstock to be too young and inexperienced. But after recording four sides with this small band, Weinstock was so impressed with Rollins that he agreed to Miles's request to use him in a quartet session. They recorded "I Know," with Miles accompanying on piano—the beginning of Rollins's long, brilliant recording career.

Although Weinstock could not pay much, Miles didn't really care. He hoped the exposure would make it easier to get club gigs, and he'd use the small advance to get high. This was another aspect of what might be called the Charlie Parker syndrome, which affected so many modernist musicians of the late forties and early fifties: making records merely to receive the immediate advance, enough to score junk. Many of these musicians look back at such recordings now with regret and distaste. Miles is one of them: "When I had a habit, I didn't care," he says today. "I do now."

He returned to Prestige studios in March 1951 to co-lead a date with his *Birth of the Cool* colleague, Lee Konitz. Miles sounds uncomfortable in this setting, since the group consisted of students of Lennie Tristano, Konitz's musical guru.

Except for these sporadic recording sessions there was little of importance happening in Miles's career. His attention was concentrated on staying alive and high; he put little energy into promoting his career. Periodically he would go back briefly to East St. Louis, but his habit and remaining hopes always drew him back to New York.

In October 1951 he again recorded for Prestige, once again using Sonny Rollins, as well as teen-age alto saxophonist Jackie McLean. Although Miles now disowns this session and others of this period, many people are not so eager to dismiss it. In Rollins, McLean, and Art Blakey, the drummer on the session, Miles had as sidemen players who would become modern-jazz leaders in the fifties. The music is indicative of the direction that jazz would take during the next decade; the excitement, the burst of energy with which bebop was born, was over. Modern-jazz musicians could no longer pull in the curious or interest the jazz audience with the "shock of the new." The "second wave" of bop musicians had to reexamine and renew their music. In addition, the adversity which had made bop almost a crusade was beginning to soften. More and more, musicians and critics, even those who were initially harsh in their response to the new jazz, began to accept it. This was due not only to familiarity but also the grow-

ing maturity of the music itself. A number of saxophonists were refining their own styles rather than simply
imitating Charlie Parker, and trumpet players were
finding stylistic avenues other than those of Dizzy and
Miles.

Miles's October 1951 session, usually known as the
"Dig" session, was a superb example of these changes.
While his style retained many of the cool nuances from
the nonet recordings, it was more rhythmically aggressive, part of the legacy of his association with Fats Navarro. His tone was increasingly becoming one of the
wonders of jazz—on the "My Old Flame" recorded at
this session, he used his sound to wonderful effect. Rollins's playing had a good deal of Coleman Hawkins's
rougher hues, but his rhythmic freedom and harmonic
sense were obviously influenced by Bird. His overall approach to the horn, however, was unique and highly
personal. McLean, an ardent admirer of Parker's, was
also developing a sound and approach that owed something to such older stylists as Benny Carter. And Art
Blakey's complex drum patterns pointed the way to the
increasingly prominent role of the drummer in fifties
jazz.

The job situation for jazz musicians continued to de-
teriorate throughout the early fifties. Miles took one gig
at a Pittsburgh bar that closed even before they paid
him. Birdland and the Royal Roost, with their high ad-
mission and cover charges, would book only musicians
with steady followings, men like Bird or Dizzy or Woody
Herman. Parker was actually banned from Birdland, the
club that was named after him. It seems that he brought
in his string unit for an engagement at the club, but
due to his increasing boredom with the concept he

would play a different tune from the one played by the string section: they would begin "Just Friends," and he would come in playing "Night and Day," totally confusing the staid string players, as well as irritating the audience.

Miles continued to depend, financially, on his father's checks, his transcription work for music publishers, and whatever recording work he could come up with. In early 1952 he played a concert sponsored by the disc jockey Symphony Sid. Also on the bill were Bird, the vibraphonist Milt Jackson, and Dinah Washington. Playing drums with Dinah was her young husband, Jimmy Cobb. Jimmy would play drums with Miles a decade or so later. He remembers the Symphony Sid concert well, for it was his first meeting with his future employer:

> Back then, Miles was just a timid little guy, real shy. He was staying with [tenor saxophonist] Zoot Sims at that time and they were both heavily into dope. Miles came out and played a little tune, and he was supposed to be followed by Bird. But Bird was fast asleep backstage. Miles had to go wake him up in order to get him onstage. I remember Bird's suit looked like a venetian blind, but when Miles woke him up, he played his ass off.

Miles at least kept a semblance of dignity; he wouldn't let himself nod out during a performance.

Shortly after the Symphony Sid show he made his first recordings for Blue Note Records. Like Prestige, Blue Note was an independent jazz label. It was started in the forties by Alfred Lion, who at first recorded only such traditional musicians as Sidney Bechet and Albert Ammons. By the late forties, however, he was recording

modern, including classic sides by Thelonious Monk and
Fats Navarro. In 1952 Miles didn't have an exclusive
contract with Prestige, and he readily agreed to record
for Blue Note. He used trombonist J. J. Johnson and,
once again, Jackie McLean. On the sides one can hear
Miles expanding his rhythmic vocabulary, playing in a
way that sounded both on and off the beat. This innovation would have a profound influence on many fifties
musicians, including Sonny Rollins and Jackie Mc-
Lean.

It was around this time that Miles became deeply interested in boxing. He had always casually enjoyed the
sport, but now that he had free time he found himself
going to gyms and learning the fundamentals. He hoped
that boxing would help keep him in shape, since playing was so physically taxing. He had already met Bobby
McQuillen, a former boxer who became a trainer after
seriously injuring an opponent in the ring. Bobby loved
jazz and spent time with many of the musicians. Miles
was immediately drawn to Bobby and began to work out
casually with him at Gleason's Gym in mid-Manhattan.
Bobby McQuillen recalls:

> I remember Miles coming into the dressing room
> at the Garden where one of my boys was fighting.
> His eyelids were drooping, his movements were
> slow, and here he was asking me to train him to
> be a fighter. "Look, Miles," I told him, "I'm not
> going to train anybody who's got a habit." "I don't
> have a habit," he told me. "Look," I told him, "don't
> bullshit me, you can't lie to a boxer. You'd better
> go home to St. Louis and kick that stuff or you
> won't be able to fight or play trumpet or do any-
> thing else. Now get the hell out of here and get
> yourself together." Miles was insistent that I start
> training him. But I was tougher.

Miles training with Bobby McQuillen (Elena Steinberg Collection).

Shortly after this encounter Miles took Bobby's advice and called his father. Dr. Davis came to New York and brought his son back to East St. Louis, hoping that Miles would settle down and regain his health once he was away from the musicians and the New York scene.

Once home, however, he immediately found a local source for dope. Every day he asked his father for money, and every day his father gave it to him, not realizing that it was for drugs. But when Miles started demanding larger amounts of money, Dr. Davis figured out what was going on and decided that he was fed up. An influential man in southern Illinois, he simply called a detective on the police force and had him put Miles in jail, with the stipulation that it not be considered an official arrest. Davis felt this was the only way to make his son come to his senses. In jail Miles for the first time went through cold turkey. But after only a couple of days his father had him released—he couldn't bear to be the cause of his son's agony. As soon as he was out, Miles convinced him that he was off drugs for good and that he had to pursue his career in New York. Reluctantly, Dr. Davis bought his son a bus ticket back to the city, and gave him, once again, enough money to live on for a month.

As soon as Miles reached New York, he went uptown and got high.

In January 1953 he played one of the most unusual recording dates of his career. At this session, once again for Prestige, Miles used two tenor saxophonists: Sonny Rollins and Charlie "Chan," actually Charlie Parker. Bird was under contract to Verve, but he recorded for other labels using this rather transparent pseudonym (Chan was the name of his current wife). Virtually everyone on the date was an addict, including a young drummer named Philly Joe Jones, who would later be a member of Miles's classic fifties quintet. Ira Gitler, the jazz critic and bop aficionado, who was supervising the session for Bob Weinstock, quickly saw that he had his hands full. Bird, as usual, fell asleep in the middle of the studio, much to Miles's displeasure. "I never did that to you when I was on your record dates," he complained after waking him. Parker simply smiled. Miles's irritation showed in his playing, and Gitler came out of the control booth and told him, "You're not playing shit." Miles immediately began packing his trumpet back into its case. "What are you doing?" asked Bird. "This motherfucker told me that I ain't playing shit," Miles replied.

"Come on, Miles, let's play some music," Bird insisted.

After this the session proceeded fairly smoothly. The results are remarkable for the excellent contrast between the tenor saxophone styles of Parker and Rollins, and a lovely rendition of Monk's "'Round Midnight."

At the end of the session Bird had fallen asleep again. "Wake up, motherfucker," Miles steamed.

"Yes, Lily Pons," said Bird, using a favorite sobriquet. As Miles stalked out of the studio, Parker called after him, reciting aphorisms in his fake British accent. "To produce beauty, we must suffer pain. From the oyster comes the pearl, Miles!" It was the last time these two would record together.

During the next few months of 1953, Miles recorded several times for both Prestige and Blue Note. Except for one strange session arranged by Al Cohn, the music that he recorded was straight-ahead bop. A quartet date with John Lewis, Percy Heath, and Max Roach produced interesting music, but the effects of the drug life were obviously taking their toll on Miles's abilities. He had always made more than his share of fluffs, but here his numerous mistakes eloquently attest to his failing spirit.

Bob Weinstock was less than thrilled by these latest recordings, and he, like everyone else, urged Miles to pull himself together before trying to continue professionally. But the habit seemed irreversible. Many thought him doomed to an early death, like Fats Navarro. Miles himself assumed, too, that "I was just going to die." But he kept on living, performing wherever he could.

In early 1954 he had a low-paying gig at the Bluebird Inn in Detroit. He had been out of the jazz spotlight for so long that his audience was virtually nonexistent. However, across town at one of the most popular Detroit jazz clubs, Baker's Keyboard Lounge, Max Roach was playing with a group that included the brilliant up-and-coming trumpet player Clifford Brown. Former Detroiter and artist Richard (Prophet) Jennings recalls:

Well, Max Roach and Clifford Brown were playing across town at Baker's Keyboard Lounge and Richie Powell, Bud's little brother, was on piano. Miles's gig was at the Bluebird and after a set he walked out and made it to Baker's. It was raining that night and Miles comes in the front door with this little coat on and the rain was in his face and hair and his clothing were all wet and the driest thing about him was the trumpet he held under his coat like a mother protecting a baby.

He didn't say anything to anybody. He weaved through the crowd and up on the bandstand and parked himself in the big bend of the baby grand piano. Clifford was blowing "Sweet Georgia Brown," I think, but anyway the tempo was way up. Totally oblivious to the group, the people, and the place,

Miles put his trumpet to his lips and began playing "My Funny Valentine." Well, Brownie stopped blowing and told the group to support Miles. A hush fell over the place and the people sat and stood like statues and they came in from off the corner and around the block. Miles just stood there playing and the rain or somethin' coursing down his cheeks.

And he seemed to be saying, "Be nice to me; smile once in a while. I know I make mistakes like everybody else but I'm only human like anybody else and I get lonely like anybody else and I need understanding like anybody else and I love you and I want you to love me just a little bit." When the thing ended, Miles reeled off the bandstand and out again into the rain. There was no sound. Then Brownie remembered what they were there for and blew a fast four.

That night at Baker's Keyboard Lounge, Miles made a major decision: "I made up my mind I was getting off dope. I was sick and tired of it. You know you can get tired of anything. You can even get tired of being scared." He went into his motel room, and "I laid down and stared at the ceiling for twelve days and I cursed everybody I didn't like. I was kicking it the hard way. It was like having a bad case of flu, only worse. I lay in a cold sweat. My nose and eyes ran. I threw up everything I tried to eat. My pores opened and I smelled like chicken soup. Then it was over."

When he left Detroit, he felt more alive than he had in almost four years. He knew that he was off heroin for good, and that he now had the determination to get his dormant career back on the track.

Back in New York Miles seemed like a different person. He was stronger, sure of himself, almost arrogant about having kicked dope on his own initiative. In early March of 1954 he made his first recordings in almost a year. The group included the new "funky" (blues-oriented) pianist in town, Horace Silver, and Miles's old compatriots Percy Heath and Art Blakey. These Blue Note records are evidence of his recovery: they are among the most aggressively rhythmic records he had produced until that time. A week later the same group recorded for Prestige. When they played "Blue Haze," a blues composed by Miles, he turned off all the lights in the studio except a small light in the control booth, in order to evoke an indigo mood. The resulting side seems to symbolize the melancholia he felt at the memory of the previous four years.

The next month Miles recorded twice again for Prestige. One of these sessions produced two classic sides, "Walkin'" and "Blue and Boogie." They are generally looked upon as the beginning of the "hard bop" movement. Both tunes are blues. The front line of the group, which consisted of Miles, J. J. Johnson, and tenor saxophonist Lucky Thompson, produced a sound that is in remarkable contrast to the cool sound of the nonet. Rather than using the impressionistic colors preferred by the arrangers for the nonet, "Walkin'" is straightforward and almost brusque, with a funky, bluesy sound that was to become a staple of much fifties jazz. Horace Silver, once again, was Miles's pianist on the date. Shortly after this session he formed a group which performed mainly blues-oriented tunes like those on "Walkin'," tunes played in typical bop format, but whose origins really precede bop and hark back to gospel music and urban blues. While "Walkin'" was probably not consciously produced by Miles as a way of renouncing cool jazz, it was nevertheless interpreted by many as a sign that jazz had to look back toward its black folk roots in order to remain emotionally cogent.

Blue Haze

Two months after the "Walkin' " session, Miles once again went into the studio with Sonny Rollins, who was now frequently recording on his own. They did three Rollins originals, "Oleo," "Doxy," and "Airegin," which would all become jazz standards. It was this period to which Rollins referred when he called Miles a star maker. Although many critics and fans were disturbed by Rollins's hard, supposedly ugly, even "angry" tone and unconventional musical ideas, his association with Miles gave him a certain respectability. In the small jazz community there is a sense of the continuity of generations; it was as if Parker had handed the torch to Miles, who then handed it to Rollins. In fact, Miles was an important influence on many, if not most, of the important musicians of the next two decades, as was Rollins.

On Christmas Eve 1954, Miles took part in another unusual recording session. Along with Percy Heath and Kenny Clarke, who had become the Prestige house rhythm section, Bob Weinstock put Miles together with vibraphonist Milt Jackson and Thelonious Monk. Miles loved Monk's compositions and his unique approach to piano, but he couldn't stand his eccentric accompaniment style. Monk would bang strange chords in back of a soloist, or play the tune in seemingly slow motion. According to Miles, "he never gave you any support," he simply distracted the soloist. Miles also insisted that Monk "lay out" (not accompany) when he soloed. But Monk could be a very stubborn man. Rumor has it there was a physical confrontation between the two men, but according to Miles, "that was all bullshit. Monk is a big motherfucker. I wouldn't try to take him on. I just asked him to lay out. That's all that happened." Nevertheless, the session quickly became jazz legend, which helped bring Miles back into the limelight.

The tensions of this session are apparent on the records. The listener can sometimes hear Miles and Monk

Sonny Rollins (Phil Bray, Institute of Jazz Studies).

quarreling musically. But in general the results are sublime. On the Milt Jackson blues, "Bags' Groove," Jackson is funky, Miles is almost ethereal, and Monk is iconoclastic, playing blues choruses that challenge every standard concept of the blues but still capture the same gritty feel of Jackson's more conventional solo. In the opening statement of "The Man I Love," Miles achieves an astonishingly beautiful sound, leaving no doubt that he was becoming one of the most moving, as well as one of the most important, jazz musicians. At the end of 1954 he had a sure sense that he was finally making it on his own terms.

The Quintet

By 1955 jazz was enjoying a renaissance. Groups like the Dave Brubeck Quartet and the Modern Jazz Quartet, big bands like those of Stan Kenton, Count Basie, and Duke Ellington, and vocalists such as Chris Connor and Ella Fitzgerald had all found large audiences, a new generation of admirers. Although there had already been a few rock 'n' roll hits—for example Bill Haley's "Rock Around the Clock"—the "Big Beat" had not yet caught on, and jazz captured the ears of many of the more sophisticated young listeners. The music had also become more accessible since the bop heyday of the forties. Brubeck, Gerry Mulligan, and trumpeter Chet Baker, among a number of others, were playing a form of jazz characterized by its rhythmic simplicity and straightforward lyricism. The Modern Jazz Quartet, which consisted of John Lewis, Milt Jackson, Percy Heath, and Kenny Clarke (all of whom played occasionally with Miles), combined jazz with a European chamber music approach. The reassembled big bands of Basie and Ellington were becoming major attractions in concert halls and night clubs.

By 1954 enough public support for jazz had materialized for George Wein, the young owner of the Storyville nightclub in Boston, to inaugurate a jazz festival in Newport, Rhode Island. It would be the first of many jazz festivals held in America. In addition, such major record companies as Columbia and RCA Victor were busily signing jazz artists in the belief that jazz had regained a large audience. New jazz clubs were opening in every major city, and jazz concerts were becoming a staple of the concert hall.

Miles, too, felt like he had started a new life. "You know," he would say later, "I don't think nothing about death. I should have been dead a long time ago. But it missed me when I was on dope. That's why I don't have any fear in my eyes." This newfound confidence is immediately apparent upon listening to his 1954 recordings.

During the making of those records he began to form ideas about the kind of permanent group he wanted. Although he enjoyed playing with Kenny Clarke, he preferred the more propulsive style of drummer Art Blakey. He needed a pianist who would give him and the other soloists support, not someone like Monk, who to Miles's ears too often seemed to be accompanying somebody in another band or on another planet. On bass he would have liked Percy Heath, since he played such strong rhythmic lines while backing a soloist and had a fine melodic sense. Unfortunately, most of the musicians that Miles wanted had other commitments. Heath, for instance, was deeply involved with the highly successful Modern Jazz Quartet, and Blakey was forming his own band, The Jazz Messengers.

However, now that word of his personal resurgence and the high quality of his Prestige recordings had reached club owners, Miles was getting a good number of gigs. He formed pickup groups with the best musicians he could put together. Sonny Rollins, Lucky Thompson, Jimmy Heath (Percy's saxophonist brother), Art Blakey, Kenny Clarke, and Percy Heath were among the men he played with. He grew especially fond of playing with drummer Philly Joe Jones, who possessed an exhilarating rhythmic drive that inspired Miles to reach for notes he hardly knew were there.

Recently, when Miles was reviewing all the great bands he had led, he admitted for the first time that there *was* one band he thought was his greatest: pianist Walter Bishop, drummer Art Taylor, Percy Heath (between Modern Jazz Quartet commitments), and two tenor saxophonists, Sonny Rollins and the young Philadelphian, John Coltrane.

It was Rollins's first meeting with Coltrane. "Coltrane always had something about him that I couldn't figure out, about his playing," Rollins recalls. "It was great: Miles used to whisper in my ear while John was playing, and then while I was playing Miles would be over there whispering in John's ear. It was wonderful to be around people who were that committed to something."

Was Miles trying to stir things up between the two tenor men, who were both still finding their styles? "Of course," laughs Miles. "I knew that if one of those guys was wondering what I was saying to the other, they would play better. But that band was a motherfucker. I would just play my little solo and then stand back and listen to Coltrane and Rollins play their asses off." Un-

Rupert "Philly Joe" Jones (Institute of Jazz Studies).

fortunately, this band lives only in memory; there were no recordings made of the group.

On March 12, 1955, the world of jazz received a severe shock: Charlie Parker died at the age of thirty-four. Bird's friends and musical associates had known that he was in grave physical and emotional condition, but they had hoped that he would regain his strength and survive. He had pulled through so many times before. "Bird had an incredible constitution," Miles remembers. "He seemed to be able to withstand everything, from drugs and booze to all those bitches."

But finally he reached the end of the line. He had been staying in New York at the home of the Baroness Nica De Koenigswarter, a wealthy patroness of jazz and jazz musicians, when his body almost literally fell apart; years of dissipation had caught up with him at last. His ironic sense of humor stayed with him to the end: when the baroness's doctor asked Bird if he drank, he replied, "I take an occasional sherry before dinner." Finally, while watching the Dorsey brothers' television show, his laughter at a juggling act turned into choking and he fell back and died. "At the moment of his going," recalled the baroness, "there was a tremendous clap of thunder. I didn't think about it at the time, but I've often thought about it since, how strange it was."

The jazz world was profoundly shaken by his passing. Charlie Mingus, upon hearing of his death, commented bitterly, "Now all those musicians at Birdland are going to have to find somebody else to imitate." Parker's influence had become so pervasive that it was difficult to conceive of modern jazz without him. Literally every musician had incorporated elements of Bird's style into his own in one way or another—everyone from trombonist J. J. Johnson to guitarist Tal Farlow to vibraphonist Milt Jackson. There were even accordionists and harmonica players who played Bird on their instruments. No one since Louis Armstrong had so changed the course of jazz, and Bird was probably even more widely imitated than Armstrong. His death left a void in the jazz world; a leader of comparable stature was needed. Miles said, "New York just ain't the same without Bird"—his only public display of emotion over the death of Charlie Parker. Miles continued, however, to have mixed feelings about Parker, and only obliquely could he display his deepest emotions about his former mentor. Max Roach ran into Miles shortly after Bird's death and Miles, remembering the days of the great Parker quintet, chuckled and said, "The motherfucker died before we could get even with him, Max."

He was too busy reviving his career to waste energy on grief. He felt strong and arrogant—he knew that he was reaching the height of his powers. His music was going through a metamorphosis, which he felt was at least partly due to the influence of Ahmad Jamal. Jamal was a pianist whose style, according to most jazz critics, veered toward "cocktail piano." His repertoire consisted of pop tunes usually associated with such crooners as Perry Como and Tony Bennett. However, no pianist since Thelonius Monk had used musical space in such a personal and sometimes eccentric manner. *New Yorker* jazz critic Whitney Balliett wrote:

Jamal is a genuine musical curiosity, whose style is vaguely akin to Count Basie's. He will play some ordinary chords, drop his hands in his lap for ten measures, reel off a simple, rhythmic single-note figure (often in the high registers), drop his hands for five or six more measures, slip in an arpeggio, drop his hands again, plump off some new chords, and so forth—all of which eventually gives the impression achieved by spasmodically stopping and unstopping the ears in a noisy room. Accompanied by bass and drums, which sustained a heavy, warlike thrumming that seemed to frown on his efforts, Jamal played five numbers in this fashion, and after a time everything was blotted out but the attempt to guess when he would next lift his hands to hit the piano. It was trying work.

In early 1955 Miles began to play gigs with Texan pianist Red Garland, who played with a jaunty slick style, which, while not really imitative of Jamal, nevertheless often also veered toward cocktail piano. Miles frequently requested that Garland use some of Jamal's techniques in his playing, such as block chords mixed with single note lines in the upper register. Garland's ability to assimilate much of Jamal's approach into his accompaniment style was especially helpful to Miles, since Miles himself was attempting to incorporate Jamal's use of space and lyricism. In addition, Miles enjoyed the exuberance of Garland's playing, which provided a sharp contrast to his own more introspective improvising.

When Prestige released some of the superb sides recorded by Miles in 1954, a number of critics began to rediscover him. His style provided a sharp contrast to that of Clifford Brown, who many critics and jazz enthusiasts thought was becoming the most important trumpeter of the fifties. Brown's style, which owed a great debt to Fats Navarro, was brassy and extroverted. He seemed to have an inexhaustible reservoir of ideas, which he played with a joyous verve. Although most of these ideas had their source in forties bebop, his music sounded exhilarating and fresh, and his fiery brilliance eclipsed Miles's more cerebral style. But Miles's deeply felt lyricism in such performances as "The Man I Love" made many critics begin to reexamine him as something more than a one-time foil for Charlie Parker.

Miles realized that it was necessary to build up momentum with his career by continuing to tour, as much as he disliked life on the road and the business details of touring. One great problem he encountered while traveling as a "single" artist (without an accompanying band) was finding a decent rhythm section to play with. Philly Joe Jones, his favorite drummer at the time, agreed to act as an advance man. He would precede Miles into each city to set up the gig, arrange a price for the band with the club owner, and locate a suitable bassist and pianist. Even this was unsatisfactory. Miles needed a band of his own in order to develop his new musical ideas. He felt he was treading water. He needed a break, a dramatic break.

In June 1955 he recorded a quartet session for Prestige along with bassist Oscar Pettiford, Red Garland, and Philly Joe Jones. This recording would be something of a microcosm of the direction Miles would take for the next several years. The quartet recorded a medium-tempo blues, a bop classic ("A Night in Tunisia"), a ballad ("I See Your Face Before Me"), which Miles played in what would become his classic Harmon muted approach, and two standards ("Will You Still Be Mine?" and "Gal in Calico"), both played in jaunty medium tempo, an approach that owed much to Ahmad Jamal. This version of Dizzy Gillespie's "Tunisia" best reflected the maturity and assurance that Miles's music had developed. Characteristically, he made no attempt to dazzle the listener with technical fireworks, as Gillespie and Parker did playing this tune, but rather used nuance and understatement.

Later that month he heard from an old colleague, Charlie Mingus. The two still regarded each other with distrust, stemming from the days with Bird in California, but Mingus had lent Miles money during the darkest days of his heroin addiction. Now Mingus wanted Miles to repay him by recording for his own record company, Debut. Miles agreed to a session, but not with much enthusiasm.

Mingus assembled an unusual group of musicians: Teddy Charles, a colleague in Mingus's Jazz Workshop, played cerebral vibraharp; Britt Woodman, who had played with Duke Ellington, played trombone; Mingus played bass; and the then unknown Elvin Jones, from Detroit, played drums. Jones would later become the drummer in John Coltrane's classic sixties quartet and would come to be regarded as the most influential drummer of his generation. Mingus dominated the session, so much so that the resulting record, titled *Blue Moods*, shows little in the way of Miles's highly personal approach.

The summer of 1955 was also the occasion of another dramatic Davis comeback appearance, at the controversial second Newport Jazz Festival. The 1954 inauguration of the festival had been met with a fair amount of justifiable skepticism. Newport, Rhode Island, had traditionally been the exclusive resort of the wealthiest and most socially prominent members of American "society." The very notion of a festival of music that came from the country's ghettos, city streets, and smoky saloons taking place in this posh community seemed paradoxical, to say the least. Many in Newport were appalled at the idea of an invasion of jazz musicians and fans, most of whom they conceived to be drug addicts, sexual perverts, alcoholics, and—worse—blacks, Jews, and Italians. However, the Lorillards, scions of the tobacco empire, strongly supported the idea. Mainly because of such musicians as Gerry Mulligan and Dave Brubeck, jazz had attained a degree of respectability among some of the upper class.

George Wein, who was sincerely dedicated to jazz, wanted the Newport Jazz Festival to be a smorgasbord of music, including a presentation of jazz from every one of its periods, from its blues roots to the latest innovations, thus appealing to both older fans and the new collegiate crowd.

Among those appearing at that second Newport Jazz Festival were Miles's early idols from Fifty-second Street, Roy Eldridge and Coleman Hawkins, who played together for a set; the big bands of Basie, Ellington, and Kenton; the Clifford Brown–Max Roach quintet, with Brown garnering raves for his virtuosic performance. At the festival Wein often put together informal groups. In a close approximation of spontaneous jam sessions, musicians who might never play together could exchange ideas: the Chicago-style clarinet of Pee Wee Russell might be followed by Stan Getz's cool tenor saxophone or Roy Eldridge's classic trumpet—all accompanied by, say, Max Roach, bassist Milt Hinton, and Dave Brubeck—a true closing of jazz generation gaps.

Miles's appearance in 1955 was actually a last-minute idea of Wein's. A motley group of modernists had been gathered to play the Sunday evening concert: Zoot Sims, Gerry Mulligan, Thelonious Monk, and the Modern Jazz Quartet's contemporaneous rhythm section, Percy Heath and drummer Connie Kay. The group needed a trumpeter, and Percy Heath suggested to Wein his longtime Prestige recording colleague, Miles. Wein hesitated at first—outside of his association with Charlie Parker, Miles was still known only to the hipper modern jazz musicians and fans. But at last he relented; after all, here was a living link to the recently deceased Parker.

When Miles received the invitation to appear at Newport, he quickly accepted. There were few gigs he would turn down at this point in his career, and even though the idea of being accompanied by Thelonious Monk was annoying, he knew the gig would gain him valuable exposure to jazz fans, the press, and the music industry.

Duke Ellington was the master of ceremonies on Sunday evening, July 17, introducing the modernist ensemble that included Miles. The group opened with Monk's "Hackensack," then followed with two bop standards, "Now's the Time" and " 'Round Midnight." Although Miles played brilliantly on every tune, it was his performance in " 'Round Midnight," which he played with his Harmon mute, that most deeply affected the crowd and the critics. Many regarded his performance as the high point of the festival. Later, when he realized the excitement he had caused, he would say, "I don't know what they're talking about. It's like I just came back from the moon. I just played the way I always do."

Fortunately, however, the critics agreed with the fans. Jack Tracy wrote in *down beat,* "[The group] opened with 'Hackensack,' on which Miles played thrillingly, and indicated his comeback is in full stride. [Percy] Heath, too, shone, as did all members on the ensuing 'Now's the Time.' It was Miles, however, who captured most ears." In *Metronome* it was noted that "Miles Davis blew beautifully, blew better than anyone else during the three nights." Shortly after Newport, the critics would boost Miles's ego even further by voting him first place in a tie with Dizzy Gillespie in the *down beat* Critics' Poll.

Among those in the audience that Sunday evening was Goddard Lieberson, president of Columbia Records and a casual jazz fan. Columbia had become increasingly interested in jazz, due to a great extent to the success of Dave Brubeck for the company. Lieberson was looking for fresh, young talent, musicians who might have the same appeal Brubeck had, especially for the growing collegiate audience. That night at Newport, Lieberson noticed not only Miles's lyrical style but also his undeniable charisma; even when he wasn't playing, the eyes of the audience were drawn to him.

When Miles received an offer from Columbia shortly after Newport, he was naturally excited and eager to accept. However, there were two major stumbling blocks: he still owed Prestige four more albums, and he wanted to have a working group together for his Columbia debut.

He decided that he wanted both Red Garland and Philly Joe Jones in his band. He would also have liked either Percy Heath or Oscar Pettiford, but both had other commitments. While trying to find a bassist, he took a tip from a friend and went to hear an old bebop colleague, George Wallington (who had composed "Godchild," performed by the nonet). Wallington was playing in a trio with a nineteen-year-old bassist, Paul Chambers. Miles was impressed by the youngster's unflagging rhythmic drive and full tone, and immediately asked Chambers to join his new group. Chambers, encouraged by Wallington, immediately agreed. Others might have been reluctant to hire someone so young and inexperienced. But Miles had his own philosophy about young players: "Coleman Hawkins told me never to play with someone older than me, and I never have. With older players, there's no force, no drive. With younger players, it's not that you know it all, or I know it all—it's I'm trying to learn it all."

Miles had tired of playing in a quartet format, especially after his years touring as a single, and he wanted another horn, a saxophonist who would provide the same sort of contrast that Charlie Parker had. His favorite tenor at that time, Sonny Rollins, joined the group with great eagerness. But Rollins's tenure in the band was to be short. At this point in his career he had severe difficulty with drugs and frequently withdrew from the jazz scene in order to pull his life together. While the makeup of the band was still somewhat in flux, Miles recorded with Jackie McLean and Milt Jackson for Prestige—a pleasant but not ground-breaking session— and continued his search for a permanent tenor saxophonist. According to Philly Joe Jones, "When Miles wanted a partner, another voice in the group, Red [Garland] and I hollered 'Coltrane.' Miles had heard him with Diz and liked him." Coltrane had also played with Miles before, in that band that Miles would later name as his greatest, but at this point he was still groping for his own style, and Miles preferred Rollins. Still, he could clearly hear Coltrane's potential, and when he lost Rollins he made Coltrane a member of the group.

Coltrane was, in more than one way, an unusual foil for Miles. To many critics his tone was as hard and harsh as Miles's was pure and lovely. Emotionally, he was introverted and quiet, certainly a contrast to the wild Bird, although he shared with Parker the same demons of alcoholism and drug addiction. Coltrane had, by the time he joined Miles's band, a wide variety of experience. He had played briefly with Dizzy Gillespie (playing alto rather than tenor saxophone) both in the big band and the Gillespie quintet. In his hometown Philadelphia he had played in a number of rhythm-and-blues bands. He had also played in Johnny Hodges's short-lived big band and in Earl Bostic's raucous R and B group. He was an intensely dedicated musician, as musically curious as Miles. Between sets of the quintet he would not leave the stage but would remain at the piano, working out chord progressions. Although Coltrane was not as accomplished a saxophonist as Sonny

John Coltrane, 1962 (Institute of Jazz Studies).

Rollins when he joined the quintet, Miles could clearly see that potentially he was perhaps even a greater player.

Miles had a great deal at stake with this new group. After his success at Newport, Birdland had signed him to a contract guaranteeing twenty weeks of work a year, as well as performances as part of a Birdland tour package. In addition, there was the deal with Columbia Records. On October 27, 1955, Miles brought his new quintet into the Columbia studios. The band recorded two bop themes: "Budo" and Charlie Parker's "Au-Leu-Cha." Thus, with his new band and revived musical career, Miles made a symbolic nod to his musical past.

In the fall of 1955 he gave an interview to Nat Hentoff, in which he expressed his new confidence, his refusal to compromise his beliefs, and his commitment to saying exactly what he felt. This provided a sharp contrast to the interviews he had given in the late forties and early fifties, when he seemed reticent about giving offense. In this interview he stated that Brubeck "doesn't know how [to swing]," that as far as Kenton went, "I can't think of anything he did original," and that popular clarinetist Buddy DeFranco "plays a lot of clichés and is very cold." Miles also criticized his future record producer, Teo Macero, for his work at Newport. About Mingus's compositions for small groups, he said, "Some of them are like tired modern paintings. Some of them are depressing. . . . Mingus can write better than that." Perhaps Miles felt that being less than totally honest with himself had been one of the causes of his drug addiction, and that the jazz world needed more serious self-appraisal.

Needless to say, many saw his new (at least publicly new) uncompromising persona as arrogant. Mingus was particularly upset, and wrote, in a long, angry "Open Letter to Miles Davis" for *down beat:*

> I know Miles and his cult of self-esteemed creators, who are convinced of their clan's mystical powers of secret formula swinging, and they're cool as long as they are together to pat each other on the back.

The Quintet

Remember me, Miles? I'm Charles. Yeah, Mingus! You read third trumpet on my California record dates 11 years ago on the recommendation of Lucky Thompson. So easy, young man. Easy on those stepping stones. . . . Truly, Miles, I love you and want you to know you're needed here, but you're too important a person in jazz to be less than extra careful about what you say about other musicians who are *also trying* to create.

But Miles would never again mince words about music or musicians, even about those who (like Brubeck) were his friends. Years later Miles would say, "Everybody calls me arrogant. I hear that all the time. I'm not arrogant. I just tell the truth." His uneasy relationship with Mingus would last until the bassist died in 1979.

Although the recordings that Miles had made for Columbia could not be released until he had settled his contract with Prestige, he received a four-thousand-dollar advance. That amount might now seem paltry, but it was a large advance for a jazz musician at that time. With his career now apparently back on the track, he settled into a large apartment on West Fifty-seventh Street. He bought a white Ferrari, a car he loved both for its speed and its European elegance. Clothes had always been very important to him, and now he indulged his love of imported Italian suits and shoes. He seemed, post-Newport, to be (consciously or not) creating an image quite distinct from that of Charlie Parker, Bud Powell, or almost any of the great modern jazz stars, who remained bohemians.

When Miles's new quintet made its New York debut at the Café Bohemia, a tiny jazz club in Greenwich Village, the visual impact of the group confused the audience. Philly Joe, Paul Chambers, and Sonny Rollins (temporarily back in the sax spot of the group) all appeared to be nonchalant, typical boppers, in both dress and attitude. The group's leader, though, was dapper enough to be a black Frank Sinatra.

There seemed a great disparity among the musical styles as well. This was further exaggerated when Rollins decided, once again, to retire from music, and Miles rehired John Coltrane as the group's permanent saxophonist. In the early recordings of the group, one can hear Coltrane struggling to define his musical style; most listeners and critics saw his playing as an amalgam of Rollins, Sonny Stitt, and Dexter Gordon, but lacking their smooth techniques. Garland sounded far too slick in contrast to the tenor man, almost as if he belonged in another group. Philly Joe was a relentlessly deafening drummer, who employed great polyrhythmic complexities, but to many of the uninitiated he overwhelmed the others. Chambers seemed young and unsure at first, and in the early days of the group, according to Philly Joe, "he slowed tempos sometimes. But it got so that tempos didn't mean anything to him after a while." The leader's sparsely melodic, often elegant approach to the trumpet seemed at greatest odds with the group, although with increasing frequency Miles was playing with great fire, more than most jazz fans had ever heard him display.

Despite these differences Miles was able, in a relatively short time, to mold these diverse musicians into a genuinely cohesive unit, making every part of it work and making the whole greater than the sum of those parts. A Boston jazz fan still vividly remembers the impact of the quintet when it first played his city:

Everybody was disappointed that Sonny Rollins didn't show up with the group. He was the hippest saxophonist since Bird, and none of us had heard of this shy young cat John Coltrane. But once he started blowing, we immediately realized that he had a new and incredibly exciting sound. And Philly Joe! I had never heard a louder, more dynamic, exciting drummer. At first nobody could put all the pieces of the group together, there was so much happening, but we knew that we had heard something special. And that week the word on the street was that Miles Davis had put together *the* group, the best since Bird.

On November 16, 1955, Miles brought his quintet into the Prestige recording studios for its first full-scale recording session. The record, which would be called simply *Miles*, contained tunes that had already become staples of Miles's repertory: some old standards ("S'posin'" and "Just Squeeze Me"), a couple of boppish tunes ("Miles' Theme" and Benny Golson's "Stablemates"), and the requisite ballad ("There Is No Greater Love"), played by Miles in his most tender, muted style.

In retrospect it might seem that on many levels he was following a conservative course, despite his association with some of the more avant-garde musical thinkers in the jazz community. There were many musicians

Miles and Paul Chambers, 1958 (Frank Driggs Collection).

who seemed, at least on the surface, more daring. Mingus, for example, was experimenting with polytonalities and unconventional instrumentation. When he did resort to more standard instrumentation, he would use it unconventionally, creating new textures through the use of special sound effects (for example, Mingus's own cries). John Lewis was using his Modern Jazz Quartet to play fugues, rondos, and other forms borrowed from European classical music. When this mixture of jazz and classical worked—which it did, for example, when Milt Jackson's bluesy vibraharp played in counterpoint with Lewis's piano—it produced a heady brew. Even the popular Dave Brubeck was experimenting with sophisticated counterpoint, dissonance, long forms, and varied meters. They and a number of other musicians realized that the bop format, once so revolutionary, could become as much of an airless trap as the swing-era clichés had been for the musicians of the generation of Charlie Parker and Dizzy Gillespie.

It may seem odd, therefore, that Miles's seemingly conservative approach led more directly to the "free jazz" of the sixties than the innovations of Mingus, Lewis, Jackson, and Brubeck. Miles's quintet had the standard bop configuration (trumpet, saxophone, piano, bass, and drums); its repertoire consisted of bop standards, pop tunes, and blues; its format was almost always the same: Miles's statement of theme, trumpet solo, sax solo, piano solo, and either bass or drum solos with the occasional trading of four bars between the horns and the drums. But the simplicity of this approach left room for complexities and variations of the utmost subtlety.

Miles rarely dictated to soloists what to play, and he would disappear from the stage after his own solo, leaving the rest of the group to its own devices. Thus Coltrane was given the freedom to expand and develop what would become his revolutionary and vastly influential style. The rhythm section evolved new modes for supporting the soloist and expanded its own role. On this point, Philly Joe Jones is somewhat ambiguous. On the one hand he states that Miles "let me have all the freedom I wanted." On the other, he complains that Miles "would not let me try all the things I wanted to. He ruled with an iron hand." This contradiction lies at the heart of Miles's musical leadership, not only of this quintet but of subsequent groups as well. Every member of the group had total freedom within the often not explicitly stated parameters of Miles's musical vision. "Freedom, but controlled freedom," he would say later in another context. Throughout his career he would play the roles of both musical conservative and visionary revolutionary, usually simultaneously. And he would lead his groups mostly through intuition, rather than by direct instruction.

A perfect example of the quintet's ability to reflect Miles's musical thinking in the absence of explicit guidelines was the performance of the rhythm section. As Joe Goldberg wrote in *Jazz Masters of the Fifties:*

At least part of the unique quality of the quintet performances lay in a particular principle which Davis grasped, a principle so simple that it apparently eluded everyone else. To put it in terms of this particular group, a quintet is not always a quintet. It could also a be a quartet featuring Miles, and, at different times on the same tune, it could be a quartet featuring Coltrane, or a trio featuring either Garland or Chambers. The Davis rhythm section, Jones in particular, was well aware of this, and gave each of the three principal soloists his own best backing. Behind Davis, the rhythm was full of space, with few chords; behind Coltrane, it was compulsive; and with Garland, it lapsed into an easy, Jamal-like feeling.

Therefore, instead of the usual bop formula of a stream of solos accompanied by a steady rhythm section, the quintet's music was subtly kaleidoscopic, changing textures and moods within the context of a unified performance.

All these factors—the apparent total freedom given to the musicians within the context of an unstated musical vision, the concern with shifting textures, the dominance and central importance of percussion and the striking contrast among soloists—would be the essence not only of all Miles's subsequent music but almost all jazz since the midfifties.

As brilliant as the group was, there was one aspect that deeply disturbed Miles: with the exception of himself, every member of the quintet was involved with drugs. His own resolve remained strong—he would never again be driven by the need for dope; his days of "being scared" were over. But its effect on the others was, for him, a continuing source of irritation. Chambers and Coltrane would often nod out on the bandstand. Philly Joe, although personally very close to Miles, was the most exasperating. He was frequently late, and rather than being cool about his habit, he had become something of the Dean Martin of junk, joking on and off the bandstand about it. Nevertheless, Miles deeply respected these musicians and liked the chemistry of the group, so he held his temper. Of Philly Joe he said, "I wouldn't care if he came up on the bandstand in his B.V.D.'s and with one arm, just so long as he was there.

He's got the fire I want. There's nothing more terrible than playing with a dull rhythm section. Jazz has got to have *that thing*. You have to be born with it. You can't even buy it. If you could buy it, they'd have it at the next Newport festival."

Sometimes, however, when a particular problem got out of hand, Miles would fire one or more of the group's members. Their work was still not that steady, so he could make changes without tremendous risk. Sonny Rollins would reappear, and then mysteriously disappear again. Miles would make these changes both for the sake of the group and for the musicians themselves— no one knew better than he how difficult it was to do drugs and remain a working musician.

Miles Ahead

If in early 1956 a casual jazz fan or tourist in Greenwich Village happened to wander into the Bohemia in order to catch the current attraction, the Miles Davis quintet, he might have been in for something of a shock. For one thing, he probably would have had quite a wait, for the group was often late coming onto the bandstand. When it did straggle on, it would have been with a nonchalance alien to show business, and more like that of laborers going back to the job after a lunch break.

All eyes are immediately drawn to the trumpet player, who is wearing an elegant Italian suit and a scarf around his neck, accentuating his striking good looks. (Many years later, while talking about another musician, Miles said pointedly, "I know why he doesn't like me. Because I've got *charisma*.") Casually, the trumpeter picks up his horn, and with his back arched and his muted trumpet pointed down toward the microphone, he begins playing the standard tune "Diane." But he seems to be leaving out almost as many notes as he is playing—distilling the melody, making the listener hear the essence of the tune, its very heart, for the first time. After this initial statement of the melody, the drummer switches from brushes to sticks and the volume of the music increases. By the time the trumpeter has finished his sighing, melodic, minimalist solo, the tenor man begins playing with a hard, almost bullying tone. The drummer's din increases, almost to the extent of drowning out the sax man. After this tune has ended, the group plays a very fast version of Sonny Rollins's "Airegin." The drummer at this point is so loud, the soloists so aggressive, that the fan might think seriously of paying his tab and leaving in order to escape what sounds to his ears like musical anarchy. He is confused not only because the music is so harrowing but also because there have been no announcements of the tunes, no introduction of the musicians, and none of the banter with the audience that one expects from performers. The leader even occasionally turns his back to the audience, and leaves the stage after playing his own solo; in fact, he acts as if the audience does not exist at all, as if the musicians are playing only for themselves.

Even though the world of jazz may be something of a mystery to the fan, still, to his mind, it is show business. After all, Louis Armstrong and Duke Ellington act like other entertainers on stage. But just as the fan has reached the end of his rope, the trumpeter puts the mute on his horn, puts the horn right up against the microphone, and plays the loveliest, saddest, and most moving version of "My Funny Valentine" that the fan has ever heard. Every single note is played so poi-

gnantly that the preceding raucous din only empha-
sizes, by contrast, the beauty of this unforgettable
"Valentine."

When the fan finally leaves the club, he may decide
immediately to buy Miles Davis's latest album, even if
he has to skip over the fast tunes while listening to it.
He has been deeply moved not only by the loveliness of
Miles's ballads but also by the undeniable, unforgettable presence of Miles himself, a man who, when onstage, can draw attention to himself by merely rubbing
his nose.

This is how a legend is made—and as early as 1956,
at the age of twenty-nine, Miles was becoming a legend. Columbia was anxious to release a record by the
group, but they were prevented by the Prestige contract. Finally, Miles and Bob Weinstock came up with
a solution: Miles would record enough music so that
Prestige could release Miles Davis albums periodically
over several years. Miles's solution here was an example of another aspect of his growing legend: that of the
astute, if eccentric, businessman. He would do things
his way, even if it meant going an unusual route in the
world of show business.

For a brief time during the course of these negotiations, he changed the personnel of the group. Red Garland was replaced by the lyrical young pianist Tommy
Flanagan, and Philly Joe was spelled by the up-and-
coming drummer Art Taylor. Coltrane had gone back to
Philadelphia, his home, and Sonny Rollins was back in
the band. Paul Chambers stayed on. During his record
company negotiations, Miles took this interim group into
the Prestige studios and recorded three tracks. They
were smoother in some ways than the original quintet,
but lacked that fire, the "sound of surprise" (to use
Whitney Balliett's phrase) that was to Miles the essence
of jazz.

However, soon after the session, Rollins disappeared once again (to join Clifford Brown in the front line of the Brown–Max Roach quintet) and Miles brought Coltrane, Jones, and Garland back in.

He had no illusions about pressuring the men in his group to kick their drug habits. As he told Nat Hentoff, "I just tell them if they work for me to regulate their habit. When they're tired of the trouble it takes to support a habit, they'll stop it if they have the strength. You can't *talk* a man out of a habit until he really *wants* to stop." Miles's compassion, his refusal to moralize about drugs, was in sharp contrast to those reformed junkies and alcoholics in jazz who acted like born-again preachers.

At one time in the midfifties Miles was in a club where Billie Holiday, his friend from Fifty-second Street days, was performing. He overheard her ask a musician to lend her some money. He refused, saying that he knew she was just going to use it for dope. Miles scowled and said, "What's wrong with you, man, haven't you ever been sick?" He promptly handed her the money without bothering to ask when she would pay him back.

In May 1956 Miles brought Coltrane, Garland, Chambers, and Jones into the Prestige recording studios to fulfill his contract. This would be the first of two marathon sessions. The plan for these sessions was simple and logical: the group would play three sets exactly as they would have performed the tunes at a club, without rehearsal or second takes—they did not need to rehearse their repertoire. At first glance this approach might merely seem to be an easy way of fulfilling the contract. But as J. J. Johnson explained, "I've recorded with Miles and I know how he operates. Most of the time he goes into the studio and one take is it! Goofs or not, there's no second or third take. That's his philosophy on the recording bit." Actually, it's no secret that when several takes are made for each tune, and the group is so rehearsed and polished that every note seems predictable, a recording will lack the edge that makes the music exciting, "that thing," as Miles calls it. He would even insist that mistakes not be edited out, saying that mistakes, too, were a necessary part of improvised music.

In this first marathon session he recorded, in addition to such bop staples as Dizzy Gillespie's "Salt Peanuts" and "Woody 'n You," pop tunes that would seem to have little interest for a jazz musician, including "The Surrey With the Fringe on Top" (from *Oklahoma!*), "Diane" (Vic Damone's hit), and "When I Fall in Love." These tunes had been performed by Ahmad Jamal, and Miles was fascinated by Jamal's ability to make them swing. Miles also realized that the harmonic complexity of certain tunes that post-bop musicians were using, tunes like "How High the Moon"—seemed to force improvisers to play the same licks and clichés over and over again in order to fit their solos into the complex harmonic structure of the song. Miles wanted to make full use of his gift for melodic invention rather than simply "run the changes" (i.e., play licks that showed off a musician's ability to handle difficult chord progressions). Such deceptively simple tunes as "Diane" provided unfamiliar chord changes and a strong melody to use as a basis for improvisation. Miles always kept in mind Thelonius Monk's advice to "use the melody"—not simply abandon it for notes that fit the harmonic structure of the tune being played.

The quintet also performed blues. Miles had gained a reputation as one of the subtlest blues players in the history of jazz, while Coltrane employed a contrasting gutsy blues approach, no doubt because of his rhythm and blues experience. The blues, too, provided a great opportunity for melodic freedom.

The ballads recorded by the band for this session, which included Rodgers and Hart's "It Never Entered My Mind" (Miles loved the poignant lyrics of this song, particularly the line "You have what I lack myself, And now I even have to scratch my back myself"), "Something I Dreamed Last Night," and "When I Fall in Love," were all played muted by Miles; Coltrane did not solo.

Joe Goldberg wrote, "When Davis plays ballads, mute tight against the microphone (he seems to play microphone as much as trumpet), he reveals an area of tenderness and sensitivity which is rarely visible in his public aspect. These performances, in the emotion they evoke, are comparable to nothing in jazz."

Such performances would also play a large part in winning Miles a larger audience, which had little interest in jazz itself. The fact that Miles seemed to his audience to be so tough, so cool, made the ballad performances even more moving. Many years later, long after he had for the most part stopped playing these ballads, he said, "I never could stand it when a bitch came up to me after I had played a ballad and wanted to ball me or something. Couldn't she understand how much it took out of me to play a ballad? It left *me* weak in the knees."

Less than a month after the first marathon session for Prestige, the quintet went into the Columbia studios. They recorded three tunes: "Tadd's Delight," composed by Miles's former boss, Tadd Dameron; Stan Getz's version of an old Swedish folk song, "Dear Old Stockholm," and the standard "Bye Bye Blackbird." "Blackbird," like "Diane" and "Surrey With the Fringe on Top," was played in a moderate tempo, which the group, and especially the rhythm section, had totally mastered. Miles's solos on these tunes presented an aspect of his musical personality that would be largely ignored by most critics. Rather than sounding like the melancholy "musical lonely hearts club" (to use the phrase of one writer) of the ballads, these tunes show Miles in a lighthearted, even humorous mood. Although many critics disparage his supposedly limited emotional range (saying he was capable of expressing only dark and sorrowful emotions), "Blackbird" and "Diane" are as joyous in their own way as anything that, say, Louis Armstrong ever recorded. In addition, Miles's solos on these tunes again demonstrated his ability to condense an apparently simple melodic line and play it in a manner that both swung and subtly suggested to the listener other melodic possibilities.

The New Yorker's jazz critic expressed this perfectly when he wrote, "Davis is capable of remarkable distillation, rather than a one-two-three outlining of the melodic possibilities; indeed what comes out of his horn miraculously seems the result of the instantaneous editing of a far more diffuse melodic line being carried on in his head." Miles would present this concept in even simpler terms. "Man," he said, "you don't have to play a whole lot of notes. You just have to play the pretty ones."

While critics were beginning to recognize Miles's musical importance, they were more often than not critical of many aspects of the quintet, especially the playing of Philly Joe and Coltrane. Although many complained that Jones was too loud, they still admitted that he was an extremely skillful drummer. Coltrane, however, was a different matter. The saxophonist seemed to have technical problems: his reed squeaked at odd moments, and he often played out of tune. His solos started and stopped in fits, and his tone seemed painfully harsh to many critics. But there was an obvious parallel between Bird's faith in Miles, despite the trumpeter's technical limitations, and Miles's commitment to Coltrane, despite those voices in the jazz community who urged him to drop the saxophonist. Even though, at this time, he was deeply affected by his drug problems, Coltrane was an extremely serious, relentlessly curious musician. Miles recalls Coltrane "having a bottle of heroin that he was supposed to be sharing—he wound up doing almost the whole thing. But he was like Bird—when you're a genius like that, you live above everything else. You're a hog." Above all he realized that Coltrane's loquacious style brilliantly offset and complemented his own understated trumpet and that the hard edge of Coltrane's tone made his own sound even more sensuous.

By the time Miles completed his first album for Columbia, in September 1956, the paradoxes of the quintet's varied repertoire and the contrasting styles of its members synthesized into a sort of mystical perfection, possessing a fascination quite unlike anything else in jazz. The first record by the quintet was called by Ralph Berton in *The Record Changer* "orthodox, middle-of-the-road conservative progressive jazz." Many of the major breakthroughs that Miles made with this group were seen clearly only in retrospect. Years later Coltrane would say:

Miles is the number one influence over most of the modern musicians. . . . There isn't much harmonic ground he hasn't broken. Just listening to the beauty of his playing opens up doors. By the time I run up on something, I find Miles or Monk has done it already.

Some things I learn directly from them. Miles has shown me possibilities in choosing substitutions within a chord and also new directions.

Perhaps the greatest paradox was that all the seeming contradictions of the quintet coalesced so frequently into a stunning whole. The recordings attest to this. They sound as fresh and exciting today as they did twenty-five years ago.

Despite the growing success of his quintet Miles was still interested in playing with larger ensembles and working with some of the brilliant arrangers who had been involved with the nonet, especially Gil Evans. Since the breakup of the nonet Evans had been making a scant living by arranging music for commercials, pop recording dates, and the like. One of the few jazz gigs he had during these lean years was arranging a bizarre session for Charlie Parker with voices—hardly the best use of his talents. Miles had remained close to Evans, and now that he had a contract with Columbia he hoped to reestablish their artistic collaboration. Miles rarely abandoned his goals. He regarded the years of dope addiction in the early fifties as merely a postponement of the logical evolution of the nonet into an even larger ensemble. Duke Ellington had long been one of his idols, and he hoped to explore, as Ellington had, the relationship between the arranger and the improviser. The quintet was the culmination of many of the ideas that Miles had expressed in his small group recordings of the early fifties, but the principles of the nonet remained to be further explored and expanded.

Shortly after completing his first album for Columbia, he was asked to participate in an unusual project, one that would enable him to record with a large ensemble. Miles's former colleagues John Lewis and J. J. Johnson, along with other composers, including Jimmy Giuffre and Gunther Schuller, had been commissioned by Columbia to compose pieces for an orchestra made up of both classically trained and jazz musicians. The project was an outgrowth of the Third Stream movement—a blend of jazz with European classical music. Such musicians as Gunther Schuller viewed a combination of the two as being a way of revitalizing western music. Stravinsky in the early forties had experimented with jazz idioms in his music (for example, his *Ebony Concerto* for Woody Herman's orchestra), and of course in the twenties George Gershwin had attempted to "make a lady out of jazz" with his *Rhapsody in Blue* and other works. But these pieces, and others like them, were essentially classical pieces and ignored some of jazz's most significant components, especially improvisation. Unlike Stravinsky and Gershwin, Schuller, as well as John Lewis and Teo Macero, had some experience with jazz and a genuine understanding of it. Miles appreciated their ambitions, but he thought that this music was somewhat dry and overly cerebral. Later he would say about Third Stream, "It's like looking at a naked woman that you don't like."

Nevertheless, he was intrigued by the pieces that were being composed for the *Music for Brass* album, especially those by Johnson and Lewis, and readily agreed to play on the sessions. Johnson's piece "Poem for Brass" (the title wasn't the only thing pretentious about it) turned out to be rather ponderous. However, Lewis's "Three Little Feelings" was light and melodious and it was sparked by Miles's lovely solo—for some the highlight of the entire project.

If *Music for Brass* was not altogether successful, it further convinced Miles that he wanted his own large ensemble. He expressed to Gil Evans his interest in exploring the varied tonal colors that could be produced with an orchestra constituted of primarily brass instruments. Evans was also intrigued. Instead of the cool, pastel sound of the nonet, their new band would have layers, depths, of sound.

Before Miles could fully concentrate on the Evans project, he still had to complete the albums due on his contract with Prestige. His method remained the same: simply to go into the studio and record the quintet's repertoire. This second session was extremely relaxed, which is obvious not only from the recorded results, but also from extraneous comments picked up during the recording. At the beginning of "If I Were a Bell," which was played at that medium tempo the group handled so brilliantly, Bob Weinstock can be heard asking "What's the name of the tune, Miles?" "First we'll play it, then I'll tell you," is the reply. One can almost hear a shrug from Weinstock as Miles begins playing. At the end of "Oleo," Coltrane can be heard asking, "Where's the beer opener?" This was the spirit of jazz recording before the age of overdubbing, sophisticated production, and the striving for aural perfection instead of spontaneity.

"I have to laugh when I hear about people taking months to make a record," Miles mused recently. "I can make a record in four hours and it will be a *mother-fucker*." The sheer excitement audible on the quintet records bears this out. They contain striking evidence of Miles's increasing subtlety as an improviser. If one compares the recording of "Oleo" that he made with Sonny Rollins in 1954 with the version recorded with the quintet in 1956, his evolution is particularly striking. On the first version his solo is neatly organized, his ideas balanced, logical, and melodic—but there is a certain predictability to the solo. The later version of "Oleo" seems to burst through the confines of the tune, with unexpected rhythmic accents and a compelling and unpredictable lyricism. He is doing here what great improvisers do: building his own complex composition, an outgrowth, both melodically and harmonically, of the original tune.

In early 1956 benign nodes were discovered on Miles's vocal cords. A minor operation was performed, and the nodes were removed. There were no complications, but Miles's doctor warned him not to speak above a whisper for the following two weeks or he would irreversibly damage his vocal cords. Miles, in his headstrong way, put little stock in the doctor's words—he considered doctors overcautious and square. The day he got out of the hospital he ran into a promoter with whom he was having a business disagreement. Miles became enraged (this was common in his dealings with promoters and club owners) and began screaming at the man. Needless to say, the doctor was right: Miles permanently damaged his vocal cords, which reduced his voice to a hoarse whisper and forced him to have to concentrate on articulating every word. He found this condition infuriating, frustrating, and embarrassing. Already a shy man, he became very self-conscious about his voice. One night he was discussing the styles of various singers that he admired, from Al Green to'Sinatra to Maria Callas. Then a melancholy look came into his eyes and he muttered, "Of course, I could never sing." But his trumpet, especially with the increasingly vocal shadings of his playing after 1956, was an eloquent surrogate voice.

In the fall of that year he sent a letter to George Avakian of Columbia describing the record he wanted to make with Gil Evans. At the end of the letter Miles wrote, "If you can't do it that way, please recommend me to a company that can." Of course, this was a bluff, since he was under contract to Columbia. But it would set the tone for his continuing love-hate relationship with the record company.

Actually, Avakian was pleased that Miles was working on an album with Evans. He had long been a fan of the nonet, and as he later wrote:

When Miles Davis signed with Columbia, we found in each other a mutual interest in furthering the ideals of the nine-piece band. What direction this desire would take was uncertain, beyond the conviction that Gil Evans was the arranger we wanted. A series of discussions with Gil followed, out of which grew the basic conception (largely Miles's).

Work on this album began to take up most of Miles's time. Procedures were set up that would be followed on all his subsequent projects with the arranger.

Once when describing Evans's working method, Miles said, "You know, in New York we go over to each other's houses, but we don't drop our problems on each other. When Gil is writing, he might spend three days on ten bars of music. He'll lock himself up in a room of his house, put a Do Not Disturb sign on the door, and not even his wife Lillian can come in. It's torture for her when he's writing. It's like he's out to lunch. Sometimes he'll get in there and play the piano for twelve hours." Miles, on the other hand, wrote very quickly, often "taking what Gil handed me and showing him how it could be done a lot simpler—in just a few minutes!"

The contrast between the two men was sharp: Miles short and stealthy, Evans tall and patrician; Miles a volatile, continuous source of inspiration and ideas, Evans the deliberate, slow-working intellectual. Yet, Evans had stated, "We think alike. We are complementary in that we are opposites. My inclination is less extroverted than his. We both love the same kind of music."

Miles agreed, adding, "I just let Gil write. I give him an outline of what I want and he finishes it. I can even call him on the phone and just tell him what I got in mind, and when I see the score, it is exactly what I wanted. Nobody but Gil could think for me that way. He just has a gift of being able to put instruments together. Some people have it, some don't. Gil has it."

In early 1957 Columbia finally released its first Miles Davis album, *'Round About Midnight*. The record garnered excellent reviews and, due to Columbia's steady promotion, it jumped to number seven on the chart of jazz best sellers. Writing in *down beat*, Ralph J. Gleason gave the album five stars (the highest rating) and raved:

> This is the kind of album to which one returns time and time again, because it is in its way a perfect thing; a slice of modern jazz conceived and executed in the very best style. . . . [Miles's] solos build beautifully to logical climaxes and Coltrane, who customarily enters after Miles, seems here to have more of the melding of Prez [Lester Young] and Hawkins and less of the bad tone which has been his lot up to now.

The most celebrated cut on the album was Miles's very personal version of the Monk classic " 'Round Midnight," the tune with which he had impressed the critics so much at his comeback performance at Newport. The cover of the album, which shows Miles sitting glumly in a red light, wearing bebop shades, did much to further his image as the jazz maverick, the lonely man with the horn.

Although he was now receiving national attention, he was becoming increasingly frustrated with the group that had done so much to bring him this fame. Philly Joe and Coltrane were more erratic than ever. Many observers thought, at this time, that Coltrane would never live to see thirty-five.

Still, Miles knew that this group was his ideal vehicle. Critics were not nearly so sanguine. The reviews the group received when performing at nightclubs were often less than glowing. Harry Frost, writing in *Metronome* of a performance in early 1957 in Miles's hometown, East St. Louis, complained:

> There is no doubt that Miles has today surrounded himself with some superb musicians. There *is* considerable doubt as to whether he will ever again head an important group as he did in 1949 [the nonet]—unless his attitude undergoes a pronounced change.
>
> Twice within seven months Miles has come home to appear at Peacock Alley in St. Louis. Both times he has tendered his music on a "here it is—if you don't like it—so what" basis. A feeling of cold independence rules this group. It's as if these guys are too *good* to try. Their approach is careless and almost deliberately sloppy. . . . The drummer is the redoubtable Philly Joe Jones. Joe has a lot of flash and flexibility. He provides a penetrating beat and plays with fiery vigor. He also plays at a dynamic level that obscures most of what's happening in the group, behind a wall of cymbal-clatter. . . .
>
> Sharing the front line with the Davis trumpet is tenor man John Coltrane. A typical unison piece

will find Miles on one side of the stand and Coltrane on the other. There is no attempt to blend the horns and each is content to play his part as though the other man had left for the evening.

As a soloist, Coltrane appears to have the equipment but indulges too often in extended double-time flurries that are notable for their lack of direction. . . .

As an artist, Miles Davis has a right to a certain amount of temperament. As a musician of the cool school, his audience is conditioned to his aloof, emotionless facade. The implicit danger is that this coolness will degenerate into indifference. Then the music degenerates.

This review was not untypical. But despite such opinion the quintet prospered, becoming one of the most successful and sought-after jazz groups in the country. In a way, reviews like this even helped foster the image of Miles as Ultimate Hip, Ultimate Cool—an attractive image to the young of the late fifties, though he himself did not consciously assume it. And of course, the uncompromising spirit of the music itself did little to hurt the image. The jazz fans drawn to Miles would have been shocked had he started to make long announcements to his audiences, crack jokes like Dizzy did, or smile and bow after every number. His audience expected him, even wanted him, to turn his back (although he actually did this to hear the drummer better), and to leave the stand (he thought there was no reason to hang around the bandstand after a solo). His hipness, as perceived by many of his fans, was an extension of that of the beboppers, but it was also something more. Miles, to them, was too cool to be involved (any longer) with drugs and too much the sensitive artist to clown around on stage. In the late fifties, when interest in the Beats and the existentialists was growing, Miles Davis suddenly found himself at the height of fashion.

He didn't have to look too far to see so-called hipsters dressing like him, scowling and cursing like him, and even trying to talk like him with the raspy whisper that was for him an embarrassing affliction. These types, especially if they were white, were often sarcastically dubbed "hippies" by the musicians—a term that took on a different connotation in the middle and late sixties.

An ad placed in national magazines in the late fifties by the phone company opened with the line, "I was listening to Miles playing 'My Funny Valentine,' and I started thinking about you." He appealed to a variety of people on a great many levels; his brand of hip could be understood easily by squares. One night at a club he took an unusually short solo and walked casually off the stand. Backstage the club owner threw up his arms and started shouting about Miles's shortcomings as a performer—his refusal to announce tunes or the names of his sidemen, his frequent lateness, etc. Finishing up, he said, "The trouble is that everybody *likes* you, you little son of a bitch." Miles could only smile.

In March 1957 he could no longer contain his growing disgust with the unprofessional behavior of Philly Joe and Coltrane. In Baltimore he walked off the stand while both of them were nodding out. "How can I play with musicians in that kind of condition?" he told the exasperated club owner. He brought the band back to New York to play a long engagement at the Bohemia, the club which had nurtured the group since its inception. One night early in the engagement he left the club at the beginning of the two A.M. set, again because Philly Joe and Coltrane were too drugged-out to play. The club owner promptly fired the band, and Miles announced that the quintet was officially disbanded.

While most of the members took this in stride, to Coltrane it was a shock, a slap in the face. But he desperately needed a shock. Miles hated to lecture his sidemen, but he knew that Coltrane, with his heavy use of alcohol and heroin, was headed for certain disaster. When Coltrane returned home to Philadelphia, he came to the same conclusion. One morning soon after the disbandment he quietly announced to his wife, "I am going to quit drugs, alcohol, and tobacco." Coltrane would later say that he had had a religious revelation that brought him to his senses. But for whatever reason, he did manage to kick both alcohol and drugs on his own—in much the same way that Miles had. Again like Miles, he resolved to concentrate totally on music, and began to practice twelve hours a day or more. When he returned to the jazz scene, nobody would be calling him a bad-toned imitator of Dexter Gordon.

Although Miles was deeply involved with Gil Evans on the big-band project, he felt restless after dissolving the quintet. He needed the excitement of improvising with a small group, and so he readily accepted an invitation to make a quick tour of Europe with pickup rhythm sections. He had not been there since 1949.

Paris was his second stop after an initial engagement in Switzerland, and once again he found his spirits lifted by the City of Light. He got together with Juliette Gréco there and met one of his staunchest supporters, André Hodeir, who had declared in print in 1953 that Miles was the brightest hope of the post-bop musicians. Hodeir introduced him to a number of musicians who had a deep intellectual respect for him that Miles was not used to back home. He also met Louis Malle, a young French filmmaker with a special love of jazz. Malle asked Miles to return to France later in the year to record a soundtrack for the film he was directing, *L'Ascenseur pour l'échafaud* ("Elevator to the Scaffold"). Miles was aware that few jazz musicians had ever been asked to score a film in America, and impressed by Malle's enthusiasm he agreed to work with him.

He returned to New York mainly to record the bigband album with Gil Evans. Once back, he also played several club dates, trying to find musicians of the caliber of those who had been in the original quintet. Sonny Rollins again teamed up with him and once again disappeared after playing for only a few weeks. Red Garland and Paul Chambers were frequently on the dates. Daniel Morgenstern, reviewing an appearance by Miles at the Bohemia with a group that included Garland, Chambers, and Rollins, stated: "At the time of the Newport Jazz Festival, I was amazed that any human could achieve such distillation of pure sound from an instrument so often thunderous. If anything, Miles has gone on making his tone purer and purer until it now is the gentlest of whispers when muted, and a subtle but somehow forceful and glowing sound on open horn." In addition Morgenstern praised every member of the group.

He also mentioned that "Miles was in a buoyant mood, strolling down into the audience after his solos to chat with friends."

In May 1957 Miles and Gil Evans finally had their recording session. The nineteen-piece band, which was conducted by Evans, resembled the nonet in that it included tuba and French horns, but now there were more instruments, creating a larger sound. Miles and Gil wanted the album to be as innovative as the original work on *Birth of the Cool*. One unusual feature was the piecing-together of tunes with segues, making the album into one continuous composition. Also, Miles was the only soloist, playing flugelhorn rather than trumpet.

The music was among the lushest jazz has ever heard, so much so that some critics would complain that the album, *Miles Ahead,* was dangerously close to "mood music." Whitney Balliett wrote in *The New Yorker:*

> There is . . . too much port and velvet, and Davis, a discreet, glancing performer, backslides in these surroundings into a moony, saccharine, and—in "My Ship"—downright dirge-like approach. The result is some of the coolest jazz ever uttered. Despite its technical innovations, *Miles Ahead* seems almost an epitaph for the cool school, whose beginnings are often dated by the Davis-Mulligan records, and which has recently shown signs of wilting away.

Despite this critique, *Miles Ahead* has worn well and is a record of remarkably subtle ingenuity and beauty. André Hodeir wrote in the liner notes to the album:

> Miles Davis in this album confirms what we already knew about him—that he is the most lyrical of modern jazzmen. But whereas the lyricism of Charlie Parker, in his great moments, seemed to want to burst open the gates of delirium, Miles's lyricism tends rather toward a discovery of ecstasy.

Although there could never be any single street as alive with the spirit of jazz as Fifty-second Street had been, Greenwich Village and lower Manhattan as a whole were becoming a haven for the music. The Village Vanguard, the Village Gate, the Café Bohemia, and the Half Note had all become favorite clubs for modern musicians by the late fifties. They were also frequented by the artists and writers of the area, and became gathering grounds for some of the avant-garde of the time, including writers such as Frank O'Hara, Jack Kerouac, and LeRoi Jones (Imamu Amiri Baraka), and artists such as Larry Rivers, Franz Kline, and Willem de Kooning.

One of the favorite clubs in this milieu was the Five Spot Café, which was originally located on the Bowery. In the summer of 1957, after years of being denied a cabaret card due to an arrest for drugs, Thelonious Monk opened a summer-long engagement there with a group that included John Coltrane, now clean and healthy, Philly Joe Jones, and the brilliant bassist Wilbur Ware. The group, according to J. J. Johnson, "was the most exciting thing I've heard since Bird and Diz." Monk had long been a jazz phenomenon, but it was the rejuvenated and drug-free Coltrane who so astonished everyone who heard him. He was no longer the groping, unsure player who had been a member of Miles's original quintet. Rather he was playing the intricate music of Thelonious Monk in a style of saxophone that no one had ever really heard before, a style that critic Ira Gitler would later dub "sheets of sound"—notes which poured over one another in a fountain of music, each note following the next faster than the ear could follow, but in a pattern that made complex, overall, sense.

Miles became a regular at the Five Spot, fascinated by Coltrane's complex harmonic sense, his mature, brilliant saxophone style. Here was the flowering of the potential he had always seen.

He also realized that Coltrane was now one of the few musicians who could understand some of the concepts that were brewing in his own mind. He had no doubts—Coltrane belonged back with him. By now, however, Coltrane was emotionally and intellectually involved with Monk's music. "Playing with Monk," he said once, "is

sometimes like walking into an empty elevator shaft."
But the challenge excited him.

In the meantime an altoist named Julian "Cannonball" Adderley had appeared, and he had been dubbed
the "New Bird." This was somewhat unfair, since it
aroused such great expectations. Adderley was no in-
novator; he had incorporated much of Bird's style into
his own sound. However, he had also been influenced
by such altoists as Benny Carter, and in his bluesy style
there was more than a touch of such rhythm-and-blues
saxophonists as Earl Bostic. Miles immediately liked the
young saxophonist: "He had a certain spirit. You
couldn't put your finger on it, but it was there in his
playing every night." When he first heard him, Cannonball was playing in his own quintet, co-led by his
brother, cornetist Nat Adderley:

I had gotten an offer from Dizzy to go with his
small band. I was opposite Miles at the Bohemia,
told him I was going to join Dizzy, and Miles asked
me why I didn't join him. I told him he never asked
me.

Miles had helped me when I first came to New
York. He told me whom to avoid among the record
companies, but unfortunately I didn't take his advice. Al Lion of Blue Note was one man he recommended and Miles also told me about John Levy.
Miles began telling me something musically about
chords, but I sort of ignored him. I was a little arrogant in those days. Then about three months later
I saw an interview in which Miles had said I could
swing but I didn't know much about chords. . . .

Well, Miles kept talking to me for two or three
months to come with him, and when I finally cut
loose in October 1957, I joined Miles. Not that Dizzy

John Coltrane, Cannonball Adderley, Miles Davis, Bill Evans, 1958 (Institute of Jazz Studies).

isn't a good teacher, but he played more commercially than Miles. Thank goodness I made the move I did.

The obvious influence of Miles on Adderley was made apparent by a recording session supposedly led by Cannonball in early 1958. As a favor, Miles agreed to play trumpet on the date, in a rare appearance as a sideman. However, it would be clear from the resulting record, titled *Something Else,* that Miles was its true guiding spirit. Everything from the choice of tunes (including an especially tender version of "Autumn Leaves") to the arrangements, which were reminiscent of those for the original quintet, strongly bears Miles's stamp. But perhaps most telling is Adderley's own playing, far more tasteful and thoughtful than on any other records he made, except those with Miles. As extraordinary as it may seem, the simple fact that Miles was at a session had an effect on musicians—he could make them play with intelligence and luster by simply looking at them and making what appeared to be the simplest suggestions. A look of disgust or sigh of impatience from Miles made a good musician want to be great. To use an epithet applied to him in *Rolling Stone* much later in his career, Miles was becoming the *brujo* of American music, the great teacher, even the alchemist of jazz.

Modes

Julien is trapped in an elevator; he must escape in order to save himself from implication in the murder of his mistress. Like a rat in a cage, he surveys the possibilities for escape.

The scene is a Gallic version of Hitchcock. On the soundtrack, the most mournful trumpet ever heard gives Julien's plight an element of tragedy that it never would have had otherwise. For his music to Louis Malle's film *Elevator to the Scaffold,* Miles used an all-star French group, including the superb bassist Pierre Michelot and the young tenor man Barney Wilen. The one non-Frenchman in the group was Miles's cohort from Fifty-second Street days and the Paris Jazz Festival of 1949— Kenny Clarke, now an expatriate. Although all were experienced musicians, no one was prepared for Miles's method of making a film soundtrack.

Rather than sit down and compose music, he brought the group into a darkened studio and had a projectionist run the film as he led the group in totally improvised music—thereby giving the suspense drama an added edge.

The result was strong enough to stand on its own and eventually won the highest French award given to records. Most of the music was blues-based, with no motifs, just a set of simple guidelines for the players, streamlined chord progressions that would give them the maximum amount of freedom for improvising. That the music turned out to be so deeply stirring gave Miles encouragement to pursue similar directions, which for some time had been gaining importance in his musical priorities.

In January 1958 he officially became an American cultural icon—he was written up in *Time* magazine. The article hailed him as "the leader of the post-bop generation of boppers." (*Time*-ese could be especially obnoxious when it tried to be hip.) Miles denied to the *Time* interviewer that he was a cool musician, and informed him that, "If you play good for eight bars, it's enough—for yourself." (Later he would say, "I just never tell which are those eight good bars. That's my little secret.") Perhaps with his elegant clothes and repertoire of pop tunes Miles seemed *Time*'s idea of the jazz musician. But a few years later the *Time* people would get a shock. When they tried to do a cover story on him and modern jazz in the early sixties, Miles refused to cooperate. He threw their photographers out of the Village Vanguard, telling them, "I wouldn't come to where you work and blow my horn." At that time he had little interest in getting publicity, especially in a magazine that he disliked. Eventually *Time* did a story on Thelonious Monk instead.

In the spring of 1958 Miles was interviewed by Nat

Hentoff for *The Jazz Review*, a new and very intelligent jazz magazine. Hentoff conducted the interview by playing records for Miles, who made comments. At one point he stated:

> I think a movement in jazz is beginning away from the conventional string of chords, and a return to emphasis on melodic rather than harmonic variation. There will be fewer chords but infinite possibilities as to what to do with them. Classical composers—some of them—have been writing this way for years, but jazz musicians seldom have.
>
> When I want J. J. Johnson to hear something or he wants me to, we phone each other and just play the music on the phone. I did that the other day with some of the Khachaturian scales; they're different from the usual western scales. Then we got to talking about letting the melodies and scales carry the tune. J.J. told me, "I'm not going to write any more chords." And look at George Russell. His writing is mostly scales. After all, you can feel the changes.
>
> The music has gotten thick. Guys give me tunes and they're full of chords. I can't play them. You know, we play "My Funny Valentine" like with a scale all the way through.

These concerns would begin to dominate Miles's musical thinking and they would in turn be a part of a major evolution in jazz, the first real shake-up since the advent of bop in the forties. Jazz was at a crossroads. Although the ideas of bop were still predominant, the rebellious spirit had died. Dizzy Gillespie, Thelonious Monk, Max Roach, and Miles himself were now the jazz establishment. There remained little excitement in the jungle of chords that had become the essence of modern jazz, and Miles, for one, was bored with the clichés that had replaced original ideas among so many of the second-generation musicians.

For him the answer was simpler harmonic structures, freeing the improviser to use his ability for melodic invention. However, only the finest musicians—the ones who were extremely sophisticated harmonically and had the imagination and self-assurance of someone like Coltrane—would be able to take on this new challenge of no longer relying on old licks or a stream of notes that fit neatly into the harmonic pattern of a tune.

In early 1958 John Coltrane rejoined Miles's group, making it a sextet (Cannonball remained in the group). In a 1960 interview Coltrane recalled his surprise at the evolution taking place in Miles's musical thinking:

> On returning to [Miles's group] this time to stay until I formed my own group a few months later, I found Miles in the midst of another stage of his musical development. There was one time in his past that he devoted to multichorded structures. He was interested in chords for their own sake. But now it seemed that he was moving in the opposite direction to the use of fewer and fewer chord changes in songs. He used tunes with free-flowing lines and chordal direction. This approach allowed the soloist the choice of playing chordally or melodically. . . . Miles's music gave me plenty of freedom. It's a beautiful approach.

And it would be the approach that would profoundly affect the direction of Coltrane's own music during the sixties.

Among the musicians whom Miles met in Paris was a young composer-arranger named Michel Legrand. Legrand would later become famous for such pop tunes as "The Windmills of My Mind" and his score for *The Umbrellas of Cherbourg*. But at that time his passion was jazz. In response to a recording offer from Columbia, Legrand put together an all-star band. When asked about Miles, he had stated, "Ah, Miles. For me, the most important musician." Miles, who was friendly with Legrand and feeling generally indebted to the French, agreed to play on the album. In addition, he wanted to compare Legrand's orchestral approach to that of Gil Evans. Eventually he came to regard the French arranger's work as clever and frothy, especially in versions of such hoary jazz standards as Fats Waller's "Jitterbug Waltz," but it seemed retrograde after the innovations of *Miles Ahead*.

Miles and Gil had talked about several ideas for projects—they did not want to simply repeat themselves. Columbia executives suggested they record a version of Gershwin's folk opera, *Porgy and Bess*. Samuel Goldwyn's big-budget film of the opera was due to be released later that year, and everyone from Mel Tormé to Louis Armstrong was recording the score. Miles's initial reaction was negative—he wanted to record music, not execute marketing concepts. But after consideration he decided that *Porgy and Bess* was an ideal score, after all, for a new collaboration with Gil. They could use Miles's trumpet as an operatic voice, as they used it for their version of Kurt Weill's "My Ship" on *Miles Ahead*. Gershwin's music seemed almost designed for the orchestral timbres and textures with which Evans was experimenting. In addition, it would provide a special challenge, precisely because so much of it was almost overly familiar. Miles and Gil were determined to make the score of *Porgy and Bess* their own—indeed, to give Miles the opportunity to capture several of the characters of Gershwin's folk opera on his horn.

By this time not only had *Miles Ahead* become a best-selling record but the music trade magazines were hailing the new collaboration of Miles and Gil as a brilliant step forward for orchestral jazz. Ralph Gleason gave the album five stars in *down beat* and wrote:

> This is an extraordinarily well done album with absolutely no point at which you can wish for more if you, like John Lewis and so many others, have wished for a big band with delicacy. If so, here it is, playing ten beautifully arranged selections and sounding a good deal like the best of Claude Thornhill with Miles. . . . This is not, by intention, an lp to raise you off your chair screaming. It is one to bring you close to almost unbearable delights in music in much the same way the Modern Jazz Quartet does, and which only Duke consistently has been able to do with a big band. The handling of the brass, with its muttering, spouting,

Miles and Gil Evans, 1957 (Frank Driggs Collection).

rolling figures, is a thing of liveliness that grows with each hearing. . . . This is some of the best mood music produced since Duke.

Almost every critic would refer to *Miles Ahead* as sophisticated mood music. This could be attributed, at least partly, to the fact that Miles played flugelhorn instead of trumpet. The flugelhorn has a much rounder, more satiny tone than the trumpet, and Miles was, at this point, fascinated with the larger horn, much as he would be with the electronic wah-wah pedal for his trumpet in the seventies. However, the two collaborators wanted *Porgy and Bess* to have a more pronounced rhythmic fire than *Miles Ahead*. The project would dominate Miles's musical thinking throughout 1958.

In 1958 Miles was reaching the height of his fame, and he was richly enjoying its rewards. Among those rewards were women. With his superb wardrobe, white Ferrari, and macho image, he was no longer the celibate student of his Fifty-second Street days. After his divorce from Irene, beautiful, glamorous women were a constant in his life. In a *Rolling Stone* interview he would say about these years, "All the money, cars, clothes, the bitches—all that was to match my ego."

Miles's love of clothes sometimes almost seemed to supersede his love of music. Once in the sixties after a concert he asked a friend, "How was I?" "You sounded great" was the reply. "No," Miles said, "I don't mean my music. What did you think of my suit?" Indeed, Miles's clothes often reflected subtle changes in his music. While tight Italian suits were almost his trademark in the late fifties and early sixties, colorful shirts and scarfs reflected the more aggressive textures of his music in the middle and late sixties.

Miles refused to be told by anybody what he should wear. Once when he was appearing at Birdland with his sextet, Oscar Goodstein requested that Miles have his band dress in uniforms, as many groups were doing at the time. According to Nat Adderley, Cannonball's brother, the next night Miles kept the group in the dressing room until it was time to go on. When the group went on stage, they were wearing the same disparate clothes they had worn the night before. Miles pulled a rack of uniforms that he had obtained from a nearby clothing store onstage and told the audience, "Oscar Goodstein wanted to see uniforms onstage so here they are. If that's what you came for, to look at uniforms instead of music, that's what you got. Now we're going to leave so you can enjoy these uniforms." Needless to say, Goodstein quickly backed down on his demand, and the group played in their usual clothes.

Women found Miles fascinating, charismatic, witty, and intelligent. But he was also totally unpredictable, and when angered, he could be violent. "He could be so sweet at times," said one of his ex-girlfriends, "and then at other times go completely off. He often frightened me."

Also in 1958 Miles met Frances Taylor, a young dancer whom he had seen perform at the Apollo Theater with the Katherine Dunham troupe. Not only was Frances exceptionally beautiful, she also had grace and intelligence. Miles was entranced by her, and found himself, for the first time since he was a teen-ager, actively courting a woman. Frances had recently been divorced and had a small son by her first husband; she had no desire to jump into another marriage, especially with a man as notoriously volatile as Miles. But Miles was persistent, all the more so because Frances was truly hard to get. Soon she began to be deeply touched by the shyness and vulnerability she glimpsed beneath

Miles's angry shell. Eventually, *she* asked him to marry her. According to Miles, he never could turn down a sincere proposal of marriage: "Every time I got married," he said later, "it was because the bitch asked me. I didn't want to hurt their feelings, so I would say yes." In mid-1958, Miles and Frances were married.

In April of that year Miles took his sextet, which now consisted of the original quintet plus Cannonball Adderley, into the Columbia recording studio. In addition to Monk's "Straight, No Chaser" and the bebop standard "Two Bass Hit," they also recorded a tune titled "Miles" (he originally called it "Milestones," perhaps forgetting that he had already recorded a different composition with the same title on a Charlie Parker date in the forties). The simple melody was an experiment inspired by an evening Miles had spent with the jazz composer and arranger George Russell, who at the time was working on his theoretical "Lydian Concept of Tonal Organization." Basically, this was a method for the jazz composer and improviser to use modes rather than the traditional tonal chord progressions and tonally responsive melodies. Modes are actually a very old concept in western music, dating back to ancient Greece, and modal concepts were used, in different incarnations, in the "primitive" music of Africa and in the art music of India. Miles was fascinated by Russell's approach. Here was a means of breaking free from tonal clichés—while maintaining some amount of restraint. "George," Miles told Russell that night, "if Bird were alive, this would kill him."

Shortly after his evening with Russell, Miles recorded his new composition demonstrating Russell's basic principles. Cannonball Adderley played a fine solo on the tune. Coltrane's solo sounded less assured—his musical mind was deeply involved in the incredibly complex harmonic structure with which he was still obsessed—but he was immediately intrigued by Miles's new tack. And Miles's own solo, played through a felt mute, was a perfectly structured improvisation, remarkable for its melodic invention. The tune itself, with its repeated vamp played on piano, its changing meters midchorus, and the steady, repetitive rhythmic figures played expertly by Philly Joe, would become a model for the jazz-rock that was to become so predominant more than a decade later.

Although the album would eventually be considered a classic, the sessions for the *Milestones* lp were chaotic. Once again Philly Joe was becoming difficult to work with. He didn't like recording for Columbia; at Prestige, he had been able to walk out of the studio with cash—now he had to wait, sometimes for weeks, for his check. For a junkie, even a day's wait is too long. Cannonball, realizing that Philly Joe was becoming undependable, brought in Jimmy Cobb, who had played briefly in his quintet, as well as with Dizzy Gillespie and Dinah Washington. Eventually Jones did reluctantly show up, but then Red Garland vanished. Miles had to take Garland's place at the piano to accompany the other soloists after taking his own solo on the blues "Sid's Ahead" without piano accompaniment, something he had done many times before (most memorably, on the equally chaotic all-star session with Thelonious Monk). When the session was over, Garland finally showed up. As Jimmy Cobb remembers, "Red walked in and started to play the piano. But the shit was over! Miles was pissed, but he knew what Red and Philly Joe were about; he had been through that junkie bullshit himself. And Red and Philly Joe, in turn, felt that Miles didn't care about their problems, that he could just go home to his great home, he didn't have to scuffle on the streets like they did."

Milestones marked the final breakup of the great

Jones-Chambers-Garland rhythm section. Shortly there-
after, Cannonball brought Jimmy Cobb to play a
date with Miles at a club in Brooklyn. "And," as Jimmy
remembers, "I just found myself in the group."

Bill Evans, a young pianist with George Russell's
group, had impressed Miles very much. Evans's touch,
his rich harmonic sense and lyricism, had already come
to the attention of many musicians. In addition, he was
interested in and actively exploring the same new harmonic horizons as Russell and Miles. Soon after hiring
him, Miles would say, "Boy, I've sure learned a lot from
Bill Evans. He plays the piano the way it should be
played. He plays all kinds of scales; can play in 5/4; and
all kinds of fantastic things. There's such a difference
between him and Red Garland, whom I also like a lot.
Red carries the rhythm, but Bill underplays, and I like
that better."

Evans was invited by Miles to record music for the
flip side of the *Elevator to the Scaffold* album. The date's

Miles and Jimmy Cobb (Frank Driggs Collection).

personnel was the same as for *Milestones,* except that Cobb and Evans were respectively playing drums and piano. The group recorded three tunes: "On Green Dolphin Street," the children's song "Put Your Little Foot Out," and the standard "Stella by Starlight." This recording session, held one month after *Milestones,* shows a marked contrast to the previous sessions. The jaunty piano of Garland is replaced by Evans's warm and romantic playing, which has more than a touch of Debussyesque impressionism. Cobb's drumming, while not as dynamic as Philly Joe's, has a cleaner sound and is less complex.

As brilliantly as Bill Evans played, his hiring still caused controversy in jazz circles. Evans was white, and conservatory-trained. In the late fifties, there was a growing phenomenon tagged "Crow Jim." Many black musicians refused to hire or play with white musicians, which was somewhat justified considering the decades of discrimination and rejection they had received from the white musical establishment. Although Miles often made comments such as "all those white tenor men sound alike," he had worked closely with white musicians since the late forties. He became annoyed when musicians said to him about Evans, "Miles, what are you doing with that white boy up there? You know he can't swing." As Miles would say later, "I remember when I hired Lee Konitz, some colored cats bitched a lot about me hiring an ofay in my band when Negroes didn't have work. I said if a cat could play like Lee, I would hire him. I didn't give a damn if he was green and had red breath." Although Miles would continue to talk about white and black approaches to music, he would always hire the musician that best fit his musical needs at the time, regardless of race.

Even though Bill Evans added a lyrical influence, the

group was still playing fiery, bristling music, and many critics were still perturbed by its unabashedly loose structure. Coltrane was becoming even more of a puzzle for the critics. His solos were getting longer and longer, employing labyrinthine scales and arpeggios delivered with a fervor that many found overwhelming. A *down beat* critic called the group's front line "working egos. Coltrane erupted in a fantastic onrush of surrealism and disconnected musical thought best appreciated within the dark corridors of his personal psyche." As for Miles, the reviewer simply stated, "Miles's bearing resembles more and more that of Frank Sinatra." To many critics the image was becoming more important than the horn.

Three weeks after appearing at the 1958 Newport Jazz Festival with his sextet, Miles began recording *Porgy and Bess* with Gil Evans. He played both flugelhorn and trumpet on the date, and as in *Miles Ahead,* he remained the only soloist. The sessions were the most difficult challenge Miles had encountered as a player up to that point. "I had to *think* like Bess, and then like Porgy, in order to play with the right feeling," he recalls. " 'Bess, You Is My Woman Now' is the single hardest thing I ever played, because I had to think the lyrics, repeating the refrain over and over again in my head. I mean, how many times can you say 'Bess, you is my woman'? You can say, 'Bess you is my woman, Bess you is my bitch, Bess you is my whore' . . . . it fucked me up."

Evans and Miles continued experimenting with simpler harmonic progressions. At the time of the recording of *Porgy and Bess,* Miles told Nat Hentoff, "When Gil wrote the arrangement of 'I Loves You, Porgy,' he only wrote a scale for me to play. No chords. And in

Miles at ·a recording session for Porgy and Bess (*Frank Driggs Collection*).

'Summertime' there is a long space where we don't change the chord at all. It just doesn't have to be cluttered up (with harmonic complexity)." Indeed, their version of "Summertime" is unusual in many respects; they make one of the most recorded and familiar of all popular tunes sound fresh again. Playing muted trumpet, Miles blows sweet variations of the melody while the orchestra, in response, echoes his improvisations in subtly changing orchestral colors. While the song is usually performed as a languid lullaby, Miles and Gil play it at a moderate tempo, but somehow Gershwin's original rueful emotional substance remains.

(153)

Although always fascinating, and often beautiful, there is an occasional cerebral coldness about Miles's version of the passionate folk opera. When the record was released in 1959, most serious critics found *Porgy and Bess* a revelation. Martin Williams in *The Jazz Review* wrote:

> Gil Evans has taken Gershwin's melodies and has made them his own. The arrangements in this album give as much meaning to such arias as "My Man's Gone Now" as did the original score. Evans's ability to project powerful emotion in amazingly sensitive ways is beautifully matched by Miles, whose solos approach being magnificent. Davis is the first instrumentalist I've heard play a recitative that is convincing and completely devoid of burlesque.
>
> There are so many wonderful moments of beauty and swing, so many ingenious turns of phrase; there is so much that is good in this lp, that it would take thousands of words to describe it fully.

Meanwhile Miles's small band not only was continuing to become an exciting whole—its separate musicians were all finding their individual ways. Bill Evans was the most articulate about his experience with the band. He recalls:

> It was a personal as well as a musical experience, and it probably brought me back to myself quite a lot. I had felt the group to be composed of super-humans, and it helped my perspective to know how human they are and to experience the real and beautiful ways in which they deal with musical problems.

There wasn't much said in Miles's band, but things happened. We never had a rehearsal. Everything was done on the job. On the record dates, half or all of the material might be all new and had never been rehearsed before. We'd talk it over, run through certain chords, and often we'd use the first take. Even though the performance might not have been perfect, it had something else.

A beautiful thing about that band was how little was said about the music. That makes you rely on yourself; it makes you a person. It was a good social lesson and pointed up how good a way that is for a person to live.

Miles brought Bill Evans, a shy and introspective man, out of himself. When the band was together and discussing some subject, Evans would try to interject his own comments. Miles would often look at him disdainfully, say drily, "We don't need any of your white opinion," and follow with one of his croaked chuckles. At first Evans was taken aback. But after a while he realized that this was Miles's caustic sense of humor, and its intent was to make Bill actually *relax* about being the only white in the group by making it a running joke.

Miles occasionally became perturbed by the increasing length of Coltrane's solos. Coltrane was exploring the heights and depths of music every night, sometimes in solos lasting fifteen or twenty minutes or longer. One night Miles asked another musician to ask Coltrane why he soloed for so long.

Questioned, Coltrane responded, "I don't know how to stop."

When Miles heard this he said, "Tell him to take the horn out of his mouth."

But Miles remained committed to Coltrane. He told a critic around this time:

I don't understand this talk about Coltrane being difficult to understand. What he does, for example, is to play five notes of a chord and then change it around, trying to see how many different ways it can sound. It's like explaining something five different ways. And that sound of his is connected with what he's doing with the chords at any time.

As can be seen from a review in *down beat* written at this time, Coltrane's fierce explorations were dominating the attention of most of the band's listeners, who were often disturbed by what they heard. Coltrane, a reserved, modest man, was puzzled by accusations that he was playing "angry saxophone." "I guess," he told a writer, "that's because I play the horn hard."

Cannonball and Coltrane were learning from each other, each encouraging the other saxophonist's growth and curiosity. Miles encouraged this as much as possible, just as he had done when both Sonny Rollins and Coltrane were in his midfifties band. When Cannonball was playing, Miles would whisper to Coltrane, "Listen to how Cannonball gets in all his lyrical ideas without playing as long as you. You should learn how to edit your ideas from him." And when Coltrane was soloing, Miles would tell Cannonball, "Listen to Coltrane's harmonic ideas. You should learn to play with his type of harmonic thinking." After the gig, Coltrane and Adderley would each tell the other what their boss had said about him and laugh—they both appreciated the accelerated learning experience that Miles was providing.

While most of the band was equally engrossed in Coltrane's nightly evolution, his long solos often left the rhythm section exhausted. But he would explain that he needed to play at such great lengths in order to "get it all in." Jimmy Cobb recalls one night: "My hands were so sweaty from playing behind Coltrane that one of the drumsticks came flying out of my hand and missed Coltrane's head by about an inch. After the set was over, Coltrane came up to me and said, 'Well, you almost got me that time.' We both laughed—he knew that I loved his playing." Few recordings of the time show the power of Coltrane's solos, but the live recording from the 1958 Newport Jazz Festival gives the listener at least some idea. And there is an as yet unreleased recording of the band (without Adderley) in Japan that Miles has in his archives, which clearly demonstrates how Coltrane's music could make some people walk out of a club in disgust, while making other listeners' hair stand on end.

If there was one goal Miles had by this point, it was not to wind up like Charlie Parker, living like a bum in the twilight of his career. He had learned from his predecessors that he could not depend on the good graces of either his public, agent, or record company in order to remain living in the manner to which he was becoming accustomed. His friend Harold Lovette, an attorney, became Miles's personal manager, handling the business aspects of performing, which Miles hated to deal with. In addition, he began to invest his money in stocks, bonds, and public utilities. Miles was constantly talking to his stockbroker, although he used his own expertise and intuition to choose his investments.

In addition he had become adroit in dealing with record executives, club owners, and concert promoters. Around this time (late fifties) he was scheduled to play New York City's Town Hall for two shows on the same night. The custom of the time was to pay the musicians the full price—in this case $1,000—for the first show, and half that price for the second. When Miles heard of this arrangement he told the promoter, "Wait a minute, I don't get this. You bring in an audience for the first show, I play my ass off and I get a thousand bucks. Then you empty the place, bring in a new audience, and I only get $500. What kind of bullshit is that?" He told the promoter that he would agree to play at those rates if he would rope off half the theater for the second show. The promoter finally agreed to pay him $2,000. Miles's insistence on being treated fairly encouraged other long-exploited jazz musicians also to demand their just due.

This business acumen helped make Miles one of the richest men in jazz. By the end of the fifties his band commanded between $3,500 and $5,000 for a week's engagement at a club, more than any other modern jazzman with the exception of Dizzy Gillespie. Jimmy Cobb remembers playing a hotel in Chicago where there was a long line of customers waiting to get in. A fire broke out in another part of the hotel, but the customers remained waiting to hear Miles and his group. "They even put up with the smoke in order to hear our music," he recalls.

Despite his increasing affluence, Miles never forgot his days of scuffling. He was one of the softest touches in jazz, always helping out musicians and friends. When pianist Wynton Kelly's father died, Kelly worried about not having enough money to cover the funeral expenses. Miles came up to him during his solo and whispered, "Pick up the money after the set, and don't worry about paying it back, forget it." Kelly became so flustered that he missed a note. This prompted Miles to mutter, "Damn, you motherfucker, you can't even play." He walked off the stage before Kelly could thank him.

Miles did not rest on his popularity. He remained continually involved in developing new approaches. "If there's one thing I always hated," he would say later, "it's being bored by my music." Along with Bill Evans, he was working on the most radical music of his career up to that point, an album that would be almost entirely modal. In March 1959 he recorded the first session for what would be one of the most important, as well as sublimely beautiful albums in the history of jazz, *Kind of Blue*. Miles brought his working sextet into the studio, as well as Wynton Kelly. Kelly's style was bluesy, often funky, hard-swinging, and a marked contrast to the impressionism of Bill Evans.

"When Wynton came to the date," remembers Jimmy Cobb,

> he was puzzled. He said, "I thought I was the pianist on this date." He was wondering what Bill Evans was doing there. So I told him not to worry, that this may be different from what he was used to, but that Miles did things differently. Miles liked to fuck with musicians' heads like that, get them worried and nervous. He thought it would make them play better, and I guess he was usually right. And on *Kind of Blue* it worked out, because the tune that Wynton played on ["Freddie Freeloader"] fit in perfectly with the rest of the album, like it was all part of the same piece.

The recording in and of itself was an experiment. None of the musicians had ever played any of the tunes before; in fact Miles had written out the settings for most of them only a few hours before the session. They also incorporated features different from almost anything that the musicians had ever encountered before. The tune "So What" was based on a simple but effective modal progression. "Flamenco Sketches" was, according to Bill Evans's liner notes, "a series of five scales, each to be played as long as the soloist wished until he has completed the series," and "All Blues" was a "6/8 twelve-measure blues form that produces through only a few modal changes." In addition, Miles stuck to his old recording procedure of having virtually no rehearsal and only one take for each tune. As Jimmy Cobb remembers this recording date: "It must have been made in heaven. All Miles did was tell each musician 'You play like this up to here and then you modulate to here and then you come back to this. Okay, let's do it.' And we just went ahead and did it."

Evans tried to elucidate the philosophical concept behind the record:

There is a Japanese visual art in which the artist is forced to be spontaneous. He must paint on a thin stretched parchment with a special brush and black water paint in such a way that an unnatural or interrupted stroke will destroy the line or break through the parchment. Erasures or changes are impossible. These artists must practice a particular discipline, that of allowing the idea to express itself in communication with their hands in such a direct way that deliberation cannot interfere.

The resulting pictures lack the complex composition and textures of ordinary painting, but it is said that those who see will find something captured that escapes explanation.

Evans understood, on the profoundest level, Miles's working procedures—and why they were so effective.

"So What" (one of Miles's favorite expressions, incidentally) contains an astounding solo. Although some critics would describe it (as well as several others on this album) as melancholy, there is a clear underpinning of joy, even ecstatic joy, which is the hallmark not only of Miles's most outstanding solos but also of the finest improvisations of Louis Armstrong, Lester Young, Charlie Parker, and other jazz greats. In the best performances of the blues, the emotions of joy and sadness exist side by side. However, many critics who reviewed *Kind of Blue* complained: "Miles's playing throughout is morose"; "his playing verges on maudlin"; "the playing is sluggish and low in energy output." But *Kind of Blue* has survived as a classic, one of subtlety and shifting shades of emotions. On "So What," "All Blues," and "Blue in Green," his solos are poignant and have a remarkable sense of structure, balance, humor, and rhythmic nuance that have rarely been matched. On "Freddie Freeloader," he even surpasses those superb numbers. For this traditional twelve-bar blues (named after a persistent hanger-on to the jazz scene), his solo is, arguably, the best constructed of his career. It sums up all his best blues solos, but with an economy of notes and a subtle rhythmic precision that is equaled only by Louis Armstrong's "West End Blues" and Bird's "Parker's Mood" in extending the emotional richness that can be brought to the deceptively simple blues form.

On *Kind of Blue* Coltrane also played perhaps the greatest recorded solos of his career until that point— his style is a hybrid between the explorations he had begun with Monk and the lyrical modality that would dominate his playing in the early and mid sixties. On "Freddie Freeloader" he plays the blues with a joyous but fierce abandon, a harbinger of his groundbreaking blues solos on such classics as "Chasin' the Trane" (recorded with his own group in the sixties). Adderley's solos are attractive for their funky ebullience and serve as something of a respite for the listener. Only he sounds

rather uncomfortable on the modal pieces, and on "Flamenco Sketches" his solo sounds incongruous after the
serene statements of Miles, Evans, and Coltrane. Shortly
after these sessions Adderley left the sextet to re-form
his own group, which played funky jazz mixed with
hard bop. Bill Evans also left after these sessions, for
personal reasons as well as to form his own trio. His
playing on *Kind of Blue* demonstrates the maturity he
had developed playing with Miles. He does not "swing"
in the conventional sense, but then the same thing has
often been said about Thelonious Monk and Miles himself. However, his playing on this record, especially on
the delicately lovely "Blue in Green," shows how effective impressionism could be in a jazz idiom. His playing
would influence countless pianists, including such future Miles sidemen as Herbie Hancock and Chick Corea.

Kind of Blue served as an inspiration for aspiring
young musicians. One was Larry Willis, who would
eventually become a leading jazz pianist, playing with
Cannonball Adderley, Jackie McLean, and Blood, Sweat
and Tears. Listening to *Kind of Blue* made him decide
to become a serious musician. He says about this record, "It showed me not only what jazz could be, but
what art itself was all about."

Two events occurred in 1959 that would profoundly
affect Miles's attitude toward his music and his career.
The first was personal and took place while he was
playing Birdland in August. Between sets he left the
club with a white female friend. After hailing a cab for
his friend, he was casually smoking a cigarette with another friend outside the club. A police officer, for no
apparent reason, walked up to him and told him to move.

His friend told the officer that Miles was working at the club and that he was taking a breather between sets. Miles said nothing, feeling that since his name and face were on a poster right outside Birdland, this was fairly obvious. He also was certain that the officer was annoyed because he had been with a white woman. He looked down at the sidewalk, refusing to say anything or to move. "Are you a wise guy?" asked the cop. "If you don't move I'm going to take you in." According to Miles, the cop pulled out his nightstick and held it threateningly. Miles, using his training as a fighter, immediately moved closer to the officer, so as not to be hit on his mouth. Apparently he moved rather sharply, because the cop lost his balance and fell to the ground. Before Miles knew what was happening, a plainclothesman who happened to be nearby jumped on top of him, bashing the trumpeter's head with a nightstick. A passing squad car stopped at the site of the melee. The patrolman, now back on his feet, told the cops in the car, "Take him to the precinct, that black motherfucker. Don't let him get away free. Get that son of a bitch out of here." Miles, seething, muttered, "I'll punch him right in the nose, so help me." He was taken to the precinct station, where an ambulance surgeon attended to his battered head (which required several stitches). He wound up spending the night in jail, and was charged with first-degree assault for attacking the patrolman.

The incident generated a great amount of publicity. Not only were there headlines in many metropolitan newspapers, there were even international repercussions. The British press took the attack as an example of American racism. The British music journal, *Melody Maker,* published a picture of a bloodied Miles on its front cover with the headline, "This is what they did to Miles Davis." Although all charges against him were eventually dropped, the ugly encounter deeply embittered him.

Immediately after the incident he announced to *down beat*, "I'm never working in New York anymore, especially Birdland." Two weeks later he was playing there again, but the incident did stir up his not-so-latent hostile feelings toward the white power structure. Obviously, celebrity made little difference to racists, even in supposedly cosmopolitan Manhattan. Miles and his lawyer lodged a million-dollar suit against the city but later dropped it (Miles always hated going to court for any reason).

The other crucial event was musical and it affected not only Miles but every other progressive musician. A former rhythm-and-blues saxophonist named Ornette Coleman was booked with his pianoless quartet at the Five Spot Café and created the greatest sensation in jazz since Charlie Parker. Coleman's music was immediately labeled "free jazz"—that is, it frequently had no tonal harmonic structure at all, the rhythms played by the bass and drums were often deliberately off-center, never swinging in a conventional manner, and the soloists—Coleman and the trumpeter Don Cherry—often used sometimes harsh vocalized effects in their playing. Although other jazz musicians, notably pianist Cecil Taylor and composer George Russell, had been experimenting with atonality, Coleman's seemingly anarchic music had a blues-based strength that clearly announced it was a new avant-garde phenomenon in jazz. Coleman played with an ingenuous approach, and his often strangely melodic improvisations were clearly part of the jazz tradition—this is apparent at least in retrospect. If Coleman was an atonal Charlie Parker, then

Don Cherry played a surreal version of Miles's late for-ties–early fifties style. Together they brought back eerie echoes of the years when Charlie Parker, whose music was now the mainstream, was shaking up every musi-cian in America.

However, in a reverse of the situation encountered by Parker, critics were more immediately drawn to Cole-man than musicians, who were deeply disturbed by his music. Roy Eldridge told a critic, "I listened to him all kinds of ways. I think he's jiving, baby." Red Garland said, "Nothing's happening. I wouldn't mind if he were serious. I like to see a struggling cat get a break. But Coleman is faking." Coleman's chief champions among musicians were John Lewis and Percy Heath; Lewis proclaimed that Ornette was the first important jazz in-novator since Parker. And another musician from a dif-ferent musical world, Leonard Bernstein, announced that Coleman was a genius.

Whatever else he did, Coleman made most members of the jazz community reexamine their music. Miles was ambivalent. He told Nat Hentoff that musicians were jealous of Ornette because he was giving them all an aesthetic kick in the pants and creating such enormous controversy. "I like Ornette," said Miles, "because he doesn't play clichés." Coleman was, with careful listen-ing, obviously a mesmerizing player. He was able to make cries, blue notes, vocalized smears, and bizarre scales into coherent solos that often made one think one was hearing genuine improvisation for the first time. But when some of Coleman's followers claimed that his music had a deep spirituality, Miles commented acerb-ically, "Hell, just listen to what he writes and how he plays. If you're talking psychologically, the man is all screwed up inside." Coleman's music made Miles's own more cautious approach to extending harmonic and melodic freedom seem conservative. Nonetheless he continued to adhere to his belief in "freedom, but freedom with control." Although both intrigued and disturbed by the music of Ornette Coleman, Miles continued to play many of the same tunes that had been in his repertoire from the time he formed his original quintet. Coltrane, however, was becoming increasingly restless playing these tunes and was interested in exploring some of the ideas engendered by Ornette's music.

In September 1959 Miles filmed a television special for CBS's *Robert Herridge Theater* with his quintet and an orchestra led by Gil Evans. This was a rare appearance, as Miles despised TV and as a matter of course turned down offers for video performances. Once he had agreed to appear on the Steve Allen Show, on the condition he only had to play and not talk with the host. As he remembers, "I finished playing when I looked over and there's Steve Allen coming over to shake my hand and talk to me. I thought, 'Oh, shit.' He reached out his hand, I grabbed it and pulled hard, making him go flying off into the wings. Then I just left the stage." Nevertheless, Miles agreed to the Herridge program because it would consist of all music and no dialogue at all. The program turned out to be a fine presentation of jazz on television. Miles and his group played a moving "So What" followed by performances of pieces from *Miles Ahead* with Gil and the big band.

By the end of September the group was once again a quintet—Cannonball Adderley had left and Wynton Kelly replaced Bill Evans. Although Coltrane was recording regularly for Atlantic Records, he still did not feel comfortable about going out on his own and Miles was insistent that he stay.

In 1959 Miles was preoccupied with a new collabora-

Miles on the Robert Herridge Theater show, 1959 (David Chertok).

tion with Gil Evans—their most ambitious project yet. It germinated one night when Frances persuaded Miles to attend a performance of a flamenco troupe of dancers and musicians. Miles, who rarely left home when not working, went reluctantly and found himself deeply affected. He had already felt a deep affinity for Spanish music (as demonstrated in his performance of "Blues for Pablo" on *Miles Ahead*) but the flamenco performance heightened his interest ("Flamenco Sketches" on *Kind of Blue* was the immediate result of this experience). Later, when Miles was on tour with his group in California, a friend played him a record of *Concierto de Aranjuez* for guitar and orchestra by the modern Spanish composer Joaquin Rodrigo. "I couldn't get it out of my mind," he would later say. "Then when Gil and I decided to do this album, I played him the record and he liked it. As we usually do, we planned the program first by ourselves for two months. I work out something; he takes it home and works on it some more; and then we figure out how we're going to do it. He can read my mind and I can read his." The instrumentation for the album, which would be called *Sketches of Spain,* was another departure from that of the traditional jazz orchestra. The orchestra was divided into groups for much of the music, Miles playing within a brass quartet at one moment and being accompanied only by percussion at the next. The rhythm section included not only Jimmy Cobb and Paul Chambers but also Elvin Jones, who played a variety of percussion instruments, including castanets and tambourine. In addition, there was a large woodwind section, playing such instruments as bassoon and oboe which were rarely, if ever, used as jazz instruments. Gil Evans also made innovative use of a harp and produced some wonderful effects.

In addition to the *Concierto* Miles and Gil recorded a bolero, "Solea"; a portion of a Spanish ballet, "Will o' the Wisp"; and reworkings of some traditional Spanish songs, "Pan Piper" and "Saeta," which was a song for a dead matador. Many critics and listeners would find the relationship of *Sketches of Spain* to jazz tenuous. But to Miles's mind the only relevant point about the *Spain* album was that the music was good. He and Gil were not creating Third Stream hybrid music, nor were they "jazzing the classics." They had made an album of personal music that fit into no rigid category.

About the *Concierto* Miles said, "You know, the melody is so strong, there's nothing you have to do with it. If you tried to play bebop on it, you'd wind up being a hip cornball." Many years later, he admitted some even more profound difficulties in playing this music; "Here I was, a black man from East St. Louis, trying to think like a Spaniard, like a matador in Spain. I had to think like he would think for every note I played." Even twenty years after its release, Miles would consider *Sketches* and *Porgy and Bess* as his greatest recorded achievements.

Shortly after the album's release he and Gil consented to a press conference, since they agreed with Columbia that the record was a significant musical event. The first question was asked by a reporter who had not heard the record. Miles rolled his eyes, got up from the table, and said, "That's it. Back to the bar. Nobody has heard the record and this conference does not make sense." After being assured that other reporters had listened to the record, he fielded another question: "Mr. Davis, do you feel this new work of yours is jazz?" Miles immediately bristled. "It's music," he said, "and I like it. I'll play anything I take a fancy to, if I feel it is possible for me to do it. Anyway, flamenco is the Spanish counterpart of our blues." The final question was "Is *Sketches* a new direction?" Miles had to smile. "If you mean am I going to Madrid and marry a Spanish girl, the answer is no. Gil and I are interested in doing an African ballet album. I think that will be the next direction." (Unfortunately, that album was never made.)

In his review of *Sketches of Spain,* Bill Mathieu, one of *down beat*'s most perceptive and musically astute critics, wrote in an astonishingly enthusiastic review:

> [*Sketches of Spain*] is one of the most important musical triumphs that this century has yet produced. . . . It brings together under the same aegis two realms that in the past have often worked against one another—the world of the heart and the world of the mind. . . . To Davis and Evans goes not the distinction of five or ten or a zillion stars in a review rating but the burden of continuing to show us the way.

That was quite a task for Miles, especially after completing *Kind of Blue* and *Sketches of Spain* within one year. And he knew that with the advent of Ornette Coleman's "free jazz" there were fresh, and disturbing, challenges on the horizon.

Sorcerer

One night in the early seventies at a club where Miles was playing, somebody casually mentioned to him that for his new, multidirectional electric music he really needed five or six saxophonists. Miles sighed and muttered, "I once had six saxophonists," referring in his enigmatic parlance to John Coltrane.

Coltrane, who by 1960 was playing with a staggering brilliance, had left Miles's band during a world tour. The group was playing in Stockholm when Coltrane decided that he had to go on his own. This infuriated Miles, not because he hadn't realized, at heart, that Coltrane had grown enough in stature to form his own group, but simply because he couldn't find another horn man who could play at anywhere near the level Coltrane approached every night he played. Miles found him thrilling to listen to, positively mesmerizing, as did his audiences. He had always discouraged Coltrane's fascination with Ornette Coleman's free jazz, and now he was severely disappointed by Coltrane's need to expand his musical explorations with a group of his own.

When Miles returned to the States, his first concern was to find a new horn man for his group. The rhythm section still consisted of Wynton Kelly on piano, Paul Chambers on bass, and Jimmy Cobb on drums. Kelly had become an unusually resourceful accompanist, giving solid support to the soloist. His solo work was also gaining depth. The rhythm section itself had become a cohesively swinging unit. Cobb might have lacked the verve and fire of Philly Joe, but like Kelly he was a superbly sensitive accompanist; his playing did not dominate the group, as Jones's had, but complemented the other players in subtle ways.

Surprisingly, Miles chose Sonny Stitt as his new sax man. He had initially met Stitt in East St. Louis, when Sonny had urged the young Miles to join Tiny Bradshaw's band. Stitt was an up-and-coming saxophonist at that time, but during the late forties and early fifties he had lived in the shadow of Charlie Parker. Although he claimed to have been playing basically the same way before ever hearing Bird, his playing was very clearly influenced by Bird's style; in fact, it was sometimes difficult to tell them apart. In the early fifties, however, Stitt began specializing in tenor instead of alto saxophone, in order to clearly establish his own identity. His playing might have lacked the often unsettling originality of Rollins or Coltrane, but it was solidly professional and hard swinging, perfect in front of the driving rhythm section.

In the fall of 1960 Miles toured Great Britain for the first time. His visit was eagerly awaited by English jazz fans. During the tour most of the British critics were thrilled by the music but, predictably, appalled by Miles's stage manners. Articles immediately appeared in the British press with titles such as "Miles Davis: Boor or Businessman?" Ridiculous security precautions were taken by the British to keep reporters and jazz fans away. The whole thing irritated Miles: "Who the hell do they think I am," he said, "the Congolese ambassador or something?" Humphrey Lyttleton wrote that Miles made his British audience feel "like locked-out members of Parliament in a state of indecision and bewilderment," and Allsop of the *Daily Mail* called him a "sour and surly sorehead." Actually, Miles had presented his music as he had everywhere else. The British simply expected showmanship, although some argued that Miles's apparent lack of it was actually supreme showmanship, calculated and self-conscious. Some critics *did* notice the actual music that Miles was playing. Bob Dawborn, in *Melody Maker,* proclaimed, "I have never heard such sustained brilliance as Miles Davis's playing at the Gaumont, Hammersmith, last Sunday. He is a genius."

A famous but anonymous drummer said about Miles's music in 1960: "A certain vitality isn't there anymore. He lives a pretty lush life and his music gets kind of lush." While most listeners of the time would have seriously disagreed with the drummer about Miles's music, there was no doubt that his life was becoming comfortable. In 1960 he bought an apartment building on West Seventy-seventh Street that had once been a Russian Orthodox Church. Its baroque exterior led Nat

Hentoff to dub it "an architect's nightmare." Nevertheless, the first two floors provided plenty of room for Miles, Frances, and their two children, and the upper two floors were rented out for extra income. When Miles first moved to the neighborhood, he recalls, "everybody raised hell because they thought a black family would lower the value of their property. But then they realized that I owned this building, and there was nothing they could do. A lot of people come here thinking I'm the janitor. Then they find out I own the damned building." Actually, many of Miles's neighbors were proud that a celebrity lived on their block, and he took tremendous pride in his house, outfitting the basement with a small gym in order to train his sons in boxing (Gregory would eventually become an amateur boxer in the Army), and refurbishing the top floor of his apartment in a manner that would cause Hugh Hefner envy—a huge circular bed, fireplace, a gigantic, semicircular couch, a bathroom with bathtub large enough for three, etc. It was perfect for Miles's increasingly reclusive nature; there was no reason for him to leave home other than to play a club or a concert, or to record.

Even if one didn't consider the music as merely "lush," it at least appeared, by the end of 1960, that Miles was settling into a fairly conservative role as a preeminent jazz personality. His group briefly became a sextet when J. J. Johnson joined for several appearances, but basically Miles was playing the same music that he had since the midfifties, such as "Bye, Bye, Blackbird," and "My Funny Valentine." Coltrane had quit the band primarily because he felt that Miles was unwilling to confront the musical challenge of Ornette Coleman and the other Young Turk musicians who were beginning to emerge in the early sixties. However, without Coltrane, Miles's terse trumpet statements once again became the focal point of the group. Perhaps his use of Johnson and Stitt, musicians solidly associated with bebop, was his way of answering the "New Thing," freeform musicians. But it soon became apparent that Stitt, who had a severe drinking problem, was unreliable, and Miles hired Hank Mobley to replace him. Mobley had been one of Art Blakey's Jazz Messengers, and although he was scarcely a surprising or fiery soloist, he played a bop mainstream style that seemed to be a cross beween Sonny Rollins and the early bebop tenor man, Wardell Gray. Miles was not entirely satisfied with Mobley. Often, in the middle of one of his solos, Mobley would hear Miles's hoarse whisper telling some bystander how "I sure wish I could get Sonny Rollins back in the group." This might have been another of Miles's attempts at psychological manipulation, but its effect was merely to depress and discourage Mobley.

In March 1961 Miles brought the group into the Columbia studios for his first small-group recording date since the *Kind of Blue* sessions of 1959. They recorded a blues song Miles had playfully named after his wife, "Pfrancing," and another tune called "Drag-Dog." Miles was not altogether happy with the results, and he contacted Coltrane and asked him if he could play at the next session for the record. Coltrane was at the time busily rehearsing his own group, and he told Miles that he couldn't make a firm commitment. On that next date Miles decided to record "Some Day My Prince Will Come" (a waltz from Disney's *Snow White*). Hank Mobley was having particular difficulty with the changes, even after a period of agonizing rehearsal. Then, totally unexpectedly, Coltrane showed up. As Jimmy Cobb recalls:

The red light was on in the studio, and we were right in the middle of the tune when Trane showed up. While we were playing, he put together his horn while Miles showed him the changes for the tune on a piece of paper. Coltrane put his horn in his mouth and blew that solo you heard, that incredible solo. To this day, I don't know how he was able to immediately play in exactly the right key, right in tune with the rest of the band, and handle changes which baffled Hank, never having even seen the sheet music for the song before.

The solo is stunning, waltzing arpeggios displaying a lyricism that was becoming the core of Coltrane's music. Coltrane also recorded the one modal tune of the session, "Teo," which had a fascinating eastern flavor. The tune was very similar to much of the Indian-influenced modal music that would become his main avenue of musical exploration in the first years of his quartet. At the same session, Philly Joe also unexpectedly showed up, and he replaced Jimmy Cobb for a blues number. Cobb might have been a subtle, skillful, and thoughtful drummer, but Philly Joe's unabashed exuberance always had an uninhibiting effect on Miles. "Jazz has got to have that thing," he loved to say. And Philly Joe was always sure to provide it. As did Coltrane—his playing always challenged Miles to find new ways to complement his favorite saxophonist. But these sessions would be the last time the two would ever play together. And they would also be the last sessions in which Miles recorded with Philly Joe.

When the record was released (without the blues with Philly Joe) the album was titled *Some Day My Prince Will Come*. Miles put his wife Frances on the cover. He was tired of seeing albums with only white women on them, and after all, as he stated, he was Frances's "prince." There were no liner notes on the back of the album, only a picture of Miles, because, as Miles insisted to

Columbia, "There's nothing you can say about the music."

"I'm going to retire," Miles announced to a startled reporter. "I'm retiring and moving my family to Europe." He talked about how sick he was of putting up with club owners, record companies, persistent fans, and undependable musicians—and then explained that he already was retired anyway, "since I only play when I feel like it."

One of the places he enjoyed playing was San Francisco's Blackhawk, a small, dark club not far from the seedy Tenderloin section of the city. A month after the *Some Day My Prince Will Come* sessions, Miles recorded with his group at the club, live for the first time. The results, while hardly extraordinary, show that he was a somewhat more daring improviser outside the recording studio, taking more chances and trying to expand his technical resources. One cut in particular, Monk's "Well You Needn't," demonstrates Miles's ability to take difficult material and make it his own. He shows a rare understanding of the piece and takes fascinating, unexpected melodic twists and turns. He sounds bored on "So What" and "Bye Bye Blackbird"; however, "Oleo," another old staple of his repertoire, is played with a cerebral brilliance, further expanding the ideas which he had been developing since first recording the tune in 1954. "I never resolve anything in my playing," he said many years later.

The Blackhawk set is marred by Mobley's playing, which was, to put it bluntly, dull—and Miles was becoming increasingly dissatisfied. Jimmy Cobb recalls that "Miles didn't like it when a guy like Mobley played behind the beat; he knew that it fucked with the rhythm section. Maybe because he used to play that way himself during those cool years he understood its effect." Apart from Miles's group, Mobley played with far more vigor, but these records, *Friday and Saturday Night at the Blackhawk,* show not only how uninspired Mobley was in Miles's group, but also how a less than exciting sideman could dispirit Miles's own playing. But if Mobley was dull, Wynton Kelly could get Miles to swing harder than perhaps he ever had. In the midst of a Kelly solo Miles would often lean over Jimmy Cobb and mutter in his ear, "Damn, I wish I could swing as hard as he does." Whitney Balliett compared the simpatico musical relationship between Miles and Kelly to the classic duo of Louis Armstrong and Earl Hines. Similarly, in reviewing the Blackhawk set, Martin Williams wrote, "More than any other single player, Miles Davis echoes Louis Armstrong. Hear his paraphrase of almost any standard theme. And that is particularly worth saying because, beneath his sophistications and through his transmutations, Davis's horn echoes something of Armstrong's exuberant, humorous, forceful, committed, self-determined joy as well." But the comparison with Armstrong unintentionally said something else about Miles's position in jazz. Like Armstrong, and later Dizzy Gillespie, Miles seemed at this point in his career to be simply repeating himself. And at a Carnegie Hall concert, recorded a month after the Blackhawk stint, he did little to discourage such thinking. In addition to the now inevitable quintet renditions of "So What" and "Oleo," he also performed with Gil Evans and a large orchestra. Except for one new piece, a short, tortuously slow but achingly lovely "Spring Is Here," Miles performed pieces ("Lament" and "The Meaning of the Blues") only from his first record with Gil. Like Armstrong performing "Sleepy Time Down South" and "St. Louis Blues," and

Gillespie playing "A Night In Tunisia" and "Manteca" at every performance, Miles seemed to have fallen into a comfortable rut, honing his playing and the craft of improvising, but apparently caring little about further advancing the possibilities of his art.

He had begun working out regularly at Bobby Gleason's gym, then in the Bronx, believing that it would help his playing, in addition to keeping him fit. A young black writer began hanging out at the gym, trying to get Miles to consent to an interview. At first he refused as usual. But the writer, the then unknown Alex Haley, who had been sent by *Playboy* magazine, was persistent. He even got in the ring with Miles and worked out with him for a few rounds. This so impressed Miles that he finally agreed to the interview.

Playboy had chosen Miles to be the first subject of a new feature that would be called "The Playboy Interview." The idea was to obtain controversial interviews with public figures who rarely gave interviews, and whose point of view or life-style would be of interest to "the man who reads *Playboy*." Miles was a perfect choice for the first subject: he was well known for his truculence with the press, and his reputation for having beautiful women, stylish clothes, and expensive cars perfectly fit the *Playboy* fantasy.

However, even *Playboy*'s editors were somewhat shocked by the resulting press. Throughout his conversation with Haley, Miles vented a militant racial hostility which, in 1961–62, was extremely radical:

> When it comes to human rights, these prejudiced white people keep on acting like they own the damn franchise! And, man, with the world in the mess it's in now, we trying to influence on our side all them Africans and Arabs and Indians and

Chinese. . . . You know two thirds of the people in the world ain't white? They see all this crap with Negroes and supposed to feel white people really think any different about them? Man, somebody better get straight! . . . Prejudiced white people ask one another, "Would you want your sister to marry a Negro?" It's a jive question to ask in the first place—as if white women stand around helpless if some Negro wants to drag one off to a preacher. It makes me sick to hear that. A Negro just might not want your sister. . . . What makes me mad about these labels for Negroes is that very few white people really know what Negroes really feel like. A lot of white people have never been in the company of an intelligent Negro. But you can hardly meet a white person, especially a white man, that don't think he's qualified to tell you about Negroes.

Although Miles softened his remarks by adding "When I say some of my best friends are white, I sure ain't lying," Miles also told Haley that the complaints about his supposed lack of showmanship resulted from the fact that white people simply refused to take a black man seriously as an artist.

Few if any major black performers had ever been so outspoken. But Miles knew what he was doing. Rather than simply giving a routine interview, he sought to awaken a few consciences.

In early 1962 he heard a record featuring a Brazilian singer named Joao Gilberto, on which most of the tunes were composed and arranged by Antonio Carlos Jobim. Miles was immediately taken by the music, which was apparently a combination of samba rhythm with the harmonic vocabulary of jazz. It would later be tagged "bossa nova." Gilberto sang in a penetrating whisper, and yet with a compelling emotional thrust that would lead Miles to say later, "He could read a newspaper and sound good!" Gil Evans also liked Jobim's music, and once again the two began planning a new project.

Evans and Miles wound up recording seven tunes for a new album: two or three Brazilian numbers, the others with the same Latin flavor as Jobim's pieces.

The sessions proceeded slowly—Evans's notation was becoming increasingly complex—and midway through its completion the project was aborted. Miles had a major disagreement with Teo Macero, who had become the producer for all his recording sessions, and he simply refused to proceed. The sessions were eventually released, although there was less than half an hour of music on the album, called *Quiet Nights* (after a Jobim song that they had recorded). Most critics found the music to be disturbingly similar to *Sketches of Spain,* and since the record was not released until 1964, it seemed an attempt by Miles and Gil to cash in on the then-current bossa nova fad. But these recordings were probably the first actual bossa nova recordings made in this country, produced before the Stan Getz–Charlie Byrd collaboration, which would set off the public's brief fascination with the lovely music of Brazil.

Using virtually the same instruments as on *Sketches,* Evans seemed to bring his use of slowly moving orchestral colors to its ultimate consummation, and Miles's playing was so polished, and yet so careful, that the music could not be separated into components of melody or harmony or rhythm. It was pure, gorgeous *sound* for its own sake.

One night in 1962 Miles was listening to a familiar complaint from two of his sidemen, Wynton Kelly and

Paul Chambers. "We just can't live on what we make from playing with you. You pay us well, but you don't pay us well enough." To them, he had it easy—he owned a brownstone, had money from his investments, and received regular royalty checks. Miles had been thinking about this himself, and he suggested, "Why don't you collect unemployment when the band's not working?" He meant this sincerely, but Kelly and Chambers were insulted—they detected in the remark something of a "let them eat cake" attitude. The group was scheduled to play Chicago, but the two disaffected musicians wound up not going. Miles announced that the men were fired and he was looking for replacements. (In addition, he fired Mobley, whose playing he had long been dissatisfied with.)

He immediately found a young, brilliant bassist, Ron Carter, to take Chambers's place. A graduate of the Eastman School of Music, Carter turned out to be an excellent replacement. Miles also hired a tenor saxophonist named George Coleman. Coleman had worked with Max Roach; his style was lyrical although not overwhelmingly original, and at times he sounded like Sonny Rollins. He played on the beat with more rhythmic vitality than Hank Mobley had displayed during his stint with the group. Miles took his new sidemen, as well as Jimmy Cobb, and flew to the west coast for an engagement at the Blackhawk. Once there he also hired alto saxophonist Frank Strozier and pianist Harold Mabern. After a brief rehearsal period the band played a two-week gig.

The new group had a revitalizing effect on Miles. Russ Wilson in *down beat* wrote:

The presence of unfamiliar associates turned up the burner under Davis. So pronounced were his fiery forays into the upper register, some listeners wondered if he was using a new, smaller mouthpiece. [He wasn't.]

Strozier was in particular a provocative player; although firmly in the Charlie Parker bop tradition, he played with a passion and daring that was reminiscent in feeling of the growing contingent of New Thing saxophonists.

As successful as this band apparently was, it lasted only a few weeks. Jimmy Cobb decided to join Wynton Kelly and Paul Chambers in the trio they were forming, and Miles took Carter and Coleman to Los Angeles for a recording session. For this date he used the Australian pianist Victor Feldman instead of Mabern and the West Coast drummer Frank Butler. And although Coleman was present during the session, Miles did not use him.

Playing in a quartet for the first time since the mid-fifties, Miles recorded three ballads, two of which were associated with, of all things, New Orleans jazz: "Baby, Won't You Please Come Home" and "Basin Street Blues." This might have seemed like a further retreat from contemporary jazz trends. But his renditions of these tunes, along with the standard "I Fall in Love Too Easily" are, once again, miraculous transformations of the overly familiar. Miles treated "Basin Street Blues" as a slow elegiac ballad, playing with a muted poignance that seemed to be a melancholy meditation on New Orleans and its greatest son, Louis Armstrong. Both from his playing with his short-lived sextet, and from these profoundly moving ballads, it was clear that Miles was setting his direction: his music for this period of his career would not explore new theoretical frontiers, but he would continue to shape and extend his style profoundly.

When Miles returned to New York, only Carter and Coleman remained in the band. But Miles had been tremendously impressed by a new, very young drummer. He had heard Anthony Williams play with Jackie McLean near the end of 1962, and thought he had a unique style, combining polyrhythms as complex as Philly Joe's with some effects of the New Thing drummers. Even more amazing was that Williams's style was so genuinely mature—he had taken the fundamentals of modern-jazz drumming and advanced them with surprising and explosive results. Perhaps no other drummer had better represented Miles's concept of "controlled freedom."

For his new pianist Miles chose Herbie Hancock, a Chicago-born musician in his early twenties who had been in New York since 1961. He had played with trumpeter Donald Byrd, Jackie McLean, and J. J. Johnson and had recorded under his own name "Watermelon Man," a tune that became something of a hit. His playing was almost a compendium of the styles of Miles's former pianists: it was as slick and melodic as Red Garland's, as funky as Wynton Kelly's, and showed the obvious imprint of Bill Evans's impressionism. Technically, Hancock was superb, and he was not a mere eclectic—he had honed these influences into a personal and often exciting style. In addition, he was an uncanny accompanist, who always seemed to anticipate a soloist's train of thought. Hancock's initiation into the group was so casual that he didn't even realize that it had taken place. Hancock told *down beat:*

> Miles called me up. He asked me if I was busy, if I was working. I was at the time, but I told him no; so he asked me if I would come over to his house the next day. I told him sure, but he hung

Tony Williams (Institute of Jazz Studies).

up without giving me his address or anything. Luckily, I had gotten it from Tony Williams.

Next day I went over. Tony was there with Ron and George Coleman. We ran over some things while Miles walked around and listened. Philly Joe Jones stopped by, too. Then Miles called up Gil Evans. He said, "Hey Gil. I want you to hear my new drummer."

After we rehearsed the next day, he told us we were going to do a record in two days. I was wondering what was going on; he hadn't even told me whether I was in the group or not. So I didn't say anything, and we did the record *Seven Steps to Heaven*. Then we had another rehearsal, and he mentioned a job at Bowdoin College. I said, "Wait a minute, Miles. You haven't even told me if I'm in the group or what," and he said, "You made the record, didn't you?" So I said, "Yeah, okay." That was fine. I was jumping through hoops.

Playing with Miles Davis was more often than not a tremendous boost to a young musician's career. It was certification that a musician had arrived among the select circle in jazz.

Miles used his new quintet to record three tunes for the *Seven Steps to Heaven* album, all with brisk tempos in order to contrast with the ballads he had recorded in Hollywood. The sense of unity in the band is truly astonishing considering the limited amount of rehearsal. And those few rehearsals were, characteristically, perfunctory. "Philly Joe, show Tony how to do this," he would tell his former drummer. "Okay, Herbie, now play these chords here. Okay, that's it." A few years later Miles explained how he would deliberately plan to make his sidemen rely on their own resources: "[This is] what I tell all my musicians: I tell them be ready to play what you know and play above what you know. Anything might happen above what you've been used to playing—you're ready to get into that, and above that, and take that out."

Miles had an immediate and surprising problem with his new band: since Tony Williams was only seventeen, the band could not perform in clubs where liquor was served. Therefore, the clubs where the band played simply did not serve alcohol during the group's engagement. This did not faze many club owners, since Miles still drew more customers than virtually any other modern-jazz performer. Customers simply had to get used to the idea of doling out $2.50 for a Coca-Cola. Another solution for Miles was to do more concerts, although he preferred the ambience of the nightclub, which had a looseness that befitted the spontaneity of the improvising jazz musician.

Despite these inconveniences, Miles could not conceive of letting his new drummer go. Williams was a supremely musical drummer, using his entire drum kit to create a constant onrush of astonishing rhythmic sound. This inspired Miles to play his horn with a new virtuosity, extending his range further than ever before.

Except for some of the tunes from the *Seven Steps to Heaven* album, Miles was still playing basically the same repertoire. However, this new band was shaping the familiar standards in strange and unexpected ways. Almost every night, the rhythm section was finding new ways not only to work as a unique and cohesive unit but also to redefine the basic post-bop rhythm section itself. The more they played together, the more startling their effects. They would change meter midtune, stop the rhythmic flow with near free-form bursts of energy, and spontaneously slow and speed up tempos. Sometimes the three men would, just for a moment, stop playing altogether, often along with Miles—taking Miles's concepts of the use of space to their logical conclusion: making silence itself a part of the new quintet's music. "They enjoy playing together, that's why they sound good," Miles said. "That's the same thing as with Red, Paul Chambers, and Philly Joe." All three of Miles's new young players were finding their way. The conservatory-trained Hancock often found himself confused. "Sometimes, Miles," he told his boss, "I feel like I shouldn't play anything." Miles replied, "Then don't play; just sit there and look funny."

A concert recorded at Lincoln Center makes plain the incredible strides this group was making. "So What" is played at a breathtakingly fast clip, with Miles taking a solo that bears no resemblance to his original solo on *Kind of Blue,* while Hancock's solo uses modes to extend his melodic line. The high point of "Walkin' " is Williams's solo, which uses the simplest rhythms, silences, crescendos and decrescendos, to produce an amazingly *musical* drum solo. Around this time Miles made the statement, "After all these years, I've finally figured out how to play 'My Funny Valentine.' " In this rendition with his new group he turns the tune inside out, using only fragments of Rodgers's original melody. The group begins it as a slow dirge, then moves into a medium tempo. The meter changes into quasi-Latin, and then back again to the medium swing. There seems to be no readily apparent logic to Miles's solo, but miraculously, he gives this love theme dimensions that no one has been able to give it before.

Nevertheless, Tony Williams began to feel restless. He told an interviewer, "I'd rather be playing with Cecil Taylor." Pianist Taylor was experimenting with extraordinarily virtuosic atonal music, which exhibited influences ranging from Horace Silver to Stravinsky. His music and that of other revolutionary jazz musicians of the mid-sixties seemed more than just another step in the evolution of jazz. It was firmly tied to the growing anger of American black people. Free jazz had an extramusical meaning for both its musicians and many in the audience. The horn players had gone beyond Ornette and were using their instruments to howl and cry and scream and shriek. "It's not about notes anymore," said one of its great practitioners, saxophonist Albert Ayler. Those who expressed distaste for this music were seen not only as musical conservatives but as political conservatives as well.

It is not surprising, then, that at seventeen Williams

felt it was time to move on from the post-bop of Miles Davis, no matter what refinements of that genre he was achieving. Hancock and Carter, while not committed to or associated with the more radical avant-garde, were nevertheless making records with musicians such as Eric Dolphy and Sam Rivers, Young Turks interested in changing the very nature of jazz (the term *jazz* itself, incidentally, was increasingly distasteful to these young musicians, who preferred calling their music "black classical music" or "Afro-American music").

The man who was becoming the father of the new avant-garde was John Coltrane. Although his music still heavily relied on the modal theory he had learned with Miles, he encouraged many of the new breed. Eric Dolphy served a stint in Coltrane's band, and Coltrane recorded with Cecil Taylor and Archie Shepp. He actively encouraged the most radical of these musicians, and began working the vocalized effects and screams into his own playing. Now, with his own group, his solos sometimes lasted a half hour or longer.

Miles had remained personally close to Coltrane, and continued to respect his playing. But he forthrightly condemned many of his new associates. In a 1964 Blindfold Test, Leonard Feather played records by both Dolphy and Cecil Taylor for Miles. About Dolphy, Miles said, "That's got to be Eric Dolphy—nobody else could sound that bad! The next time I see him, I'm going to stomp on his foot. You print that. I think he's ridiculous."

About Taylor's record, Miles exclaimed:

Take it off! That's some sad shit, man. Is that what the critics are digging? Them critics better stop having coffee. If there ain't nothing to listen to, they might as well admit it. To put the loud pedal on

Miles with Tony Williams and Ron Carter, 1964 (Institute of Jazz Studies).

the piano and make a run is very old-fashioned to me. Just to take something like that and say it's great, because there ain't nothing to listen to.

Miles was steadfast: he would not embrace music that he didn't like, no matter how fashionable it had become. "Look," he said at the time, "you don't need to think to play weird. That ain't no freedom." Nevertheless, the latest trends in jazz spurred him on to actively rethink the evolution of his own music, using the new and fresh ideas of the young members of his band.

By the mid-sixties Miles had become an international celebrity. He was able to command high prices for overseas concerts and continued to tour extensively. However, he was deeply bitter that the State Department had never asked him to tour as a representative of the United States. After all, he had won polls in every country that had a jazz magazine. He told Leonard Feather:

I'd rather have somebody curse me out than ignore me. Anyhow, I don't want them to send me over just because I'm a Negro, and they want to woo Africa. . . . If I ever went on one of those tours, they'd have to give me a badge to wear over here. A platinum badge. It would have to say on it that this man did such and such a thing for his country and his government.

Miles's anger was perhaps the real reason that the State Department avoided sending him—he was never one to mince words when it came to his opinions of the government and its social policies.

Actually, Miles was never keen on protocol wherever he traveled. He was particularly feisty when he traveled to Germany, where he was enormously popular. He recalled:

I remember one time going through customs in Berlin. The German customs man asked me to take out my passport. I pointed to the pocket of my jacket and told him, "Take it out yourself. We won the war." I didn't like the Germans because of what they did to the Jews—even though they expected everybody to forget about it. Once I was there with a Jewish girlfriend. Some government dignitary shook our hands and smiled, but I knew that he was a Nazi when Hitler was in power. Later, the government had a state reception for me. I sent Tony Williams and told him to say that he was me. I know what they really thought about me and my Jewish girlfriend.

In Japan Miles was, and is, an especially beloved and respected figure. There is even a street named after him in Tokyo. However, the Japanese often did not know what to make of his sense of humor. On one tour the editor of *Sing Journal*, the Japanese jazz magazine, asked Miles for an interview. "Get me ten thousand dollars and I'll do it," he told the editor. Shortly before Miles left Japan, the editor sadly told him they could not raise that amount of money for an interview. "Then how about a bowl of noodle soup?" he asked. The editor promptly took Miles to a Japanese restaurant, bought him a bowl of noodle soup, and got his interview.

By the summer of 1964 Miles had dropped George Coleman from the quintet. Although Coleman was a lyrical and technically proficient saxophonist, his playing did not suit the musical direction that the group, as a whole, was heading in. Tony Williams suggested Sam Rivers as a replacement. Miles hired him for his Japanese tour, but he immediately became dissatisfied. Although Rivers played fairly conservatively in Japan, he was committed to the new jazz avant-garde, and Miles knew that having a musician so dedicated to free jazz would never work out. He wanted to replace Rivers with Wayne Shorter. Miles had already recorded with Shorter in 1962, before putting together the new band. But Shorter was now playing with Art Blakey's Jazz Messengers and serving as musical director of that band as well, a position he did not want to relinquish. Miles was insistent, though, and would constantly call him, asking him to reconsider. Tony Williams and Herbie Hancock also urged Shorter to join, and in the fall of 1964 he finally relented and toured Europe with Miles's group. His initiation was similar to that of many other of Miles's sidemen—it included no rehearsals at all.

With Blakey, Shorter's style had been very obviously influenced by Coltrane. His writing, however, was idiosyncratic and often took unusual melodic directions.

Miles immediately asked him to write for the band. After only a short period of time playing with Miles and his unique rhythm section, Shorter began to find a more personal voice as an improviser as well. Coltrane had once told an interviewer that in his first year with the quintet he tried to play like Miles but decided that he had to find a style more suited to the saxophone. Shorter, however, began to bend his notes in a way that uncannily did sound like Miles. Even his tone began to sound like Miles's trumpet, so much so that in later years it was often difficult to differentiate between the two in ensembles. However, Shorter's playing still reflected Coltrane's influence, especially in his more lyrical improvisations.

With Shorter the group coalesced into a cohesive and brilliant musical unit, but it was overshadowed by the group that had become the dominant jazz unit of the sixties, John Coltrane's quartet. Coltrane's virtuosity had become stunning, his forays into the shattering sounds of the avant-garde were totally convincing. His music was in a constant state of flux, as if he were in continuous search of some cosmic lost chord. Elvin Jones, his drummer, was expanding the polyrhythms of such post-bop drummers as Philly Joe and Art Blakey, often sounding like three drummers playing together in ferocious concert, so loud that he often rendered the rest of the group inaudible. Coltrane was constantly bringing young musicians into his group and playing together with them in screaming group improvisations. Although many found this music profoundly disturbing, it was an overwhelming force in jazz and blotted out almost everything around it.

Though Coltrane made few direct political comments, he was often tied to militancy and Black Nationalism. Actually he never thought of his music as political, but viewed it as deeply religious. His albums had such titles as *Meditations* and *A Love Supreme,* and his pieces such titles as "Love" and "Peace." Whatever Coltrane's intentions, his music certainly mirrored the turbulent sixties, and to its followers it was as relevant to their time as the concurrent acid rock.

In this context Miles's first studio album with Shorter and the rest of the quintet seemed tame, if not staid, despite the inclusion of modal pieces and tunes with interesting construction, like the unusual blues "Eighty-One." Miles was more actively involved in the music of the group than he had been in the early sixties. While almost all the pieces were written by other members of the quintet, he got cowriting credit. Although he didn't actually write the tunes, he acted as editor, as he did when working with Gil Evans. He reduced the harmonic complexity and simplified the melodies to their most basic elements. "Miles likes music *slick*," Herbie Hancock recalled. "He used to take our compositions in the studio, tear them up, and then put them back together again."

The group had evolved a type of ensemble thinking that made the album's title, *E.S.P.,* appropriate. The most exciting moment is Miles's solo on the title cut, notable for its form and unexpected climaxes. Wayne Shorter's style, his sense of irony and lyricism, was at this point still in its formative stages, and the rhythm section was still finding new ways to appropriately accompany the increasingly elastic styles of the horn men.

The cover of *E.S.P.* shows Miles gazing at his wife Frances with a mixture of love and something like curiosity, almost as if he had not yet figured out this beautiful woman. As much as Miles loved women, they remained a mystery to him. This often led to behavior that the women in his life found difficult to cope with.

His temper was volatile, and he could be childishly possessive and jealous. He made no excuses for his behavior. "I don't care what a bitch does, as long as she doesn't lie about it. I can always tell when they're lying, and I hate that. I hate the lies." However, his emotions were more complex than that would indicate. Once, in Hollywood, he was at a nightclub with Frances. When a man asked her to dance, she turned to Miles, who immediately encouraged her to accept. But when she got back to the table he slapped her. To his way of thinking, he had no choice but to let her dance with the man, and vent his anger when she returned. As deeply as Frances loved Miles (and in unguarded moments, Miles would admit that Frances was the great love of his life), she began to lose her patience with such unpredictable behavior. Their marriage began to falter, and Miles's response was to become even more deeply involved in music.

The band began to tour more extensively, and although they were playing some newer pieces, their staples still remained tunes like "On Green Dolphin Street," "Walkin'," and "Milestones." The group had made these tunes their own, and after the initial statement of theme would tear them limb from limb with ferocious abandon. Fans of Miles's fifties music might have been disappointed to hear him take a ballad like "On Green Dolphin Street" at a breakneck tempo, but he loved the energy of the band at this pace, and sometimes almost every tune was played that way. Tony Williams had become, along with Elvin Jones, one of the most thunderous drummers in jazz, building climaxes of percussion that overwhelmed almost everyone else; he almost seemed to be the center of the band. The way Miles and Shorter were using space and elliptical melody, their method of playing both on and against the beat was complemented by the primal function of Williams's drums. Indeed, the incredible tempos coupled with the splash of the cymbals nearly eliminated the beat.

By the time the group returned to the Columbia recording studios in October 1966, they had achieved a state of cohesiveness that rivaled that of any other group in the history of jazz. By this time Shorter had emerged as the principal writer. The perverse lyricism of his enigmatically melodic compositions made them singularly provocative for improvisers. While not harmonically rich, they were constructed to give soloists the maximum amount of freedom. In the sessions for *Miles Smiles*, Miles and Shorter had mastered playing *above* the rhythm of Tony Williams's drums, in solos that were streams of sound, far different from the solos in fifties bop. Another salient aspect of these sessions was Herbie Hancock's frequent laying-out during the horn solos. This gave the horns greater harmonic freedom (in much the way that lack of piano in Ornette Coleman's group did).

However, as fresh and exciting as these mid-1967 sessions were, Miles was exploring even more experimental directions for the standard jazz quintet. For instance, on "Sorcerer," a Wayne Shorter piece, Miles and Shorter trade sixteen bars apiece, rather than each simply playing a complete solo. This results in a unique ensemble feeling of group improvisation. "Masqualero" changes, in mood and tempo, from a ballad to an almost totally free, even aggressive feeling. "Nefertiti" receives an even more radical treatment. The horns simply repeat Shorter's theme over and over again; there are no solos as such—the rhythm section plays intricate patterns in response to the theme. As one listener observed, "I kept on waiting for the music to happen, and then I realized it was happening all the time." These and other innovations gave new life to tonal, post-bop jazz. Unfortunately, few groups that played this type of music adopted these new approaches—they still played the modern jazz of the midfifties.

Once, in the late seventies, a friend suggested to Miles that he watch a TV show featuring some prominent post-bop musicians, a few of whom had played in his groups. "Why should I?" he replied pointedly. "They're playing the same shit I was playing in 1951." Indeed, when post-bop once again regained center stage in the mid and late seventies, there was little difference between it and, say, Miles's first recordings for Prestige.

During this time his life was going through major changes. Frances had moved to the West Coast, and Miles had become involved with the actress Cicely Tyson. Tyson, beautiful, intelligent, and sensitive, was a steadying influence on him, and for a while they lived together. Once again, this time on *Sorcerer,* Miles put the lady in his life on the cover of an album.

The albums Miles made with the sixties quintet are among the most important work of his career. But the subtle innovations that the quintet developed were largely overlooked because of the extremely radical music being created by Coltrane, Taylor, Shepp, Sanders, and others. While the New Thing jazz was reacting to the ossification of post-fifties bop, Miles's quintet took that music and helped it evolve beyond clichés. Although all the members of the group contributed to its unique sound, this quintet, with its "controlled freedom," shows the imprint of Miles the auteur as much as any group he had previously had, if not more so.

Bitches Brew

In June 1968 Leonard Feather visited Miles in a Hollywood hotel suite in order to tape another Blindfold Test for *down beat*. He was astonished to see the particular records and tape cartridges Miles had with him: the Byrds, Aretha Franklin, the Fifth Dimension, James Brown, and other funk and pop recordings. There was nothing in the room that came even close to being jazz. Feather interpreted Miles's choice as meaning "when you have reached the esthetic mountaintop, there is no place to lie down." He was wrong. Miles was finding in the pop music of the sixties the new source of inspiration he could no longer find in jazz. When Feather played a Freddie Hubbard record for him, Miles complained, "I don't dig that kind of shit, man; just a straight thirty-two bars. . . . It's formal, man, and scales and all that. . . . Freddie's a great trumpet player, but if he had some kind of other direction to go . . . you [should] place a guy in a spot where he has to do something other than what he can do, so he can do that." About an Archie Shepp record, Miles fumed, "If something sounds terrible, man, a person should have enough respect for his own mind to say it doesn't sound good. It doesn't to me, and I'm not going to listen to it. No matter how long you listen to it, it doesn't sound any good. . . . [White people] go for anything. They want to be hipper than any other race and they go for anything ridiculous like that." Obviously Miles's opinion of the now-not-so-new New Thing had not changed over the years. Actually, of all the albums that Feather played for him, the only two he professed to enjoy were one by the Fifth Dimension and another by the white psychedelic blues group Electric Flag. Miles's increasing fascination with pop music would eventually place him once again at the center of a new storm of controversy.

In the summer of 1967 John Coltrane died, totally unexpectedly. By the time of his death he had become the most pervasive stylistic influence in jazz since Charlie Parker. Almost every up-and-coming saxophonist was playing like him, and just like Parker and Louis Armstrong before him, he was imitated by musicians on every other instrument. When asked years later about Coltrane's death, Miles muttered sadly, "Coltrane died from taking too much LSD." He meant this metaphorically, since Coltrane died from a liver ailment dating back to his severe alcoholism of the early and mid fifties. Miles felt that Coltrane had used his tremendous talent to create music that was unlistenable, chemically induced pseudocosmic confusion. "Anyway," Miles said, "who do you think taught him those Khachaturian chords that he used? He learned all that modal shit from me." But his real feelings were made clear by the fact that a pensive photograph of Coltrane was the only picture of a musician that remained in his bedroom by the end of the seventies.

The death of Coltrane was a severe blow to the avant-garde, since he was its major supporter and commanded a large audience of dedicated listeners. In his wake many musicians overextended their talents, playing twenty-minute solos, using the drone of modes or totally free improvisation, but lacking Coltrane's genius to pull it off. The public was growing restless with the avant-garde, and many of its fans were listening instead to the adventuresome new rock. The Beatles, Cream, The Grateful Dead, The Jefferson Airplane, Mothers of Invention, and other groups were incorporating electronic music, sound collages, jazzlike improvisation, techniques borrowed from classical music, and other modes into rock, creating fascinating new music for a wide audience. Miles was interested in many of their ideas, as well as the rhythm and blues of artists like Aretha Franklin, Sly and the Family Stone, and especially James Brown. "Jazz," Miles declared, "is getting too far from its folk roots." The new pop music was much closer to those roots, in his opinion, than Cecil Taylor or Archie Shepp.

In January 1968 Miles demonstrated his new musical interests for the first time, in a very limited fashion, by recording with the guitarist George Benson. At that time Benson could hardly have been considered a pop player, since his style was heavily influenced by Wes Montgomery and Kenny Burrell. But there was a heavy blues flavor to his playing, and Miles was able to experiment, however tentatively, with the use of a funky electric instrument. The session, which also included his quintet, produced two tunes, "Paraphernalia" and "Side Car." On both numbers Benson's improvising is courageous in the challenging context of the group, and Miles's use of Benson's guitar for some light riffing gave an indication of things to come in his music.

In February 1968 Frances was granted a divorce. Miles was living with Cicely at the time, and that relationship, too, was in trouble. "I have a sixth sense," Tyson would tell *Ebony* years later, "and it used to drive Miles crazy; I could always tell where he had been and what he had been doing." When Miles read this, he joked, "She didn't have any sixth sense. If she did have a sixth sense, she would have known when I was going to throw her down the stairs." Actually, Miles was gentle to his women most of the time, and he cared deeply about Cicely. A decade later they would be drawn together again.

Right now he felt it necessary to complete the direction that his quintet had been exploring during the four previous years. In May he recorded a piece called "Country Son" that summed up many of these innovations. It begins with Miles improvising at fast tempo, then switches to a ballad, and then changes to a quasi-Latin, semirock feeling. The piece continues to go through these changes for every soloist, creating a true sense of freedom, a continuing flow of surprise for the listener.

Two days later, after recording "Black Comedy," a piece by Tony Williams, Miles made his boldest move toward the new type of music he wanted to play. Herbie Hancock remembers this session:

"I walked into the studio and there was a Fender Rhodes electric piano sitting there. I asked Miles what I was supposed to do and he said, 'Play it.' " Not only did

Hancock play electric piano on this piece ("Stuff"), but Ron Carter played electric bass. On this tune, while the rhythm section played a beat that sounded like something in between rock and a tango, the horns played a melody with contours not unlike many of Wayne Shorter's pieces for the band. Both Hancock and Carter acquitted themselves well, Hancock immediately seizing upon the special effects he could make with the electric instrument.

Despite these significant strides, this was not the birth of jazz-rock. Vibraphonist Gary Burton, flutist Jeremy Steig, saxophonist Charles Lloyd, guitarist Larry Coryell and others had been experimenting, at least on a limited level, with a fusion of the two idioms. Musicians from the jazz milieu knew that they were able to play with more sophistication than the rock 'n' rollers, and thus were better able to meet the special challenges of the repetitive rock beat.

Miles's interest in rock came directly out of his interaction with the young musicians in his group, and their innovations. Playing on and over the rock beat created a static sound similar to the one he and Shorter had perfected by playing against the incredibly fast tempos of their rhythm section. Miles loved James Brown and especially the way Brown made rhythmic repetition swing—swing so mightily that the beat itself had a percussive character, not unlike Indian musicians' use of the tabla (an instrument that Miles would later incorporate into his band). Hancock and Williams were also interested in the sound of rock and rhythm and blues, and they encouraged Miles to explore a fusion of sixties pop and jazz. When the record of these spring sessions was released with the title *Miles in the Sky,* the cover displayed a psychedelic abstract in fluorescent colors.

One month after recording "Stuff," Miles brought the

band back into the studio in order to record a new project, his first real collaboration with Gil Evans since the aborted *Quiet Nights.* This was Miles's first full-scale venture into a fusion of rock and jazz, and he and Gil had composed all the tunes. The album's French title, *Filles de Kilimanjaro,* indicated its contents: all the pieces had French titles and a Gallic flavor in their melody lines. Gil supplied only the bass lines and some harmonic suggestions, but the session retained the conceptual approach of Miles's and Gil's previous orchestral collaborations.

For the first time since 1964 Miles had made major changes in the band. Both Herbie Hancock and Ron Carter decided to leave and form their own groups. Miles chose the British bassist Dave Holland to replace Carter, and brought in pianist Chick Corea, who played in a style similar to Hancock's. It was Tony Williams who initially contacted Corea, asking him to join the band. Corea remembers that when he telephoned Miles to accept, he was surprised to learn how much artistic freedom his new boss would allow him:

> I had looked at some of Wayne Shorter's music that I didn't know and it looked interesting and open to a lot of different ways of being played. [Miles] said, "Yeah, it should remain that way." Then there was a little silence and he said, "I don't know what else to tell you except that we'll go and play, but whatever *you* think it is, that's what it is."
>
> Miles has a discipline, but it's unspoken. It's a magical thing that you hardly see anymore—the way family units used to be. The father would inspire the rest of the family, and they would try to become like him. The people that play with Miles respect him so much, and knowing that he knows,

they humbly put themselves at his disposal and learn from him.

Both Corea and Holland fit perfectly into the band for the *Filles de Kilimanjaro* cuts that they played on—so much so that it is difficult to tell them apart from Hancock and Carter. The resulting record is highly inventive jazz-rock, or "fusion." The rock aspects of the music (particularly the rhythmical ones) are hinted at rather than crudely pronounced. The electric instruments blend with the acoustic instruments, in tunes which often change in mood, texture, and rhythmic feeling. This is particularly evident on "Mademoiselle Mabry," a blues that sounds, at its beginning, like an after-hours funk combined with a lazy rock rhythm. The piece increases in intensity but never loses its blues feel, nor does this interfere with the thoughtful improvisations of Miles and Shorter.

In addition to this collaboration, Miles and Gil worked on some orchestral pieces for the Berkeley Jazz Festival and for a play called *Time of the Barracuda*. The music for the play has never been publicly performed, but the performance at the jazz festival surprised many listeners who were not aware of Miles's latest musical directions. Between sets of the quintet Miles and the orchestra played a lovely piece composed by Shorter, and a unique version of Aretha Franklin's hit "You Make Me Feel Like a Natural Woman." A third piece was based on Indian ragas, with a rhythmic feel unlike anything Miles and Gil had created before. Unfortunately, this piece has never been recorded.

When Miles recorded "Mademoiselle Mabry" he was not using a title he had pulled out of the air. He had become deeply involved with Betty Mabry, and was thinking of marrying her. Betty, who was twenty-three at the time, was a beautiful, accomplished woman. She had posed for *Jet,* operated a rock club, and written a hit for the Chambers Brothers called "Uptown." She was vivacious and social, which, of course, was a contrast to Miles's reclusiveness. Miles was dazzled; calling from Chicago in September 1968, he told her, "Sweetcakes, get your stuff together and come to Chicago, we're getting married." Betty announced to the press:

> One of the sexiest men alive is Miles Dewey Davis. We're going to be married forever, because I'm in love and Mr. Davis can do no wrong as far as I'm concerned. He's experienced all facets of life, has terrific taste in everything, loves only the best, and has taught me many things. I was never really a jazz fan because I lean mostly to rhythm and blues and pop, but Miles's *Sketches of Spain* and *Kind of Blue* really sock it to me. But Miles is the teacher, so I'm going to be cool, stay in the background, and back up my man.

Despite these sentiments this marriage proved to be short-lived. It is inconceivable that Miles himself would have ever made such a statement to the press about his private life.

Nevertheless, Betty would influence Miles musically perhaps more than any of his previous women. Through her he came to listen to a steady stream of pop and soul music, and he began to be aware of the nuances of rock and rhythm and blues. Jimi Hendrix, one of Betty's favorite musicians, particularly fascinated him. Hendrix was able to make his guitar sound like an entire band; he created astounding effects with electronics and then segued into down-and-dirty blues. To Miles it was irrelevant whether you labeled Hendrix "rock," "blues," or "jazz"; he was creating a new world of sound, still based on the folk roots of black music.

In November 1969 Miles ventured further into the new areas of music that he had begun to explore. In a particularly bold move he added two keyboardists to the quintet. One of them was Herbie Hancock, who returned to the band; the other was Joe Zawinul, an Austrian musician who for several years had been playing with Cannonball Adderley. Jack DeJohnette replaced Tony Williams on drums, since Williams was involved in putting together his own group. The three keyboardists created a kaleidoscope of colors, using acoustic piano, electric piano, and organ. Zawinul and Miles were beginning to work closely together in developing a new "electric-fusion" music. The group recorded two pieces by Zawinul, "Directions" (two versions) and "Ascent." Using the tone-color possibilities of the electric keyboards, Zawinul was able to create shifting patterns and textures similar to those created orchestrally by Gil Evans. Only these musicians were able to react spontaneously to the soloist, improvising new patterns and textures. With this session Miles was beginning to perceive a method of bringing together what had been seemingly disparate elements: the use of electronics and the freedom of improvisation; the music of the moment—that "thing" that was to him the essence of jazz—and the multitextured colors that in the past had been possible through scores written for the orchestra. This first session did not seem to him completely successful, but it opened up new possibilities.

One decisive factor that accelerated the changes was Tony Williams's exit from the band. For Williams this was a purely musical decision: "I knew I was going to leave Miles. . . . When Dave Holland entered the quintet, the group started going in another direction. We had come together at a certain point, a V, and when we started using Dave Holland the V started going in another direction, like an X."

A Scottish guitarist named John McLaughlin was at that time combining many of the possibilities of rock guitar with a jazz sensibility. When he heard a tape of McLaughlin, Miles immediately realized he had found a guitarist who understood the language of Eric Clapton and Jimi Hendrix as well as that of John Coltrane. As soon as McLaughlin arrived in New York, Miles invited him to join the band.

McLaughlin, as might be expected, was elated about playing with his idol Miles Davis. "Here I was," he recalled, "a British jazz musician who suddenly is playing with Miles. You cannot understand how excited and nervous I felt." The session, which resulted in *In a Silent Way,* again used the same three keyboard men as the "Directions" session, and Tony Williams played drums instead of DeJohnette. Two pieces were recorded: "Shhh/Peaceful" and a medley of Zawinul's "In a Silent Way" and Miles's "It's About That Time." Both pieces use ostinato bass patterns played by Holland on the acoustic bass, and repetitive, rock-influenced drum patterns. The low-key music is dubbed "opium music" by one listener, and is indebted to the more lyrical side of rock. The three keyboardists play lines, electric sounds, and riffs resulting in a rhythmically active collage of timbres and colors. McLaughlin's playing is tentative and relatively conservative. Both Miles and Shorter (who for the first time in public played soprano sax instead of his customary tenor) play solos with lovely melodic contours and straightforward lyrical lines. Miles's playing, at least in terms of mood and lyricism, recalls his work on *Kind of Blue*, although there is less concern for structure.

Perhaps the most striking aspect of *In a Silent Way* is how accessible it is, although it is in many ways highly adventurous. Upon its release, in fact, many long-time Miles fans were convinced that he was finally selling out, pandering to a youthful audience. But listening to the evolution of Miles's music from 1966 provides ample evidence that he had been carefully building toward this new style of music.

This dramatic change was limited to the recording studio. The music Miles played in person continued to be pretty much what he had been playing since the midsixties. However, with DeJohnette he began to see the possibility of using rocklike rhythms before live audiences. In addition, he began having Chick Corea play electric piano. Corea at first despised the instrument, which seemingly made irrelevant his development as a pianist—touch, subtle use of dynamics, the very sound of the piano itself, all were totally altered or obliterated on the Fender Rhodes. He began to play solos that sounded like electronic versions of Cecil Taylor's atonal thunder, partly to reflect his interest in tonal freedom and partly to vent his frustration at playing the electric instrument. When someone asked Miles why he was using the electric piano, as well as having Dave Holland occasionally play the electric bass, his response was "So they can be heard." This was to some degree true, but Miles was also interested in the textural possibilities of these instruments, especially in combination with the quasi-rock beat he was increasingly using.

Some writers and critics believed that Clive Davis, then president of Columbia, was responsible for the new trends in Miles's music. Davis, of course, would never have told Miles what to play, but he *was* concerned that his record sales had dropped drastically since the mid-sixties. He suggested that Miles play at places that attracted the young people who accounted for the great majority of record sales, such places as Bill Graham's Fillmore East and Fillmore West:

> From my point of view, Miles was playing only before small audiences in small jazz clubs, and word of mouth is such a strong factor in selling records. So, after an initial blowup, where he asked for his release, because he didn't want to play places like the Fillmore, which was just a short-lived burst of feeling, and marvelously Miles in nature, he called me and said he was prepared to embark on this route, which has proven beautiful for him, for us, for people, for music.

At first Miles did not like the idea of playing places like the Fillmore. For one thing, he would not be paid as much as he was usually paid for a concert. Then, too, he hated the idea of playing before a white rock audience—his group was *not,* he insisted, a rock group. Finally, he did not get along with Bill Graham, which was understandable, since both men had volatile tempers. "You play the Fillmore," Miles said bitterly, "and they come up and give you a reefer, as if that's some big deal."

Nevertheless, in mid-1969, Miles appeared at the Fillmore East with his quintet on a bizarre triple bill, which also included a San Francisco psychedelic group, The Steve Miller Band, and Neil Young and Crazy Horse. The audience of rock fans was, in the main, confused by Miles's complex music, even though he was using electric instruments and a rock beat. However, he got to play first, after which he could immediately leave the theater—something that had always been specified in his contracts for concerts, even when he was the star attraction. (He always hated waiting to go on.) "But I'm never again working for that Bill Graham," he said afterward.

In the early summer of 1969 Miles's wife Betty threw a party for Jimi Hendrix at Miles's brownstone. She invited several women friends who were anxious to meet the rock star. Miles, who hated parties, especially ones for men at his home, conveniently arranged to be working at a late recording session and never showed up at all. However, he left a score for Hendrix to look at, and called him from the recording studio. Unfortunately, Hendrix could not read music, but the two had a lively musical discussion anyway. Miles was thinking about recording Hendrix with Gil Evans and an orchestra. Hendrix liked the idea, but both men were too involved in their individual careers to connect. The idea was bandied about for some time, and finally Alan Douglas convinced Hendrix to record with Miles. Miles demanded a fifty-thousand-dollar advance—which was totally out of the question. Hendrix had never thought of himself as a jazz musician and was deeply flattered that Miles was so taken by his music. But he and Miles were not comfortable with each other, since both were kings of their respective fields. Just before he died so unexpectedly, Hendrix had made definite plans to record with Gil but without Miles. Evans did, eventually, make an album of Hendrix tunes.

In August 1969 both Miles and Hendrix were involved in musical enterprises which would add tremendous luster to their legends. That month Hendrix played at the Woodstock Festival before a half-million rock fans, and Miles was recording *Bitches Brew,* the album which would be his most ambitious foray into a new musical future. For the sessions he assembled what amounted to a small electric orchestra: three keyboard players (including Corea and Zawinul), McLaughlin on guitar, and electric rock bassist Harvey Brooks. In addition, he used Holland on acoustic bass, three drummers and a percussionist, Wayne Shorter's soprano sax, and gifted reed man Benny Maupin on the bass clarinet. This band recorded six pieces in three days, each in one take, all with a sound unlike anything that had been heard before. Miles used the three electric pianos to play melodies and create unusual textures, as he had on *In a Silent Way*, but he also had the guitar and bass clarinet improvise to create even greater density. The three drummers and percussionist gave this music a rhythmic complexity comparable to African drum ensembles, or to some Latin American music. Over all this Miles and Shorter played horn solos that had tremendous freedom, stretching the limits of tonality.

Most critics seized on the electric instruments and quasi-rock rhythms as proof that Miles was playing something very close to rock. But the real breakthrough accomplished with *Bitches Brew* was the creation of an improvising orchestra through the use of electronics. Maupin's clarinet was used as another color in the brew, rather than simply as a solo instrument, and McLaughlin's guitar both soloed and played in the ensemble. Collective improvisation had been explored by many avant-garde musicians, including Ornette and Coltrane, but Miles used it in such a way that every instrument worked together to create great kaleidoscopes of sound a la Gil Evans.

Down beat gave *Bitches Brew* five stars but found it difficult to describe this new music. (The title, incidentally, came from a menu describing some sort of stew. When Miles saw the phrase "Bitches Brew," he instantly realized that it described the sensual music he had recorded.) The reviewer wrote, "Listening to this double album is, to say the least, an intriguing experience. Trying to describe the music is something else again. Though electronic effects are prominent, art, not gimmickry, prevails and the music protrudes mightily." However, many critics and musicians were confused and disappointed.

Brew went gold (that is, it sold over 500,000 copies) and went on to become the most successful jazz record of all time (as of 1970). The music was "spacey," even psychedelic, but it was certainly far more complex than even the most ambitious acid rock of the time. The sales of the record were helped by a striking surreal cover and an ambitious advertising campaign, especially in such periodicals as *Rolling Stone*. The ad copy read, "A Novel by Miles Davis," and featured a photograph of the apocalyptic cover art.

In October 1969 Miles was the victim of a bizarre incident. While sitting in his Ferrari he was shot in the legs by hoodlums for a reason that has never been revealed. This aggravated chronic trouble with his knees he had been having since the early sixties, and he was hospitalized and forced to cancel his engagements.

While Miles was recuperating, Wayne Shorter and Joe Zawinul began developing ideas for a cooperative band. Shorter was the last remaining member of the great sixties quintet, and he now felt the urge to be on his own. He and Zawinul, who had known each other since the early sixties, wanted to use many of the ideas that had been developed in the *Bitches Brew* sessions and play music that would not be jazz or rock but a new mutant form. The group would be called Weather Report, and of their music Zawinul would say enigmatically, "We will be soloing all of the time and none of the time." He was referring to the concept of group improvisation, stemming out of improvised-sounding melodies.

Tony Williams's group, Lifetime, which consisted of Williams, John McLaughlin, and organist Larry Young (who had also played on *Bitches Brew*) was the first and probably the best group to play what would be called fusion music. Like Miles's sixties quintet, the group changed tempos, meters, moods, and rhythms midtune, playing a mixture of hard rock and flowing, inventive jazz, in a framework that seemed totally improvised. And Herbie Hancock, who had originally led a fairly mainstream sextet (heavily influenced by Gil Evans) and who had gone back to playing acoustic piano, was experimenting once again with the Fender Rhodes, as well as with rock-funk rhythms. He would eventually use various synthesizers and electric bass, blending with the three horns of his front line. Gil Evans put together a band that incorporated electronic and acoustic instruments for a brilliant album that showed he was once again on the same musical wavelength as Miles. But most of the post-*Brew* fusion music used only the shallowest aspects of this new approach, the funk rhythms and the electronic sounds.

Boxing had become part of Miles's daily routine, and no matter where he was, he would find a gym where he could work out. He even took his trainer, Bobby McQuillen, with him on a European tour in 1969. McQuillen remembers that Miles was deeply involved at this time in improving himself physically. He gave up drinking, didn't touch any sort of drug, and for a while became a vegetarian. During the tour, which lasted about two months, he even remained celibate, believing that this would help his thinking and not distract him from the rigid discipline of getting in top shape. Now that Miles was in his forties perhaps he was worried about losing his ability with his horn, but he was playing with more energy than ever.

His electric music and his appearances in such halls as the Fillmore were attracting the type of media attention that sells records. In 1969 *Rolling Stone* did a cover story on him. However, as one might expect, Miles refused to pander to the magazine's white rock audience:

Rock is social music. There's two kinds—white and black, and those bourgeois spades are trying to sing white and whites are trying to sound colored. It's embarrassing to me. . . . White groups don't reach me. I can tell a white group just from the sound, don't have to see them. I listen to James Brown and those little bands on the South Side. They swing their asses off. No bullshit. All the white groups have got a lot of hair and funny clothes— they got to have on that shit to get it across. . . .

Jimi Hendrix can take two white guys and make them play their asses off. You got to have a mixed group—one has one thing, and the other has another. . . . For me a group has to be mixed to get swing, you have to have some black guys in there.

Not long after this interview Miles put together a band that was actually dominated by white players. When Wayne Shorter officially left the group in early 1970, Miles replaced him with a Coltrane-influenced saxophonist named Steve Grossman. Another addition to the band was Brazilian percussionist Airto Moreira, who played a number of South American percussion devices that blended well with the electronic effects. Moreira filled in the spaces, often using instruments he dubbed "nothings," objects he had found on the street with which he made interesting, and frequently bizarre, sounds.

Miles also added another white musician, keyboardist Keith Jarrett, to the group. Years later he would say that Jarrett was "the best pianist I ever had." Jarrett's technique was awesome, but his imagination was often annoyingly eclectic. Left to his own devices, he would show off all the styles that he had mastered. He could play bebop one moment, then switch to a Bill Evans romanticism, and then suddenly leap into a frantic, "outside" Cecil Taylor pandemonium. He could also be extraordinarily lyrical, playing what Miles called "those beautiful Irish melodies." Under Miles's tutelage Jarrett became part of the band. Although Jarrett hated the electric instruments, Miles insisted he play electric piano (after he left Miles, he never touched one again).

Once again Miles was taken to task by militant members of the black community for using so many white musicians in what they condemned as a blatant attempt to appeal to white audiences. But Miles had never, no matter how much he discussed it, judged a musician by race. If this confused many in the black community who knew how militant he was about racial matters, in his way of thinking that was just unfortunate.

He brought his new band into the Fillmore East for an engagement second-billed to Laura Nyro, although he had sworn never to play the Fillmore again. The band played four nights in a row and recorded enough music for a double set—perplexing the audience, who had come to hear Nyro's pop tunes, not some band apparently from outer space. As had been Miles's wont, each tune segued immediately into the next, creating the illusion of a single piece of music. Most of the tunes were from *Bitches Brew,* but they sounded different with this band. Using ring modulators, wah-wah pedals and other electronic devices, as well as Airto's array of percussion, the group created a jagged, often dissonant, crackling wall of sound, against which Miles played declamatory solos, often using staccato notes in a highly dramatic fashion. Many observers, particularly those critical of this music, pointed out that the band was dressed not unlike many of the white rock musicians whom Miles, at least in his *Rolling Stone* interview, publicly disdained. Even Miles himself was wearing a tie-dyed shirt and bell-bottom pants. In addition, members of the band lit incense at the beginning of the set.

Miles performed with the same group about a month later in New York's Central Park. After a set that incorporated Stockhausenesque electronic sounds, Coltranesque free form (in which Jarrett duetted on soprano sax with Grossman), and polyrhythmic Afro-rock, Miles walked onstage and signaled for the entire band to lay out. He then proceeded to play, totally unaccompanied, a gorgeous chorus of " 'Round Midnight." No, Miles was saying musically, I have not forgotten about lyricism or my musical past.

By 1970 Miles had begun to spend a tremendous amount of time in the recording studio. It was only there that he could explore all the new sounds that he was developing. He used a wide variety of musicians: the members of what would be called the Fillmore Band, including McLaughlin, Hancock, Zawinul, Sonny Sharrock, and percussionist M'Tume. All were used in various and sundry combinations, in music which had its own immutable logic. By now Miles was not con-

cerned with chords at all; he was using key centers rather than any formal harmonic system. The sounds were often bizarre, but he was relentless in exploring every conceivable combination of electric effects, third-world percussion, and improvisation.

There were many who speculated that Miles's new musical style and dress were psychedelically induced. But although he had tried mescaline once or twice, he disliked the experience for many of the same reasons that he had never cared for marijuana. During one psychedelic experience he thought he was having heart palpitations and vowed never to try drugs again.

Perhaps the disintegration of his home life partly accounted for the inordinate amount of time he was spending in the studio. His marriage to Betty was falling apart. She was spending quite a bit of time with Jimi Hendrix, and although Miles was a jealous man, he gave up trying to control her. After their divorce Betty made her own record, on which there was a song entitled "He Was a Big Freak." The lyrics mention that the "freak" liked to be whipped with a lavender belt. When asked about it, Miles laughed. "Well *she* was the biggest freak I ever met, but the song wasn't about me, it was about Hendrix. I'm a big freak myself, but I don't want anybody beating me with a lavender whip."

In the summer of 1970 a rock festival, supposed to be some sort of metropolitan Woodstock, was held in New York on Randall's Island. Scheduled acts included such Woodstock heroes as Hendrix, Sly, and the group Ten Years After. The promoter, wanting to appeal to as many music fans as possible, arranged to have Tony Williams's Lifetime play with Miles and Eric Clapton as special guests. John McLaughlin was an up-and-com-

◄   *Miles, 1971 (Elena Steinberg Collection).*

ing guitar hero, and the combination of his jazz-rock style and Clapton's rock, along with Miles's jazz genius, seemed like a potent idea. But in an interview in *Rolling Stone,* while discussing this "super-jam," Clapton mentioned that "Miles [was] trying to become a pop star." When Miles read this, he immediately called off the gig. Coming from Clapton, he felt, this was an unforgivable insult. Eventually, the festival fell to pieces due to financial problems resulting from the "Woodstock mentality"—the insistence by rock fans that such festivals be free.

Clapton's assertion might have arisen from a statement Miles made that he could put together "the best rock group in the world." But this was a misrepresentation of his real musical goals, which transcended any such rigid categories. However, in 1971 a record was released that gave some idea of how a Miles Davis rock band would have sounded; it contained pieces from a couple of the many sessions he was recording at that time. The group consisted of McLaughlin, Grossman, Holland, drummer Billy Cobham, and Keith Jarrett on organ, playing music that was used for a documentary about the great boxer Jack Johnson. The first side is almost a straight-ahead jazz-rock jam, with little evidence of the multiple textures Miles was using in his music. Miles plays a long solo, full of a joyous blues lyricism not heard on his other recent recordings, while McLaughlin plays guitar riffs not unlike those used in such groups as Cream and the Hendrix group. The other side is far more bizarre and uses electronic effects to create genuine "space music."

By 1971 Chick Corea and Dave Holland had left Miles's group. Miles was having Keith Jarrett play both electric piano and organ, often simultaneously, and he had hired Michael Henderson, who had played in Stevie

Wonder's band, to play electric bass. Steve Grossman had been replaced by Gary Bartz, who, while also heavily influenced by Coltrane, had developed his own bluesy style on alto and soprano saxophones. The group recorded live in Washington, D.C., with McLaughlin sitting in for the session. For the first time Miles used a wah-wah pedal attachment, which made him sound almost like Hendrix playing the trumpet. He used the wah-wah to create gradations of trumpet sound just as he had used the Harmon mute in the fifties and early sixties. While many critics complained, Miles felt that his music was a genuine breakthrough in improvised sound. As always he ignored the critics; to him they were still living in the fifties.

However, Miles also found himself increasingly under attack by other musicians, even those he had worked with in the fifties and sixties. Percy Heath, the superb bassist who played with Miles on many of the classic Prestige sides, told a reporter that Miles's new style was a desperate attempt to try to stay young. "I was in his early bands," Heath stated, "and very proud to be, but in his later bands I would not have been. It's his choice to make and I'm not putting him down, but it's not the person that I knew and loved and appreciated, no matter how rich and famous he got after that." Thad Jones walked out of his concerts and publicly complained about his new direction. There had always been some resentment toward Miles because of his success, which was unprecedented for such an uncompromising musician. Now with even greater success playing his new electric music, it was not unexpected when many fellow musicians, still struggling in the jazz life, expressed disgruntlement.

When Columbia asked him to play on television, he agreed, as long as he didn't have to talk to the hosts.

"The only thing I could say to those talk show hosts," Miles declared, "is 'You're a sad motherfucker.' " Miles did appear on the Dick Cavett show and played one of his typically cryptic pieces of that time. He was infuriated when Cavett announced after the performance, "In case you didn't recognize that tune, it was 'Moon River.' " Once again Miles's worst fears about the mass media were confirmed.

However, he did agree to an interview with *Newsweek*, where he gave a cogent explanation of the duties of the men in his band:

> Everyone adds, everyone responds. Sometimes you subtract, take away the rhythm and leave just the high sound. Or take out what you know belongs to someone else and keep the feeling. . . . What [my musicians] have got to do is extend themselves beyond what they think they can do. And they've got to be quick. A soloist comes in when he feels like it. Anyway, that's what he's being paid for. If it's not working out, I just shut them up. How? I set up obstacles, barriers like they do in the streets, but with my horn. I curve them, change their direction.

Throughout 1971 and 1972 Miles continued to make continual additions and subtractions to his band. He started to use an electric sitarist and the great Indian musician Badaly Roy on the tabla. This created a heady mix combined with M'Tume's African and South American percussion, the funk riffs of Michael Henderson and electric guitarist Reggie Lucas, the jazz-rock beat of DeJohnette (and then Al Foster), and the jazz improvising of a number of different saxophonists (among them the fluent altoist Sonny Fortune, Grossman, and the inventive David Liebman), and of course Miles himself. The band usually performed what amounted to one piece, with the basic structure held together by the ostinato bass line. Though this could be monotonous, Miles used the many new sounds at his disposal to create change without the traditional method of harmonic progressions. This music, more than ever, was totally spontaneous, depending on each musician's ability to hear each nuance of change and react to the other complex elements that were occurring in the ensemble. With that group Miles never left the stage but "conducted" with hand signals, looks, gestures, and eventually by playing the electric organ himself, playing chords or single notes or dissonant sounds to turn the musicians toward new directions during a performance. In describing Miles's role in the band, Dave Liebman said:

This [music] is more of a sound; it's like a continuous tone almost, and within that tone there are variables. So in order to control that tone and the tensions within it, what he actually does is he leads it, he actually brings it up and brings it down, just like a conductor does. He used to walk off the stage when he had a quintet because when he wasn't soloing there was nothing to *do*. Now he's up there leading the dynamics, in the sense of the rhythm section, because they are working as a *unit* now. The jazz conception of soloist backed up by rhythm section is definitely not happening in this band. . . . An important part of [this music] is to have a lot of cats on the stage, especially to have a lot of color instruments. All instruments have colors, but I mean that the main function of the instrument is color. . . . Miles is one of the greatest at using chords and working within that. He's a harmonic player all the way. But that has kind of exhausted itself, at least for a while, and you therefore have to treat the other elements in the same way, with the same kind of discretion and balance, like using a certain chord against a certain chord, you use a certain color against a certain color. And this is what Miles is such a *bitch* at. . . . He's always been able to do that with music, he's a fantastic molder of music.

In June 1972 Miles made *On the Corner*. This new record, he told a writer, would be "something for black people to remember me by." Over funk rhythms were Indian sounds, two keyboardists (one being Herbie Hancock), soul guitar, Miles's trumpet plus wah-wah, and young saxophonist Carlos Garnett, also using wah-wah. Probably no record that Miles ever made was so bitterly attacked by the critics. One British critic wrote, "I love Miles, but this is where I get off." Other critics complained that you couldn't even hear Miles, his electronic trumpet being just one of the elements in a shifting electronic mass of sound. This was *not*, despite the title, street music (although the cover, one of the ugliest in Miles's history, depicts graffitilike drawings of Harlem street scenes). But it was an ambitious experiment: Miles had brought together many musical cultures, everything from the electronics of Stockhausen to ancient exotic Indian classical music, to street funk—and fused them, creating a genuine *world* music. *On the Corner,* as critic Lester Bangs has pointed out, also used pure noise brilliantly, making us hear the sounds of the world in a new, collective way.

Miles thought that his breakthroughs were exciting, and he couldn't understand how confusing many listeners, including most critics, found them. One night at a club where he was listening to a rather mundane jazz-rock group he asked rhetorically, "How come people like this shit so much, but they don't get my music?" And then he answered his own question: "I guess it's because my music comes at them from so many different directions at the same time." As Ralph J. Gleason pointed out, the dimensions of this music could not be captured on stereo.

In September 1972, while on his way to a concert, Miles had a bad automobile accident that injured his legs and broke both his ankles. Supposedly, as he was being hauled out of the wreckage, he said, "That's okay. I didn't feel like making that concert anyway." He doesn't remember saying that, and if he had known at the time how this accident would affect his legs, it is doubtful that he would have been facetious about it. The accident, and the 1969 shooting incident, combined with a rare arthritic condition (that Miles claimed only affected blacks) made him a near cripple.

While he was hospitalized, Columbia issued a live recording of the group at Lincoln Center. As with *On the Corner,* the packaging was sloppy, with no personnel listed or the names of any of the tunes. At this point, though, the names of the pieces were irrelevant, since they were not "tunes" as such. When Columbia issued a recording of the Isle of Wight rock festival containing a performance by Miles's group, the record company asked him the name of the piece. "Call it anythin'," Miles told them. Which is exactly what they titled the piece, "Call It Anythin'." But with the *Miles Davis in Concert* album, the company apparently fell in line with Miles's thinking that such matters as personnel, titles, and liner notes were irrelevant—the only thing essential was the music itself. This particular recording had a muddy sound, which made the tapestry of sound more like a morass. In addition, Miles's use of wah-wah, though often brilliant when bending notes and blending in with the ensemble, often obscured the tone and timbre of the horn.

Miles was now using crutches most of the time, and the pain on his face before a performance made his musicians wince. Nevertheless he went on a Far Eastern tour, throughout which he sat while playing. During this 1973 tour *Agartha,* another two-record set, was recorded. Miles had pared his band down to two guitar players, Reggie Lucas and Pete Cosey, Al Foster on drums, M'Tume on percussion, Michael Henderson and (for this tour) Sonny Fortune on saxophones. Miles would rev himself up for performing by listening to nothing but James Brown. "Listen to that rhythm," he would tell his musicians. "It's all in that rhythm." *Agartha* is clearer than the Lincoln Center performance, due to better recording and fewer instruments. Miles was clearly refining his ideas.

In 1974 he made his last studio album of the seventies. Along with semireggae "Calypso Frelimo," a funky "Red China Blues" (recorded with a big band), and an experiment in white noise, "Rated X," Miles recorded a piece in honor of his idol, Duke Ellington, who had died that year. Ellington had once compared Miles to Picasso, since both men were in constant artistic flux. Miles's tribute to Ellington, "He Loved Him Madly," is one of the strangest pieces in his career. "It's a sound," he explained. This is minimalist music, with Miles playing long, deeply felt notes over a held guitar tone which gradually changes and moves up in intensity over the course of an entire record side. Some critics carped that this piece had little resemblance to Ellington's music.

Miles with Elena Steinberg, 1973 (Elena Steinberg Collection).

But Ellington would have understood: the beauty of pure sound was comparable to nothing else except Ellington.

Miles continued to perform, and at the end of 1974 he played one of his few small-club engagements of the midseventies. Despite the difficult demands his music made on listeners, the audience was larger than it had ever been. He was playing organ and trumpet simultaneously, cuing the band with both. He still used the wah-wah pedal, but more sparingly, and only when its effect would be most felt. His clothes were enough to throw Mick Jagger into a fit of envy: custom-made high-heel boots, fringed yellow jacket, huge sunglasses. His playing, however, still had its old emotional thrust, often reminding one, curiously, of the Spanish-tinged melancholy of *Sketches of Spain.*

Shortly after this gig Miles had to have another operation, this time on his hip. After extensive hospitalization he made up his mind to retire. The pain was too great—he could not give the music the attention it deserved with such a distraction. He decided that he could never eliminate music from his life, but instead of the rigors of touring, which he hated, and performing, he would devote himself to composing and arranging. As he would say, "My mind is *always* on music."

As Gil Evans put it, "His organism is tired. And after all the music he's contributed for thirty-five years, he needs a rest." But rest was not always easy after so many years of artistic ferment.

Miles Down the Road

For many years Miles had talked about retiring from performing, but in 1975, when he finally did stop playing and recording, it was not really a matter of choice. His deteriorating health made performing out of the question. After a particularly long stay in the hospital in 1975, Miles explained, "It's like Gil Evans was, just about the time of the *Birth of the Cool* sessions. After them, he went to the hospital and just gave up arranging for a while, he just lost his feel. Well, I just gave up my feel for the horn."

Miles rarely left his house, and even the strong pain relievers prescribed for him helped very little. In addition, Miles hated these drugs because they made him drowsy. "If I can't stay up for five days at a time," he said, "I just might as well forget about it." However, he managed to hide his constant pain from most of his friends, since he had always hated people who whined about their ailments. On one very rare occasion he confided, "If only you knew how much this hurt. It's a motherfucker, man."

Despite his illness—and unknown to most in the outside world—Miles remained unceasingly creative. For nights on end he would sit at his piano, composing. When friends came over he would play thick chords, saying, "Listen to this, isn't that beautiful?" He would also spend time composing with close friends, such as the songwriter Elena Steinberg. However, he rarely, very rarely, touched his trumpets. When a friend suggested that the horns be fixed, since they were in disrepair, Miles bristled and said, "When I'm ready to play again, I'll fix them myself." He was also constantly irritated by those well-intentioned friends and relatives who would call him and ask when he would play again. He would tell them, "When I *feel* like it; nobody has to tell me when I should play again. I'll know." But privately he would express doubts about his ability to pick up the horn again: "I don't know," he said after he had been in retirement for a long while. "I might have to start all over again, learning the basics, just like I did when I first started playing the horn."

He occasionally enjoyed his position as mentor to young players. One time a cornetist came to the house and was asked to demonstrate his style. After only a few notes, Miles grabbed the cornet out of the younger man's hands, picked up a nearby hammer, and acted as if he were going to smash the horn while croaking, "Learn how to play this damned thing." The cornetist was shocked, but Miles was trying to shake him up, to psychically slap him into becoming a better musician. Then relenting, Miles smiled and said, "Look, you've got a nice approach to the horn, but you don't have your sound right. You play with too much vibrato, and as my teacher told me when I was a kid, some day when you're old you'll be shaking and have a vibrato anyway. You need to find your sound, because that sound is the whole thing. Musical ideas are easy, but it's developing your sound—that's at the heart of it."

Columbia's president, Bruce Lundvall, regretted Miles's retirement. Although none of his subsequent records sold as well as *Bitches Brew*, all his records were steady sellers. Every record that Miles had made for the company, beginning with *'Round About Midnight*, remained in print and in demand. However, although he had made many recordings in the early seventies when he was virtually living in Columbia's studios, he had agreed to only a few releases of old material. One record, *Water Babies*, which consisted of performances by the mid-sixties quintet, was released as a favor to Tony Williams, who had composed much of the material. But Lundvall was persistent with Miles: please, he begged him, just come into the studio and record *anything*. Miles told him that he didn't know how to run a record company. "Well," Lundvall asked, "what should I do?"

"Why don't you take up jogging or something, instead?"

Finally Lundvall did something that record company presidents rarely do: he went to the house of one of his artists. While he was there, Miles played him a recording of some fascinating, hypnotic electric music he had made. "Wow, that's great," exclaimed Columbia's president. "Bruce," said Miles, "that was from *Jack Johnson*, which was released over six years ago. Now get the hell out of my house." This incident did not deter Lund-vall from releasing new Miles Davis albums. Along with Teo Macero, he went to the Columbia vaults, and while Miles was in retirement, released two albums of material that ranged from the very first sessions of the quintet in 1955 to Miles's early-seventies music.

Although Miles enjoyed seeing friends, he was inhospitable to people who thought they had some right to meet him. Once, Mick Jagger dropped by his house. Miles did not know Jagger and when he opened the door, he said to the rock star, "What do you want?"

Jagger responded, "I'm Mick Jagger, and I've always wanted to . . ."

"Get the fuck out of here. I don't care who you are."

When a friend asked Miles why he sent away such a celebrity, he replied, "I didn't care that he was Mick Jagger, no one comes here unless they're invited. I wouldn't go to his house unless he invited me. And I even like the way the guy sings!"

Nevertheless, Miles would often get depressed when former associates failed to keep in touch with him. "Why don't guys like Thad Jones or Percy Heath ever call me?" he would often wonder out loud. One Christmas he was especially upset. "After all the musicians I trained," he said, "the only one who sent me a Christmas card was Joe Zawinul." When Sonny Rollins called him one morning, Miles was delighted—he still retained tremendous affection for the tenor man.

Dizzy Gillespie got in touch with Miles for a surprising reason: he wanted Miles to teach him how to improve his tone when he played ballads. Miles laughed when he remembered this incident: "After all the shit I learned from Dizzy, he comes to *me* in order to learn! I told him that he was too set in his ways to change now. But I also told him that all that air that puffed up his cheeks when he played wouldn't do his tone any good unless it went through his horn."

One person who stayed in constant contact with Miles was Cicely Tyson, who would call regularly and try to lift his sometimes waning spirits. His trainer, Bobby McQuillen, paid frequent visits, encouraging him to keep in shape, telling him, "You're still a young man, Miles. You've got plenty left to give to the world."

Usually his pungent humor outweighed his depressions. Once a friend mentioned an orgy. Miles shook his head and said, "I don't like orgies. I'm not putting these million-dollar lips on no two-dollar pussy."

In 1978 Miles's friend Elena Steinberg invited him for a stay at her house in Connecticut. Miles appreciated the peace of the country and began seriously considering buying a house in New England. While he was there, Larry and Julie Coryell, good friends of Elena's,

Miles with Dizzy Gillespie, 1962 (Duncan Schiedt, Frank Driggs Collection).

encouraged Miles to record some of his newly composed music in their own studio, with Larry on guitar, as well as a bassist and drummer. Miles only played piano at these sessions, but the music displayed his personal musical approach. He decided, though, that the tapes were too unsatisfactory to be released, and told Larry that he could keep them as a gift.

As much as he liked the quiet of the country, he found that he needed the discordant rhythms of New York City. "New York is great," he would say. "It's got so much noise. Subways, horns, I can't stand quiet. I go nuts." Upon returning to New York, he turned to several projects he had long been thinking about. One of the most intriguing was a new collaboration with Gil Evans, this time recording *Tosca,* with Miles playing the arias on trumpet. *Tosca* was one of his favorite pieces of music. Miles has often said, "My favorite music is Stockhausen, *Tosca,* and James Brown." These represent the three essential aspects of music that are most important to him: the complex, constantly changing electronic textures of Stockhausen (to whom he often compared Gil Evans), the lyricism of *Tosca,* and the eternal rhythms of James Brown. The *Tosca* project, to date, has not been recorded, but Miles keeps the score of the opera at home and still pores over it.

All during his retirement, Miles continued to keep active. He hated rehashing his past. When somebody asked him about an incident involving Charlie Parker, he grimaced and said, "That was so damned long ago. Who cares about that shit?" Indeed, to Miles, living in the past is destructive for an artist. One night, after several days of staying up and writing at the piano, he lost track of what day it was. "It's Thursday," claimed his girlfriend of the moment. Miles made a face and growled, "You're a lying motherfucker." When a friend showed him a newspaper with the date, which was indeed Thursday, he stood up and pointed to the awards which were hung behind the piano. "Do you see those awards?" he said quietly. "I got them because my memory is so damn bad."

As time passed Miles became increasingly restless—composing at the piano was simply not as exciting as playing with a band. And he was becoming tired of public speculation about activity in retirement. Rumors circulated that he was dead, that he was back on drugs, that he was embarrassed because he could no longer play. In 1979 Miles granted a short interview to a friend's friend who worked for *Oui* magazine. When the reporter asked Miles if he was using cocaine, Miles laughed and said, "Isn't that stuff expensive?" He had little patience for such snooping into his private life, and he began to be called "the Howard Hughes of jazz." Not that Miles cared. *He* knew that he was going to return to music, when he felt he was ready. "Everybody thinks I'm dying or on drugs or something," he would tell friends, "but I'm going to surprise the world."

His return was delayed by further operations, including the removal of gallstones, another hip operation, treatment of a stomach ulcer, and an operation intended to improve his speaking voice (it helped only slightly).

In late 1980 Miles began seriously playing the trumpet again, something he found far easier to do than he had initially feared. His nephew, Vincent Wilburn, son of his sister Dorothy, started a punk band, and Miles began working in private with it, recording music with little relationship to any of his previous work. Then, with encouragement from his manager and friend, Mark Rothbaum, Miles began to put together a working band of his own and to plan a new recording. In March 1981 he recorded three albums for Columbia, which released *The Man With the Horn,* one record from the sessions. It would be criticized as being one of the least ambitious in Miles's career. And indeed, it lacks the complexities of his electric music of the early seventies. The band was composed of young, mostly unknown players (with the exception of the superb Al Foster, who had played with Miles in the previous decade).

In its simplicity the music embraced Miles's entire career, since the young musicians played straight 4/4 swing rhythms in addition to funk. Many critics failed to perceive this band's resemblance to the early sixties band with Wynton Kelly and Hank Mobley: it served as an ideal vehicle for Miles to make beautiful musical statements without distraction. And he surprised his audiences at Lincoln Center, the Savoy, the Beacon, and other places by playing ballads like "My Man's Gone Now" as well as funk and even quasi-reggae pieces. He was still playing brilliantly, using a portable-miked horn but no wah-wah pedal, playing melodically and with a sometimes fiery rhythmic attack. He seemed more relaxed than ever, sometimes joking with the musicians onstage, or offering them drinks of water. Miles was coming back with full strength.

In November 1981 Miles married Cicely Tyson at the home of their mutual friend Bill Cosby. Cicely had remained friendly and concerned about Miles throughout his six years of retirement, and the two had grown close again in the months before his return to playing.

Although he continued to have physical problems, Miles felt strong enough to announce that with the help of his new wife, he would continue playing until he died. He had always maintained that his fate remained in his own hands:

"If I want something, it just seems to happen, or I

Miles after a New York performance, 1981 (Michael Rankin).

make it happen. You know, I live in my mind, that's all I need. They can come and take away my arms, my legs, my dick, whatever, as long as they leave me my brain. As long as I have my mind, I'll always figure out a way to get it all back."

◀ *Miles, 1977 (Elena Steinberg Collection).*

Phoenix

When Miles Davis resumed his career in the early eighties, the jazz world had changed drastically. The fusion movement, which had dominated jazz when he first went into "retirement" in the mid-seventies, was no longer in fashion. When the great tenor saxophonist Dexter Gordon returned to the U.S. after years spent as an expatriate in Europe, his "all acoustic" music sounded delightful to jazz fans after years of electronic textures and thundering volume. The warmth and the straightforward swing of Gordon's music was a tonic to many ears.

At the same time a young trumpeter from New Orleans was beginning to gain notice. Wynton Marsalis first went the route of many important musicians: he played in Art Blakey's Messengers. After that he toured in a quartet led by Herbie Hancock. Marsalis was a new breed of jazz musician. He had disdain for fusion and had little interest in the free jazz of the sixties. He was devoted to the hard bop of the late fifties, playing music that had peaked before he was born. He also had a separate career as a classical trumpeter, which would greatly endear him to the cultural elite.

From early on, Marsalis was outspoken in his views. And he was especially outspoken about Miles Davis.

He greatly admired Miles's pre-electric work, but he took Miles to task for his post-sixties fusion. This infuriated Miles. He found it deeply galling that Marsalis continually criticized him for his musical direction—implying that Miles had "sold out." And whether or not one agreed with Marsalis, his rhetoric showed a lack of understanding of cultural protocol. After all, he had just entered the jazz world; to tear down somebody who had made such great contributions to that world—as well as having been one of Marsalis's prime influences—from such a position took quite a bit of chutzpah, to say the least. And Marsalis should have known enough about Miles to realize how thin-skinned he was.

Marsalis would become the most influential musician of his generation, and in his wake there would follow another generation of like-minded young jazz musicians. Most of them were, like Marsalis, quite serious, knowledgeable of jazz history, and basically conservative. Rather than innovation, they were concerned with the "jazz tradition." Marsalis led the way, reaching back even further to Ellington and the New Orleans ensembles for influences.

Of course this ran counter to Miles's concept of the nature of jazz and the role of the jazz musician. "He's too young to think like an old man," Miles said about Marsalis. "He's playing all those things we did in the sixties, and he's a young man. He should take a step and stretch out a little bit." Actually, Marsalis's music was not nearly as adventurous as that of Miles's iconoclastic sixties quintet. Neither he nor any of his fellow "neo-classicists" (as they were tagged) took the chances that Miles and Wayne Shorter and the brilliant Hancock-Carter-Williams rhythm section took every time they played. It was hard not to think of Marsalis and his acolytes as a reactionary generation of musicians playing a music that, until the eighties, had been consistently progressive and visionary.

Certainly that had been true of Miles during his greatest years, when his influence was as widespread as that of Marsalis. There was a large difference, however, between Miles's method of exerting his influence and Marsalis's. Miles led mainly by example, sounding off in interviews from time to time, but never as actively vociferous as Marsalis, who constantly made stern declarations about what is and what is not jazz. But now Miles wanted to play music again. What would he do in this environment?

Miles himself could never return to playing hard bop, not even the very free hard bop he had played with the sixties quintet. He hated even thinking about music he made far in the past. "Sure," he would say, "that music [of the Hancock/Shorter quintet] was great in its time. But now it just sounds flat." It was, after all, music that reflected its era, like all great art does. And times had changed. The future, as always, was the only direction Miles was interested in. His ideas on music were based on his profound yet earthy American brand of existentialism. He was a man who insisted on defining himself on his own terms and having the freedom to redefine himself every time he played music.

For Miles the existentialist, the physical aspects of playing onstage were as important as such abstract considerations as harmony, melody, and rhythm. Thanks to new technology, he no longer had to play into a microphone—his trumpet was wired with its own built-in mike. He could play from any place on stage rather than having to stand in the same place. Once he got used to this new way of playing, he would tell writers that even thinking about the way he formerly had to play "gave [him] a headache." Now he felt genuinely liberated.

To understand the musical route he took upon his return, one must comprehend some basic aspects of Miles's life and nature. First of all, though he surprised everyone when he returned to active playing with his seemingly undiminished ability to play the trumpet, he had been sick for a long time, and still had lingering physical problems which drained him of his energy. He no longer had the energy it takes to be truly innovative. And it does take energy, sustained mental and physical energy, to push ahead, to walk that tightrope of innovation every time you play—especially in jazz. In jazz, after all, the act of creating is as much a physical act as it is a mental process. All Miles's remaining energy went into just playing his horn. At this point he wanted to relax onstage, exult in the joy of simply playing his horn rather than stand on the razor's edge.

Another factor that strongly affected Miles—and there is no other way to state this—was his genuine love of money. To be blunt, he liked being rich and loved getting richer. It is therefore testimony to Miles's commitment to his art that never before did he pander to his audience. More often than not he took great chances that could, and often did, deeply disturb people, or even completely turn them off. Just think of the latitude he gave to such members of his bands as Coltrane, Shorter, Hancock, Corea, etc. And when he turned to the multi-dimensional music of the seventies he took the chance of losing forever those coming to hear him play "My Funny Valentine" yet again. But now, I believe, Miles decided it was time to cash in, finally, on his legend. He was, as always, highly aware of the nature of the times, and realized that it was no longer gauche to be a bit greedy. So he charged fifty to a hundred thousand dollars per concert, and he put on a crowd-pleasing show, playing music that he hoped would be at least as appealing to pop fans as it was to his long-time jazz fans. And if the jazz critics sneered, well, he never really gave a damn about their opinions anyway.

Post-"retirement" Miles backed further and further away from being identified as a "jazz musician." He never liked the word and now felt that it limited his audience. Almost every major jazz musician has spurned the word "jazz," including Duke Ellington, Louis Armstrong, Charlie Parker, and, in his own quiet way, John Coltrane. Charlie Mingus insisted that the label "jazz" was, in his words, "part of the whole 'back of the bus' syndrome." He insisted that his big-band masterpiece *The Black Saint and the Sinner Lady* be listed by the record company as "Ethnic Folk Dance Music." These geniuses disavowed the word "jazz" because they did not want to be strait-jacketed in a narrow "jazz tradition." They wanted to be free to explore music in any direction their curiosity took them. In addition—and this was especially true for Miles—jazz records only account for four or five percent of all records sold, so a record that is considered "jazz" is apt to be ignored by ninety-five percent of the record-buying public. Miles seemed to really want to be part of the pop scene and to be perceived as being in the same musical context as Lionel Richie, Prince, Michael Jackson, Sting (who would make a cameo appearance on a Miles album), and even Paul McCartney.

Besides, Miles was disgusted with what had happened to the once creatively fervent jazz scene. He did not feel spurred by the jazz environment to create innovative music as he once had been. Musicians (at least most musicians) were no longer experimenting, pushing the envelope, challenging other musicians to push their explorations even further. Jazz was no longer an adventure, and Miles had little choice but to hire musicians who were talented but lacked much originality or the ability to innovate either within or outside the environment of Miles's band.

The band played what could be called generic jazz/rock/funk, with little of the explosive daring of Miles's seventies bands. The group's saxophonist Bill Evans (no relationship to the great pianist) was technically very proficient, and a fine all-around musician. Miles had hired him by calling him and asking whether he was willing to step into the shoes of Coltrane, Rollins, Shorter, Jackie McLean, Hank Mobley, etc. But Evans was not nearly as original a musician as any of these other former Davis sidemen. The same thing was true for Mike Stern, Miles's guitarist—plenty of chops, little of interest to express. Al Foster was once again in the drum chair, although he was not very happy playing rock and funk backbeat, which is exactly what Miles wanted from him.

Perhaps these mediocre surroundings made Miles's own playing sound more brilliant than ever, like a sparkling diamond in a drab setting. Although during his "retirement" he had told friends that it would take many months of intense practice to get his lip back to where it had been, his playing in itself didn't seem affected. Of course, Miles was never known for his powerful chops—he had built his style, after all, on the limitations of his technique. His greatest strength had always been his ability to select and play the perfect note in the perfect place—in other words, his genius at self-editing. This ability, which is one of the factors that made him such a unique musician, he still had in full flower.

His music, then, while not a throwback to earlier eras, nevertheless lacked the power and personal vision that had marked his most innovative work. And fusion was no longer looked upon as brave innovation. By the end of the seventies, much of the public had decided that most of it was little more than jazz musicians vying for their share of the rock audience by showing off their flashy chops. Yet Miles, playing music that was clearly an extension of his seventies electric period, drew the largest crowds of his career now for the biggest fees he had ever received.

Why? In the eighties, more than ever, what I call the "Zsa Zsa Gabor Syndrome" held sway in this country. Those who were famous just for being famous were made creatures of royalty. Glamor and money meant everything in this age of Reagan. Miles had always had a heightened awareness of the currents of American life. And of course he had been greatly influenced by his wives—certainly this was true for his new wife, Cicely Tyson. This marriage alone helped make Miles renowned to many who had no interest in jazz. And undoubtedly she helped groom him so he could be an acceptable part of the eighties cavalcade of celebrity that paraded through magazines like *People* (which did a story on Miles shortly after his marriage). She pressured him to give up all of his bad habits—which included alcohol, tobacco, and, of course, drugs—and tamed his usually raunchy way of expressing himself. And it was from her that he was encouraged to be more "audience friendly" and present himself as a less forbidding and alienated figure.

There is little doubt that Cicely's influence caused Miles to change, to some extent, his stage behavior.

No longer did he just ignore the audience. Now he waved and smiled, posed on stage for obviously dramatic effect, ostentatiously kidded around with his sidemen, clearly played to the crowd. And he acknowledged applause, usually with a smile, a nod, and a wave. This kind of behavior, of course, was the sort of thing that Miles used to find repugnant in other performers. His attitude had been that if he was playing superb and important music, this sort of audience pandering was not only irrelevant, but detracted from the serious commitment of the musicians. After all, he had always pointed out, nobody expected a concert pianist or violinist to announce what piece he was about to perform or do anything for the audience except to play. All of the music in Miles's past required a tremendous amount of concentration and controlled energy, and pandering to the audience detracted from that concentration. It also, from Miles's point of view, cheapened the value of the music itself.

Besides Cicely's influence, I think a major reason for his warmer stage manner was that Miles did not believe that he was producing music on the same level as the great bulk of his work of the past. It simply did not call for the same kind of serious and deep involvement. He still did irritate some members of the audience when he turned his back to them, so as to hear the drummer better. But this was definitely a "new Miles" onstage.

Ever since he had left East St. Louis supposedly to study at Juilliard (but really to find Charlie Parker and Dizzy Gillespie), Miles had been a true New Yorker. He thrived on the city's energy as well as its concentration of fellow musicians, even loved its noise. But now he began staying for longer and longer periods at Cicely's Malibu house near the beach. He loved to swim and the California weather was good for his health. He no longer needed to be driven by the frantic pace of Manhattan. At this point he sought peace and some contentment, and naturally his music reflected his new mood.

I do not mean to imply that he did not produce any worthwhile music during this period. There is a buoyancy in some of his post-"retirement" music that is genuinely delightful and unlike anything in his long recorded career. And his playing remained one of the most powerful musical expressions of the century. But for the first time, he seemed to be utilizing his legendary stature more than his ability to create innovative music in order to reach the public.

What was going on with Miles? There is no doubt he had a new cadre of friends and acquaintances. Whereas once he was closest to fellow jazz musicians, now he hung out with the likes of Prince, Lionel Richie, Bill Cosby, and other celebs. And he traveled the world with Cicely, attending posh dinner parties with fellow jet-setters. Miles was surrounded now by those who sucked up to him because of his legend, which had far more to do with his bizarre speaking voice, the beautiful geography of his face, and his reputation for being simultaneously tough and "cool" than his actual accomplishments. And they were willing to take him into the upper tiers of the cultural elite. Up there, it is easy to forget the qualities that got you there in the first place.

When Miles returned to playing, he amazed those who had seen him perform in the mid-seventies with how healthy he now seemed. No longer on crutches, highly mobile, obviously in good spirits, Miles seemed finally free of the physical infirmities which had plagued him throughout most of the sixties and the seventies.

Cicely had done a lot for Miles—getting him to eat better foods, to stop drinking alcohol, even beer, and, of course, to stay far away from the drugs which had dominated his "retirement." But she went beyond this. The turnaround in Miles's health was astonishing— once again he was capable of self-renewal. But it was also somewhat misleading, for Miles was not really as healthy as he was putting on.

In February of 1982, Miles had a setback—a fairly severe stroke partly paralyzed him. He could not move his right arm, which meant he could not play his horn or write music. He was forced to cancel several major West Coast bookings, but at least initially the press, and therefore the public, had no idea of the ordeal he was going through. His doctors seemed unable to do anything, but Cicely insisted that Miles try another tack. Although he at first objected, she had him see a Chinese acupuncturist. "I didn't want to go," Miles said later, "but she said, 'Try it. If you don't like it, you're not obliged to go back.' The doctor put needles in here, and here, and here [indicating shoulders, an- kles and other acupuncture points]." Within a couple of months Miles's arm became normal. He could even play his trumpet with little difficulty.

He continued to use non-Western methods to im- prove his health, including Chinese herbs. And he be- gan to swim as often as he could—one reason why he spent more time in the Malibu house.

In 1983 there was a salute to Miles at Radio City Music Hall called "Miles Ahead." The musical acts included, besides a number of pop acts, a big band comprised of former Miles sidemen—Wayne Shorter, Herbie Hancock, J.J. Johnson, George Benson, Jackie McLean, and others, conducted by Quincy Jones—that played selections from *Sketches of Spain* and *Porgy and Bess*. Miles was constantly insisting that he had no interest in hearing jazz any more, that the music he listened to ranged from Stockhausen to Michael Jackson, but that jazz was no longer of great relevance to him. So whoever decided on the acts to play this salute chose some pop performers who had only the remotest connection to Miles's own achievements—but played the kind of music Miles purported to enjoy.

There was some hope that Miles himself would play with his old colleagues on a few numbers, but as usual he had no interest in looking back, not even on an evening like this one. Instead, he played a short set with his current band. Miles was moved by the salute, but, in his typical fashion, only said "Thank You" when asked to address the crowd at the end of the evening. When asked later how he felt about this salute, he replied, "It should have been done a lot sooner." Perhaps he was reflecting on the irony that he was receiving such honors and so much attention from the cultural "establishment" so long after the era of his greatest achievments. If he had been given such a salute during, say, the period of his early-seventies electric music it would have given him some bolstering—and some cultural political points—at a time when he really needed it.

After Miles's stroke, he was encouraged to take up some hobby or activity which would help restore the dexterity in his hands. Cicely bought him paint supplies and Miles, completely self-taught, found a new outlet for his creativity. His work was, needless to say, as idiosyncratic as his trumpet-playing, if not nearly on the same level of inventiveness, subtlety, and profundity. But Miles had a continually restless mind and spirit—which while key to the innovation of his music, had also been responsible for much of his trouble over the years.

The world got its first glimpse of Miles the painter on the cover of his second post-"retirement" studio album, *Star People*. Eventually he would actually have one-man exhibitions of his paintings at prestigious galleries both in New York and Los Angeles. And a large coffee-table book was published of his artwork, as if he were De Kooning or the man that he was so often compared to, Picasso. However, there is little doubt that his paintings would not have garnered much notice, if any at all, if they had been done by an unknown artist. Once again, the cult of celebrity came into play, and I am certain Miles knew that. As a painter, Miles was a great trumpet player. (I wonder what Miles would have said if Picasso had attempted to play trumpet.) If that judgment sounds harsh, it is no more so than Miles's treatment of trumpet players he thought talentless. He would tell them in no uncertain terms—sometimes pretending to smash their horns—that they had no talent and should find something else to do with their time. "Why," he would ask, "should I lie and tell them they are any good? That isn't doing them any favor. It's better if they know the truth instead of wasting their time trying to play the horn. Let them become plumbers or something. There's nothing wrong with being a plumber."

One also has to wonder if Miles would have been able to focus on another artform during the years his music was so demanding of his mental energy. The *Star People* album is more ambitious than *The Man With the Horn*, but it is still not on the level of his best work. Then again, what is? Miles carried a lot of baggage—some of the greatest music of the century—which made it difficult for most critics to view his current music on its own terms. The most compelling aspect of the album is that it is dominated by the blues and, of course, Miles was always a great blues player. To him, the ability to personalize the blues was a true indication of a great jazz musician.

Interestingly, Gil Evans was involved in this album, the first time the two friends had collaborated in years. Unfortunately, his participation was kept to a minimum, but he did work with Miles on developing arranged passages for the group which were far more elaborate than Miles's usually loose small group sessions. Miles would use these same arrangements in performance, sometimes stretching them out even further. Although these passages are effective on the album, they were a good deal less so in live performance, especially when they dominated the music; then they seemed repetitious and often quite pointless, destroying that sense of on-the-edge spontaneity which had always been the hallmark of Miles's groups.

For a number of reasons, the personnel in Miles's post-"retirement" bands were constantly in flux. For instance, Miles personally liked guitarist Mike Stern and was satisfied with his playing, but Stern had personal problems and Miles reluctantly let him go. Stern, like Al Foster, preferred a more straight-ahead direction than Miles, and both were somewhat frustrated by their roles in Miles's band. Miles's model for the guitar style he wanted was, of course, Jimi Hendrix, and Stern was not comfortable playing that way. As for the drummer, Miles increasingly wanted a basic rock backbeat. He would make an amazing remark late in the eighties: he stated that his favorite drummers were just about any of the drummers who played in the big rock groups. And that was the style of drumming he wanted to hear. It is difficult to explain how the man who had led bands featuring some of the greatest drummers in jazz history now wanted the type of drummer whose idol was Ringo Starr. Miles insisted that there was a sound he was trying to create with his band, some kind of meeting place between James Brown and Stockhausen.

Miles wore out his welcome a bit after the initial excitement about his return abated. The jazz world had seemed anchorless at the time Miles reappeared and there was hope that he would once again steer it into new and invigorating directions. Once it became clear that he would not or could not point the way again, there were increasingly louder voices expressing their disappointment with Miles's current music. Yet these voices had little effect on his career. He toured the world for huge sums, he won Grammies (he also played at one year's ceremony), and his career, with new aggressive agents, went in lucrative directions.

Perhaps the strangest new direction, far stranger than his new career as a painter, was as an actor. Ever since Miles's voice had been destroyed following a throat operation in the fifties, he had been embarrassed about his speaking voice, part growl and part whisper. This is one of the main reasons he never addressed his audience (recordings made before the operation show that Miles, early in his career, did announce tunes when he performed). So it was rather shocking to longtime fans when he started appearing in films and doing commercials. Now that voice was a central part of his "legend" and, weirdly enough, a commodity almost as valuable to Miles as his ability to play music.

Some of the most disturbing examples of this were his participation in various commercials as well as acting in a TV show and a movie. Miles once claimed that his hobby was cursing television commercials and he often expressed his disgust at the hypocrisy of many Madison Avenue pitches. But during this period he began doing commercials for a brand of motorcycle—I greatly doubt if Miles ever rode a motorcycle even once. He was famous for his love of Ferraris, so this commercial was as dishonest as anything else ever produced by an ad agency. And his voice, once an embarrassment to Miles, was now a full-fledged part of that "legend," just another tool to be marketed.

More troubling was his appearance on *Miami Vice*. Miles had often angrily sounded off on the fact that the parts given to African-American actors on television were either prostitutes, pimps or drug dealers. Then he turned around and played—on *Miami Vice*—a drug-dealing pimp! Many fans had admired Miles's stubborn commitment to principle and his refusal to compromise. He had been the perpetual rebel against hypocrisy and cant; that is, until his return from "retirement." One might almost surmise, sadly enough, that he had become so jaded he decided being tethered to high principles was a sucker's game. Why not cash in like everybody else?

After *Miami Vice*, he appeared in *Dingo*, a bizarre, little-seen Australian western in which he played that Hollywood cliché, the has-been gunfighter. But instead of being a washed-up gunfighter Miles, in what can only be called brain-dead casting, plays a washed-up trumpet player. The soundtrack is somewhat interesting. It was composed by Michel Legrand, with whom Miles had recorded in the fifties; Miles plays trumpet on only part of it, and another trumpeter, who sounds a good deal like Miles, plays on the rest.

Miles also made a few music videos, none of them particularly outstanding, probably with the hope of getting play on MTV. MTV had little interest in them, although its sister channel VH-1 played them occasionally. He appeared to be at times a man desperate to appear *au courant*, "with it," at all costs.

In order to gain recognition as a "pop" rather than jazz performer, Miles began to make cameo appearances on a number of pure pop albums. Pop performers welcomed Miles because of the aura of "legend" and serious musical legitimacy he brought with him. He played cameos on albums ranging from those of Chaka Khan to Quincy Jones, and even on one by the "alternative rock" group Scritti Politti (he would record a Scritti Politti tune on one of his albums). He made a similar appearance on a record called *Sun City* produced by former Bruce Springsteen sideman Little Steven. "Sun City" was a justifiably angry song attacking South Africa's apartheid in which many well known performers (including Springsteen himself) took part. Miles would also take part, along with some of the biggest names in pop, in a spectacular series of concerts aimed at aiding Amnesty International. Although his record sales were not nearly equal to even the least popular of any of the pop acts, once again it was his stature as a "living legend" and the fact that the music he played was fairly close to pop that led to his playing at concerts such as this. One wonders how many watching him in these concerts, in the motorcycle commercials, or on *Miami Vice* had heard, or even knew about, *Kind of Blue*, *Sketches of Spain*, or *Bitches Brew*.

The most interesting thing about Miles's next studio album, *Decoy*, was his new guitarist, John Scofield. Scofield was a quirky, subtle player with great harmonic sophistication. He might have seemed a perfect guitarist for Miles, except that Miles could not get the sound of Jimi Hendrix out of his head. And Scofield felt uncomfortable playing in a style so different from his own. Scofield's sensibility was quite obviously derived far more from jazz than from rock. Yet he remained with Miles longer than any other guitarist during these last years: from 1982 to 1985.

Miles would not record again until he produced, in 1985, his last recordings for Columbia, for whom he had been recording exclusively since the mid-fifties. Increasingly, his music had been driven by synthesizers, which had long fascinated Miles. He had been deeply influenced by Stockhausen and the British synth player Paul Buckmaster, who had played on and arranged several Elton John albums. This mixture of the avant-garde and pop sensibilities was a reflection of how Miles now viewed his music—except that it would be increasingly difficult to hear the Stockhausen influence as his music became more pop-oriented.

The first of the two projects was an album called *You're Under Arrest*, which was much slicker and more accessible than his earlier post-"retirement" albums. The title track, "You're Under Arrest," is with little argument the single most embarrassing moment in Miles Davis's recording career. Over a funk track typical of Miles's work at this time, Miles "stars" in what could be called a "skit." It begins with the sound of

Miles apparently sniffing cocaine, followed by police sirens. Miles says, "Uh oh," and a cop accosts him and says, "I know you've got a girl in there" (apparently that is illegal in this skit); in the ensuing dialogue, several aspects of the Miles "legend" are trotted out, from his Ferraris to his notorious drug usage, womanizing, and trouble with cops. Not one moment of this "skit" is even vaguely funny—unless one laughs out of sheer embarrassment; "annoying," "tasteless," and "pointless" are more appropriate adjectives. Apparently the aim was to show what a bad boy Miles was, perhaps as a way of attracting rap fans with their admiration for "gangstas." Miles was long famous for his ability as a "bullshit detector," both as a musician and as a man. But that ability was either completely dormant or deliberately switched to "off" when he recorded this track.

Two of the tunes on this album (there are no more "skits," thankfully) were pop hits of the day, Michael Jackson's "Human Nature" and Cyndi Lauper's "Time After Time" (not to be confused with the beautiful old standard of the same name.) The Jackson tune is given a joyous, buoyant arrangement, Miles's playing is openhearted and, for him, unusually jubilant, and it is a highlight both of the album as well as of Miles's "comeback" career. Miles plays the Lauper tune with his Harmon mute, and the performance recalls his classic ballad performances of the fifties. However, the tune has little of the harmonic richness that enabled Miles to explore so deeply such former mainstays of his repertoire as "My Funny Valentine" and "'Round Midnight." Without the lyrics and Lauper's vocalizing, this tune, like so many pop tunes, turns into lightweight material. And when Miles sighs through his trumpet here, it seems like contrived emotion, not the deep-hearted poignance of his greatest ballads.

Overall, however, this album is livelier than many of his post-"retirement" albums and to an extent the music is slickly enjoyable. One of Miles's favorite guitarists, John McLaughlin, plays on the date, the first time the two recorded together since the early seventies. But at the heart of the album are the layers of synthesizer, which gives the music a smooth and shimmering gossamer texture.

The other album Miles recorded early in '85, and the very last recording that he would do for Columbia, was *Aura*, a very unusual project for Miles. It was his first orchestral album since the last project with Gil Evans in the sixties, the aborted *Quiet Nights* (he had recorded one big band track that appeared on the mid-seventies double album *Get Up With It*). Miles recorded it when he was in Denmark being awarded the prestigious Sonning Award, which is usually presented to "straight" composers, but for Miles the presenters made an exception. The Danish trumpeter Palle Mikkelborg had written a lengthy piece of music based on a ten-tone scale which he had keyed to the ten letters in Miles's name. The movements were named after the colors that Mikkelborg supposedly detected in Miles's "aura." Mikkelborg's writing is obviously in debt to Gil Evans, but considering the subject of this piece, that is certainly apropos. Once again, John McLaughlin plays guitar, and his presence always has a positive effect on Miles's playing, challenging him to take chances and express brilliant new ideas. There is also a fascinating duet between Miles and the great Danish bassist Niels-Henning Orsted Pedersen. The piece covers a wide range of styles, most of them reflective of states in his development. Both Miles's playing and the album itself are the best of the post-"retirement" period.

From here on, the quality and importance of his records would diminish so greatly that it was as if he had walked blindly off a sandbar into the deep. Indeed, Miles's burning creativity was about to be drowned, at least in terms of recordings. And recordings are how jazz musicians are ultimately judged. Without the technology of recording, jazz could not have survived and prospered. It is almost as dependent on modern technology as that other great artform of our time, film.

Miles had been with Columbia Records since the mid-fifties and that association was, by the eighties, both a key part of his legacy as a musical "legend" and something of an albatross around his neck. Miles was trying to escape from his glorious past, and to renew himself on his own terms. He did not want to be perceived as a jazz legend, but rather as a pop star. He was savvy enough to know the difference between record companies' support (in terms of marketing) for pop and for jazz. And he felt that Columbia would always brand him and his music as jazz. He also believed that George Butler, who headed up the Columbia jazz division, was far more committed to the new trumpet star, Wynton Marsalis, than to the company's old standby, Miles. After three decades, he realized it was time to move on.

The fact that he chose Warner's Records was not very surprising since it was known for its pop acts like Miles's new friend Prince. Here he could work with Tommy LiPuma, a producer well known for his ability to make slick, commercial albums and in particular to give jazz musicians pop appeal. Probably the best example of this was guitarist George Benson's first album for the label, *Breezin'*, a mid-seventies hit. Benson had been greatly respected in the jazz world as perhaps the most formidable straight-ahead guitarist since Wes Montgomery. But after *Breezin'*—produced by Lipuma—became a top ten hit (thanks to Benson's Stevie Wonder-like vocal on "Masquerade"), Benson became a hot commercial property, more popular even than Wes Montgomery a decade earlier.

During the height of Miles's career, it was simply impossible to imagine him working with such a commercial producer like LiPuma. But Miles listened mostly to pop music during this time and this was the turf on which he wanted to stand. And I doubt that Miles was unaware of the financial rewards involved. Miles's contractual agreement with Warner was strange, to say the least. Because Warner wanted publishing rights for any of Miles's compositions that were played on his albums, Miles agreed only to play trumpet on his albums and not to contribute any of his own music. This was a ridiculous situation—it meant that whatever innovative ideas that Miles might have been experimenting with could be heard only in his live performances. After all, Miles's role as a composer, or more exactly as formal musical conceptualizer, was as much a part of his contribution as his trumpet playing. It was a little as if a film studio signed an exclusive contract with Woody Allen, but only as performer; he could not write or direct any of the films he was involved in. Miles, like Allen, was a true *auteur*, and since he could not make albums for any other company, using him only as a trumpet soloist was a ludicrous waste of genius. But Warner might have actually liked the idea—this way they were able to exert more control over Miles just in case he decided once again to be an iconoclast and take his music into less accessible areas.

The effect of this bizarre agreement was heard immediately in Miles's first Warner release, *Tutu* (named after the South African religious and political leader). The album was produced by Tommy LiPuma and one of Miles's favorite electric bassists, Marcus Miller. Miller wrote most of the music and played most of the instruments on the album (mainly on synthesizers), except for trumpet, of course. There is something claustrophobic about these shiny, slick arrangements— they seem to strait-jacket Miles and hamper him from digging deeply. One exception is his cover of Scritti Politti's hit "Perfect Way," which is played with a joyousness reminiscent of his version of Michael Jackson's "Human Nature," another ebullient pop tune. It conveys an emotion usually not associated with Miles, whose music is often described as dark and brooding. Yet such musical joy can be heard in even his earliest work with Charlie Parker, such as his solo on "Scrapple From the Apple," or later on "Miles" (from the *Milestones* album), or the near-ecstatic lyricism in his original "Someday My Prince Will Come" solo. Miles indeed always cut a wider swath of emotional territory than that for which he is too often pigeonholed.

Not surpisingly, *Tutu* was even more of a pop album than *You're Under Arrest* (although thankfully there were no "skits" or vocal paeans to Miles). Some of it had a pleasant, afterhours feeling. But for such a major artist, the first album for his new record company was generally perceived as a disappointment. To the many in the jazz world who had hoped that Miles would point the way for yet another fruitful direction, *Tutu* was at best irrelevant. Miles did little with this album to dispel the nasty criticism coming his way from Wynton Marsalis and those in his camp.

Miles's continuing fascination with the fusion of pop music with jazz was beginning to seem out of date, as if he were struggling to hold on to the seventies. Increasingly "acoustic" seemed to be as hip as the synthetic swirls of electronic sound had seemed a few years previously. There were still those playing various forms of fusion, but it no longer seemed innovative; rather it was increasingly looked on as simply a crass way of pulling in the vast young rock audience. And, unfortunately, even the greatest pioneer of this music, Miles Davis, produced little to change anybody's mind about such things.

One wonders if Miles was aware of the growing influence of his seventies "electric" music on a whole new type of musician. These iconoclasts did not fit into any pigeonhole; they were not "classical" musicians nor jazz, really, nor rock, but creators of a new type of fusion that embraced the entire world of music. Perhaps Miles predicted the coming of this breed of musician when, refusing to play the post-bop of his past, he insisted that there were "so many more worlds of music than just that." Such "downtown" musicians as John Zorn, guitarist Vernon Reid, Bill Laswell, Glenn Moore, James "Blood" Ulmer, and the members of the rock band Sonic Youth were now involved in the same fusion of rock, jazz, "serious" electronic composition, and "world" music elements that can be found in such key Miles works of the early- and mid-seventies as *On the Corner*, *Panagea*, and *Get Up With It*. Unfortunately, Miles himself was not listening to these musicians, but seemed to prefer what I think can be labelled "corporate rock and soul"—slick, superficial, and very commercial pop music.

Miles's agent got a deal with Simon and Schuster for his autobiography—with the proviso that Miles agree to publicize it. Probably it was Cicely who convinced him that good publicity resulted in big money, because Miles even consented to be interviewed on TV, something which he had previously resolutely refused to do. Of course, he was no longer self-conscious about his voice—he realized it was an important part of his legend.

The coauthor of the autobiography was the journalist Quincy Troupe. His job (as this writer knows from personal experience) must have been a daunting one, since Miles had little interest in his past and, as we have seen, boasted of his poor memory, believing that having a bad memory was essential for an innovative artist. Nevertheless, Troupe was able to put together a convincing and often fascinating book, although, as Stanley Crouch pointed out in his review, he obviously got much of the information directly from Miles biographies—Ian Carr's book, the one you are holding, and especially that of Jack Chambers. This left many suspicious of the amount of Miles's actual participation in the writing of the book. Miles, stunningly candid as ever, gave some clues when interviewed on CBS's *Sixty Minutes*. When asked a question about a specific incident in the book, Miles replied, "I don't know because I haven't read that far yet." One has to sympathize with both Troupe and his editor at Simon and Schuster; Miles's mercurial nature and his blunt, seemingly ingenuous, candor must have been the kind of thing they feared most. At the end of the *Sixty Minutes* piece, Harry Reasoner, who had interviewed him, made it clear that he couldn't stand the trumpeter and that the interview was one of the less pleasant of his career. This was not surprising—Miles was deeply distrustful of "establishment" white men in positions of influence and power, and I am sure he let his feelings be known.

Incidentally, the question Reasoner asked Miles was about Cicely—specifically whether it was true (as Miles states in the autobiography) that she took the expensive gifts that he had given her and behind his back refunded them for cash. This marriage obviously had broken down, which was predictable enough. Miles often told friends that he liked and respected Cicely for her independence and strength as a modern black woman, but that he had few romantic feelings for her. During his "retirement" he often acted with exasperation when she called him and expressed his irritation with her overly protective (from his perspective) attitude toward him.

Rumors spread that Miles was manhandling Cicely, once again venting the misogynous rage that had been part of his character since he was a kid. Cicely could not put up with this sort of thing—for one reason, she was an actress and having, say, a broken nose can be a great impediment to one's career. She was a strong and independent woman who would not play the role of victim. The marriage had been a stabilizing force on Miles, and had probably saved his life. But he was still Miles, after all, who as a boy even slapped his mother, and eventually the anger over her attempts to control every aspect of his life could no longer be contained.

According to Miles's autobiography, attending a 1987 dinner at the Reagan White House with Cicely was the final straw in his relationship with her. While she seemed to thrive in such situations, Miles felt like a hypocrite, considering his feelings toward the white establishment. There was obviously a profoundly deep gulf between them, and despite the positive balance she had brought to his life, Miles resented her attempts to re-mold him into a more "presentable" figure.

She had even pressured him to sanitize his language. Miles had always used expletives in his speech as often (or so it seemed) as he did verbs or nouns. But as with his music, he used cussing and obscenities in a way that was totally idiosyncratic; his constant use of these words can only be described as "musical." For instance, a pet phrase of his was "He/she was a lying motherfucker." But the way he said this phrase, in an upward and then suddenly downward arc of emphasis, was like a perfect little musical phrase, reminiscent of some of Monk's tunes. To try to get him to change his ways in the name of gentility was to overlook who he was. This built up resentment, day by day. When Miles found himself sitting at a table with Ronald Reagan in the White House surrounded by a bunch of uptight white people who didn't have the slightest clue who he was (and probably would not have cared much if they did) made him realize finally that this was not a relationship which was going to work. Though he realized his debt to Cicely for saving his life, that was not enough to keep the marriage together. If anything, his indebtedness to her was probably a great contributor to the breakup. Miles Davis did not like being in a position in which he was constantly reminded how much he owed to a certain person. Not if it meant being untrue to those things which meant most to him.

Despite the breakup with Cicely, Miles continued to spend most of his time in his Malibu home near the beach. More and more of it was spent painting—it had really come to fascinate him, and when Miles got involved with something he threw himself completely into it, whether it was drugs, sex, or artistic expression.

His new albums, like *Tutu*, had music written and arranged by others. 1989's *Amandla*, once again produced by Marcus Miller, is less claustrophobic than *Tutu*, utilizing the members of Miles's band at the time rather than Miller playing all the other "instruments" by way of layers of synthesizer. There are no pop hits of the day or vocals of any sort and the music is pleasant enough—jazz/funk with some hints of reggae thrown in—but it is not particularly memorable or inventive. Miles seemed to be doing what most other jazz musicians were doing—going through the motions but staying in the same place, unsure of what new direction to pursue.

The last studio album Miles recorded, which would be released after his death, was *Doo-Bop*. In the notes, written by the album's coproducer and Miles's road manager of the time, Gordon Meltzer, Miles is quoted as saying that he wanted an album that would capture the sounds of urban life and he hoped it would appeal especially to the hip-hop generation. Miles had said virtually the exact same thing about *On the Corner*— that he wanted to make an album that reflected the lives of those in the inner city. And indeed *Doo-Bop* is kind of a brain-dead version of *On the Corner*.

Instead of Marcus Miller, who had produced most of his Warner-era albums (along with Tommy LiPuma), Miles talked with a number of rap "artists" and for some reason chose a rapper called Easy Mo Bee as coproducer with Gordon Meltzer. The idea of combining jazz and rap was not new at this point—there was even a term to describe this hybrid, "Acid Jazz." But until Miles no major jazz musician had recorded a genuine rap album. As with most rap albums, "sampled" sections from other records were used as part of the rhythm tracks. Unfortunately, the rappers on the album (JR, A.B. Money, and Easy Mo himself) were far from being the most creative. The raps are unctious paeans to Miles and are mostly horrible. I think just a couple of lines will make this all too clear: "Miles Davis's style is different, you can't describe it as pacific; / He rip, rage and roar, no time for watchin' Andy Griffith." However, the idea of Miles playing against a roiling hip-hop rhythm track is an interesting one, and he plays with surprising vigor and invention. If Miles had lived he might have really made something of this concept in subsequent albums.

Interestingly, those who saw Miles play with his group during these last couple of years report that he was going in new directions that could not be heard on any of his albums (due to the nature of his contract with Warner's). The new compositions, according to some who saw him play then, bore the idiosyncratic Miles stamp. And his improvising also seemed fresh and surprising. One critic, the Canadian jazz writer James Hale, said that Miles seemed to be ". . . calling out to Bird and Coltrane," playing phrases redolent of these two musicians, without doubt the two most important colleagues in his career.

One has to wonder if Miles was somehow aware of his oncoming death when considering the next, and last, major project in his life and career. For a long time, Quincy Jones had been encouraging Miles to perform some of the great orchestral works on which he had collaborated with Gil Evans. Miles had turned down the idea, of course, since it was totally against everything he believed in as an artist—"never look back" was his credo.

It is not hard to understand Jones's motives—he is a fine composer and arranger, but not a genius like Ellington, Mingus, or Gil Evans. Evans's arrangements for those classic Miles albums are held in awe by other arrangers, and certainly Jones was among them. He was in the position of Salieri closing his eyes and conducting the works of Mozart; for one brief moment he could have at least the fantasy of being a true musical genius.

Jones finally talked Miles into performing a number of Evans's charts at the 1991 Montreux Jazz Festival. Knowing how strongly Miles felt about this sort of thing, and his previous refusal to play, for instance, a reunion concert with his brilliant sixties quintet, one has to speculate on what could possibly have changed his mind.

Only something as overpowering as the reality of death could possibly have swayed Miles. There was the recent death of Gil, his closest friend and one of his most important colleagues. And I believe that he had a sense of the nearing shadows of his own demise. I know that many might be skeptical, but Miles's prescience has always been a remarkable, and incontestable, part of his character and sensibility. It might not have been anything supernatural—he might have known that his body was rapidly breaking down and it was just a matter of time.

After all, this was the music of which he was proudest (although he would admit that only late at night to his closest friends). If there were music to which he would want to return before he died, it had to be this—to once again to play amid these gorgeous mountains of sound of Evans's arrangements and orchestrations was simply too irresistible, even though he knew, from his own deeply held beliefs on the existential nature of the art of jazz, that the music could not possess the finely wrought power of the original recordings. But for Miles, even ghostly reminders of those golden days were probably enough.

Unfortunately, instead of using the Gil Evans band, which had stayed together as a unit after Evans's death and continued to play clubs and to record, a patchwork band consisting of members of the Evans band, George Gruntz's European band, and a number of others was put together for the Montreux festival. Although they were given time to rehearse, Evans's scores are so complex that it was inevitable that the music lacked the rich attention to detail of the original recordings. It was, to use a phrase of Miles's, "flat."

Miles had shown up early enough to rehearse his parts, but it was obvious he was simply not strong enough to handle all the trumpet soloing. So Wallace Roney, a young trumpet player greatly influenced by Miles, took up much of the trumpet soloing, played mostly with his Harmon mute, Miles's own solos ranged from fascinating (especially in "Boplicity," which he had originally recorded with the *Birth of the Cool* nonet in 1949) to incoherent (sadly, on "Summertime" from the *Porgy and Bess* sessions; his solo on the original is a masterpiece of understatement and innuendo, but in Montreux his playing seems confused and directionless). Listening to Roney, whose chops were in far better shape than Miles, is as clear an illustration as one might want of all the elements missing from the "neo-classicists"—his playing simply did not have the presence and emotional authenticity Miles could breathe into even a single note.

There was much talk in the jazz world about the

Montreux performance. Some saw it as Miles's resurgence while others considered it an embarrassment. In a way, both were right. He did play convincingly in some of the pieces, but at other times he seemed to be a shadow of himself. Nevertheless, he seemed active as ever by September of 1991, still painting, planning new gigs, living now as a Californian (he maintained an apartment in New York).

But his health had been steadily declining and in late September of 1991 he checked into a Los Angeles hospital for a "tune-up." He was too late. He developed pneumonia and on September 27th he suffered a massive stroke. This was followed by a series of lesser strokes and his body finally gave out early on the 28th. Miles had been through all kinds of treatments, from Western medicine to "holistic" healing, acupuncture and the use of herbs. But his body had been taking a beating for years, much of it self-inflicted, and finally these degenerative factors overcame his iron will. There were also strong rumors that he was HIV-positive, but there seems no evidence that he had AIDS or that his death was caused by AIDS.

His death was front-page news throughout the world and a leading story on every newscast. The establishment that he had always fought against now embraced him in death, and to a degree finally rewarded him the stature that he deserved—as, quite simply, one of the greatest artists of the century. That meant he could stand next to Stravinsky, Bartok, Pound, Joyce, and, of course, Picasso, to whom he was so often compared. If he had been alive, Miles would have shrugged off all these accolades, knowing that for an artist the only important thing is his next project, the next direction his curiosity will take him.

The day of Miles's passing was of personal pain even

to those who had never actually known him. I think many felt like I did—in the darkest hours of my life, I would tell myself as encouragement that I just had to hear whatever Miles Davis would be doing on his next album. Even in the the post-"retirement" phase, we simply had to find out where he was at now. And even on the least of those albums there would be a few moments of revelation and great beauty.

Now that he was gone, we were faced with a question: who was he, really? We know Parker was a celebrant of the human spirit, and Coltrane was a cosmic pilgrim, but who then was Miles Davis?

Prince of Darkness

"Prince of Darkness," "Sorcerer," "Evil Genius of Jazz," "The Jazz Hamlet": all of these monikers—and a number of similar "misterioso" appellations—have been attached to Miles Davis. When an album of his was released with the title *Miles Smiles*, it was met with incredulity, as if such an idea was ludicrous (despite the photograph on the front of the album of a beaming Miles). And yet those who knew him well were aware of his rich and constant (albeit often blunt and profane) sense of humor. He was a constant source of gossip and speculation in the jazz world, and one of the few modern jazz musicians who aroused the curiosity and attention of the greater world outside the jazz scene. He was constantly referred to as "mercurial," "enigmatic," a magician and alchemist. In the last several years of his life, when he granted interviews on a regular basis, acknowledged his audience, and appeared on television, he seemed almost to be campaigning to demystify his image. But in so doing, he simply became more enigmatic; who was the real Miles Davis, the outgoing, smiling purveyor of pop jazz in the eighties or the introverted, often sullen, dedicated artist he seemed to be throughout his pre-"retirement" career? When he died in 1991 at the age of 65, both he and his music remained wondrous riddles, still unsolved.

Almost all the obituaries reflected the elusive nature of Miles and his art. But they also reflected the conviction of virtually everyone who knew about his music that Miles was one of the most crucial jazz musicians of the modern period. So it should not have been surprising that what I call the "Miles Myth" became such a popular method of explaining his extraordinary importance to American music. Perhaps the most egregious example of the laying out of this myth was the obituary in *Rolling Stone.*

Unfortunately, most of *Rolling Stone's* readers have little, if any, knowledge of jazz history, and they probably accepted the obit as being correct and legitimate. The fact that Miles Davis played trumpet is only mentioned at the very beginning of the obit. There is nothing in the entire piece about Miles's stylistic innovations, easily the most important since Louis Armstrong; Miles discovered a new way to play the trumpet, and his style would affect every trumpeter that came after him to one extent or another. But the reader is left to infer that to Miles, playing was of not much importance, and that he was probably like Quincy Jones, who started off as a trumpet player but of course became famous principally because of his arranging and composing.

The rest of the obit repeats in the most literal fashion the myth that has come to be accepted as scripture by many in the jazz world. Miles himself knew better, but towards the end of his life, when he basked in the attention that he garnered from being a "living legend," he began to repeat it himself. One such incident is quoted in the *Rolling Stone* obit. When asked by a woman at a Reagan White House dinner what his accomplishments were, he answered (no doubt with subtle sarcasm) "Well, I changed music four or five times." That is a succinct summary of the Miles Myth—that Miles Davis personally "changed American music" four or five times.

This is nonsense, and if anything it simply distorts Miles's actual achievement. The *Rolling Stone* obit then proceeds to detail Miles's great innovations, how he "invented" cool jazz in the late forties and early fifties, got tired of it and "invented" hard bop in the mid-fifties, then decided to give musicians more freedom and "invented" modal jazz, then with his great sixties quintet created "Free Bop," and finally, of course, "invented" fusion, the melding of jazz with rock and funk. None of this is really true, or at least it is grossly exaggerated.

None of the key innovations in jazz, like those in every artform, were created by one person. For instance, the advent of bop is usually credited to Charlie Parker and Dizzy Gillespie. Both of them had crucial roles, of course, in the birth of modern jazz. But there were countless other musicians, some famous, many not, who were part of this movement. Thelonious Monk, Charlie Christian, Kenny Clarke, Leon "Chu" Berry (for whom Charlie Parker named his son), Joe Guy, Jimmy Blanton, and numerous others were involved to same degree in the great changes jazz went through in the mid-forties.

The "cool" jazz movement was not, of course, nearly as fundamental a change in jazz as that of bop. But the advent of this movement also was due to the contributions of many, not just Miles, whose contribution was relatively small. He was the titular leader of the nonet that was of key importance in launching the movement. But the innovative aspect of this group was its arrangements, the bulk of which were written by Gerry Mulligan. Others were contributed by John Lewis, John Carisi (the classic "Israel"), and two were done by Gil Evans—one of them an arrangement of a tune that Evans and Miles had written together ("Boplicity"). And this group was not solely responsible for cool jazz. Certainly Lennie Tristano and the musicians who were his acolytes contributed as well. And without doubt, the father of the movement, if one must pick one person, was Lester Young, who was playing "cool" in the thirties. Almost all of the cool players tremendously admired Young (including Miles), and his lyrical, behind-the-beat phrasing was the heart of this movement.

This is not really taking anything away from Miles except a ludicrous myth. His playing on the *Birth of the Cool* sides is superb and it is on these sides that Miles's genius first becomes clear. The appellation of "genius" is not for the overblown claim of Miles's supposed "invention" of cool, but rather for his ability to immediately grasp the new musical areas made possible by the cool aesthetic and, in his lyrical solos, to make deeply personal, completely idiosyncratic music out of it.

The same thing was true of hard bop. Miles did not "invent" hard bop, of course. Just the idea of any one person "inventing" a jazz movement is absurd. And this is because every one of these movements have been highly elastic, resisting hard and fast definition. The musicians who are supposedly within any such movement continue to explore their own personal agendas, constantly pushing and stretching the envelope, and sometimes breaking right through it.

For hard bop, the return to a more blues-based, funkier type of jazz was to some degree a reaction of a number of musicians to the more ethereal, lyrical pastels of the cool (later called West Coast) jazz movement. If there is one group that defined hard bop, it was the original Jazz Messengers. And, as with any important jazz movement, there were a number of others, like the Max Roach-Clifford Brown group and the Art Farmer/Benny Golson Jazztet. Miles's "Walkin'" recording session was often cited as the touchpoint for the birth of hard bop. But saying that this one session was responsible for the advent of a crucial jazz movement is absurd and demeaning to all the musicians who were involved in developing these innovations.

This is also true for the modal jazz movement (actually George Russell's conception: Russell used modes in jazz as early as the late Forties and both Mingus and Brubeck experimented with modes before Miles), the "freebop" of the sixties quintet (musicians ranging from Jackie McLean and Sonny Rollins to pianist Andrew Hill were involved in these innovations beginning in the early sixties), and fusion (the melding of jazz with funk and rock by both jazz and rock musicians had been going on for years by the time Miles truly got involved). Miles was certainly in the front lines of all of these movements, and helped to define and popularize them. But most importantly, he was continually able to create personal and important music when he became involved in each of these movements, always inspired by the challenge of change.

Of course, there were those who had a very different take on Miles and his place in jazz history. Without doubt the most vociferous was the former "New Thing" drummer, writer/critic Stanley Crouch. Crouch attacked Miles with an amazing degree of vitriol over a course of years for "selling out," regularly attending Miles performances for no other reason than to once again flog the trumpeter for his aesthetic misdeeds. In a 1990 article in the *New Republic*, Crouch, in the guise of a book review of Miles's autobiography, stated very clearly the reasons for his rage toward Miles—and the word *is* "rage."

Crouch viewed Miles as a great and brilliant jazz musician until 1968 when, in order to reach the huge rock audience, he "sold out" all his most dearly held principles. He states that after *Filles de Kilamanjaro* (which is actually a key early fusion work) "came the fall. *In a Silent Way*, long, maudlin, Davis's sound mostly lost among electronic instruments, was no more than droning musical wallpaper. A year later *Bitches Brew* was firmly on the path of the sellout—and fully launched jazz rock with its multiple keyboards, electronic guitars [*sic*], static beats and clutter." This utter nonsense would become the Wynton Marsalis/neo-classicist line on Miles and it would be draped around his neck until his death, and well after. In October 1995, Peter Watrous, the *New York Times* jazz critic (and long a Marsalis apologist and supporter) wrote a piece about what he called the "Miles Davis curse," blaming Miles for the aesthetic failures of two generations of jazz musicians. This is almost the inverse of the "Miles myth"—that one musician's musical direction could have such an enormous effect on two generations of jazzmen.

In his piece, Crouch discussed all of Miles's post '68 music as if it were all of a piece, which betrays a complete lack of knowledge of this music, since Miles's seventies music is completely different from the post-"retirement" work not only in technical terms but also in its depth, power, and sheer adventurousness. He thus exhibited an inability to distinguish the important music from the banal, and the innovative from the merely craftsmanlike.

Anybody who believes that, say, *Bitches Brew* or *Panagea* are merely attempts by a musician to crassly attempt to reach the mass rock audience must either have never really listened to those albums or must have heard some pretty bizarre rock albums. The truth is, of course, that the changes of this period were not a capricious decision that Miles made in order to reach a rock audience. If Crouch and Watrous had really looked closely at the development of this music and how it evolved through careful stages, beginning with 1965's *ESP* and then continuing through *Miles in the Sky* and *Filles de Kilamanjaro*, building through a number of experimental recording sessions, much of it never released (or not released until years later), and culminating in *In a Silent Way*, *Bitches Brew* and onward, he would have seen how carefully and thoughtfully Miles reached the apotheosis of these ideas in those initial "Fusion" albums. Miles was, if anything, a conservative in many ways. He believed that jazz had gotten too "far out," and had lost sight of its folk and dance roots. Melding jazz with elements of funk and and rock—and very selective elements—was a way of bringing these roots back to jazz, making it once again a "people's music" rather than a music appreciated and understood only by an elite few. And the reason Miles was so achingly careful in the way the music evolved was that he obviously did not want jazz to lose sight of its real "tradition"; rather, he built this new musical direction solidly on that tradition. If you listen closely to the best of Miles's electric music, you can hear all of jazz history, from New Orleans to swing to bop to Ornette's *Free Jazz* and Coltrane's *Ascension*. It is unfortunate that this latest generation simply does not understand how great jazz innovators build on the true jazz tradition.

Crouch is an intelligent and learned man, and I cannot help but wonder if his rage toward Miles was based on something other than just his belief that Miles had "sold out." I think that many men of Crouch's generation, both white and black, identified with Miles in a number of ways, and had, in idolizing Miles, made many assumptions about him, both as man and artist, fitting him into the contours of their own fantasies. When he turned out to be something other, or rather something quite a bit more than that figure that they had so long held as a role model, Miles smashed those fantasies, enraging and confusing people like Crouch. To them, it was a personal blow when Miles grew, changed, and explored new territories, both musical and of the self. They felt left behind. Imagine if Elvis in the last few years of his career decided to perform only in drag singing cabaret songs. The reaction would not be based on aesthetics as much as on a *fantasy* of Elvis. For many, Miles Davis played a similar role.

I also have to add, as painful as it is, that Crouch's criticism is not without merit when applied to much of Miles's post-"retirement" music. There, as the reader will recall, I unfortunately came to the conclusion that Miles was perhaps trying too hard to reach a pop audience, sacrificing some of the subtlest and most idiosyncratic elements of his music. However, these last years are scarcely the cause of rage; sadness is a more appropriate reaction. And even with some of the weaker bands of the eighties, Miles's own playing was still very beautiful and heartfelt at times (even on the last "hip hop" album, *Doo-Bop*).

For Miles, music was a journey into the self, and in his music he could define himself on his own terms—not those of the white establishment that he so deeply distrusted, nor those of the jazz critics who tried to place him in a pigeonhole. Even to his closest supporters his attitude was, to paraphrase André Gide, "do not understand me too quickly."

The truth is that both those who promulgated the "Miles myth," insisting that Miles basically "invented" most of the major movements in jazz since the bop era, and those who, like Crouch, demonized Miles for his insistence on change, were equally unable to understand Miles on his own terms. All Miles's greatest music, from some of the early Prestige classics to the modal and free-bop periods and the most adventurous music of the electric seventies period, is stamped with a particular sensibility, a special, albeit mercurial, personal vision quite unlike that of anybody else.

If you know the French film theory developed in *Cahiers du Cinema* (a theory which has gained hold among many critics and film fans throughout the world), those great film directors able to stamp their art with their own personal viewpoint and private concerns—Alfred Hitchcock, Howard Hawks, John Ford, François Truffaut, and even Jerry Lewis—are considered "auteurs." The *auteur* theory is also true for jazz—there are a number of musicians who have created their own musical world, and even when others are soloing the music reflects that vision. Ellington, Mingus, Monk, George Russell, and Jelly Roll Morton are all excellent examples. And certainly Miles belongs high on this list.

After his apprenticeship with Charlie Parker, his years strung out on dope, his career washed up, and his agonizing self-redemption—after finally freeing himself from the dark poison which almost consumed him—Miles knew, knew as a fact, that the only thing he could trust was his indomitable will. And he also knew that to be an artist one simply had to put one's body, mind, and soul on the razor's edge, that only through the challenge of risk could an artist reach to his deepest truths.

Perhaps this is the single greatest lesson Miles learned from Charlie Parker—playing improvised music means that one uses as the grist for musical invention the plumbed depths of one's inner world. In Bird's playing one can clearly hear the battle between Parker's inner angels and demons, the striving for ecstasy and the constant need for love. At least part of Miles's intense introversion was undoubtedly for the sake of his musical imagination as an improviser.

It was this lesson more than anything else that John Coltrane learned from his tenure with Miles. Before he hooked up with Miles, he was a journeyman tenor player, talented enough, but whose playing had little originality nor that vital commitment we so associate with Coltrane. He was also, as was so typical of modern jazz musicians of that time, a junkie and an alcoholic. But it was through Miles that, according to his own testimony, Coltrane began to explore all the possibilities of this music. It was not just Miles's ideas on harmony or rhythm that so fascinated Trane. Coltrane made the great discovery of the relationship between music and the deepest currents of his life and psyche through his tenure with Miles. He learned, most importantly, that what he was doing as a musician mattered, that it had great profundity, that its effect was deep and far-ranging: that as a musician grows, he changes and therefore is able to change the world around him. And through understanding this, Coltrane too became a jazz "auteur."

It is this aspect of Miles's music—the near-confessional bracingly personal *sound*—that was so unflinchingly direct in its pleading to be heard and understood. This was to Miles, when he talked about his art late at night, the essence of everything he knew and struggled to create out of his inner life—*sound*, his *sound*, the sum total of his breath, embouchure, fingers, harmonic conception, horn, microphone. "*Sound*," he told me, "that's what it's all about. I can look at that picture on the wall and come up with musical ideas, that's nothin'. But the *sound*, that's what I spent my life working on." Interestingly, John Coltrane's widow, Alice, told me that Coltrane used to say the same thing about his own music. And of course, in some religions, the universe itself began with a *sound*. It is a simple, yet incredibly complex concept. And for Miles and Trane it was the soul of their art.

When I was about fifteen and I first started to listen to *Kind of Blue*, like most other listeners I had no idea how important this music was, how adventurous were its techniques. I had no interest in the fact that the music was based on modes rather than chords, or how influential Miles's way of using modes would be on the jazz scene (of course he learned about modal composition from George Russell). That is not what I, or most of those who were so deeply moved by this album, heard. What I heard, and felt, was a *sound*. It was a *sound* that reached me on some elemental level, the deepest part of my heart and soul. And the whole album was suffused with that personal Miles Davis *sound*, even when the other, quite individualistic, players were soloing. I know it is a *sound* that will stay with me until I die.

Of course Miles would point out that one of the primary reasons that album is so brilliant is that the musicians could not fall back on old habits and clichés, that playing modally made them think in fresh new ways and reach new musical areas. To Miles—the ultimate existentialist artist—music had no value unless the musician was willing to put his life on the line, like a boxer going into the ring to face an unknown challenger. Boxing and music had a lot in common for Miles. In both, a man had to first know who he was before he could succeed in overcoming adversity. He had to be able to adapt to the strategy of his opponents, and to change his own style and strategy if need be. Miles often talked about pushing players in his group into new areas so that they would go beyond what they knew. Like boxers, they had to have technique and inner knowledge to be so malleable. And this is how change in this music came about.

So to Miles, innovation was inevitable. A few years before he died, Miles said about Wynton Marsalis that "if he knew the theory he wouldn't be the way he was." I realize he was probably talking about formal music theory, but I also believe he was referring to a more basic "theory" of jazz, one not written down but developed and shared by all creative jazz musicians. And that "theory" is that innovation is the life-blood of jazz. But it is a theory that cannot be taught in a school or by a music teacher. It is a theory passed on through experience, through careful explaining, but explanation not through words but through more abstract means: from the arc of musical flight itself, the musical discourse on the bandstand and at jam sessions, from silence, moans, laughter, and oblique verbal hints, from certain nods, frowns, shrugs.

When Coltrane died, he was treated as if he had

been something far more than a musician—a holy man. A church in San Francisco declared him a saint and made him its patron, ascribing to him supernatural powers. And his wife, Alice, declared him a Vedantic God (Ohnadaruth), and in her California ashram he is worshipped as such.

No one, in his most fevered imagination, could imagine Miles Davis being given such treatment. He was all too human, a man who let it "all hang out," never making any attempt to cover up his flaws and weaknesses. Certainly that is one of the most amazing things about him as a person—his often blunt, at times ingenuous honesty. He did not hide the fact that he beat up women. I do not know if he should be "credited" with that or not. I hope what it meant was that he knew this was unforgivable behavior, but could not change it because he did not understand it. And maybe the only way he could live with himself was to be upfront about it, not like the hypocritical politicians or celebrities who have "nice guy" images and then at home viciously abuse their spouses.

No, nobody will form a "Church of Saint Miles the Divine" (Miles, incidentally, had had no use for religion ever since he discovered as a boy that the churches were segregated). He was definitely one of us, not some supernatural creature, although his powerful mind often performed feats that I still cannot explain. But as unusually brilliant as he was, he never claimed to be anything other than a man, unusually gifted and angry, but just a man. (I feel the same thing, actually, was true of John Coltrane. He would have been embarrassed and uncomfortable at being worshipped like a god.) And his music was about that experience—of being human.

Miles was often called "arrogant," which he resented.

What was he so angry about? I think that Miles's anger went beyond racism and went to the heart of our existence. His rage was from "the politics of experience," his war against a hypocritical society that causes us all to lose touch with who and what we really are; a society in which shallow values prevail and blunt honesty is discouraged. Miles—as a man and as a musician—often reminded me of the boy in Hans Christian Anderson's "The Emperor's New Clothes" who is the only one to point out that indeed the emperor is not wearing any clothes at all. The boy is the only one ingenuous enough—and bluntly honest enough—to shout out the truth, despite the discouragement of the crowd clinging to its fantasies.

In a piece in the *New York Times* on the current jazz scene, Keith Jarrrett made a very insightful comment about Miles. He said that Miles would rather play music that was new and innovative than play older music even if the newer music was far less perfect. For perfection was never Miles's goal. It was the journey itself that his music was about, the process of growing and constantly arriving.

Who was Miles Davis? If I believed in astrology, I would say that he was the ultimate Gemini—outspoken yet shy, brash and introspective, sensitive and self-centered, giving and selfish, kindly and (at times) violent. Perhaps it was his *humanity*, in all its varieties, reflected in his music that has made so many of us respond to him.

Miles hated the idea of death because of its finality. In the artform that was the center of his life, the phrases he played ("I never resolve any of my phrases" he used to boast), the styles which he helped to innovate, the new sonic frontiers he explored were always open-ended and contained oblique hints of further directions. He knew his mind and spirit—and all our minds and spirits—could, in his phrase, "go on forever." Listen to his music because if you listen to it carefully you will know that he is absolutely right. MILES LIVES!

Listening to Miles:
An Annotated Discography

Miles Davis's recording career lasted for almost half a century. His first important session was with Charlie Parker on Bird's first recording date as a leader. His final recording was *Doo-Bop*, an album of hip-hop jazz. In between, of course, he was responsible for some of the most important albums in jazz history. Sorting through them and getting the most important is not easy if one is a neophyte to jazz or if one is trying to come to some understanding of the magnitude of Miles's achievement.

Part of the problem with a large catalog like Miles's is that of late so many items have been going out of print or reappearing in new contexts like box sets. In this discography, I will include only items which are now available as CDs. If at the time you are reading this book, a particular album I mention is no longer available, my advice is to be patient. Especially with somebody like Miles, it will soon be back (although, as we shall see, possibly as part of a pricy multi-CD boxed set).

If you really want to trace the development of Miles's style, you might as well start at the beginning. Although his first recording session was with Herbie Fields, he did not solo. So the first session in which he solos is that Parker session, currently available on *The Charlie Parker Story* (Savoy, 1945). This album contains every note recorded at the session, including alternate takes, partial takes, some fluffs, etc. Hearing it makes it obvious why Billy Eckstine said that Miles "couldn't blow his nose." When Dizzy Gillespie plays, albeit briefly on the masterpiece "Ko Ko," the contrast with Miles is overwhelming.

However, Miles soon made tremendous strides, mainly due to his experiences sitting in with some of the greatest jazz musicians at clubs on 52nd Street— "Swing Street." Listen to him on the Parker Dials, available complete with alternate takes on a four-CD set, or as two single CD's of just the master takes (all on Stash); you will hear Miles finding himself, discovering his strengths, and beginning to develop a unique style. Bird also continued to record for Savoy, which is now reissuing all of its Bird material. The Savoys included Miles's first session as a leader, although it was just the Parker group with Bird on tenor. But Miles's own playing is worlds removed from the '45 sessions.

The next important "milestone" was the nonet sides, collected under the title *Birth of the Cool* (Capitol, 1949–1950). These are essential. They were, of course, very influential, and the Gerry Mulligan, Gil Evans, John Lewis, and John Carisi arrangements are marvels. But equally brilliant are the soloists, particularly Lee Konitz and Miles himself. Miles is superb throughout these sides, clearly charting out his innovative style. His solo on John Carisi's "Israel" is an early example of Miles's genius for improvising with a sense of architectural form.

From '51 to '56, Miles would record almost exclusively for Prestige. If you can afford it, I recommend the Fantasy set called *Chronicle*, which contains every note Miles recorded for Prestige. Listening to these recordings chronologically one can trace the development of Miles's fifties musical conception, both as a trumpeter and as a leader.

If you cannot afford this set, there are a few Prestige albums which are essential for an understanding of Miles's growth and contain wonderful music (all of these sessions have been released by Fantasy in their original format as part of its Original Jazz Classics series). *The Musings of Miles* (Prestige/OJC, 1955) is a superb quartet session, and *Miles Davis and Milt Jackson* (Prestige/OJC, 1955) is a personal favorite of mine, with fine work from Jackie McLean and Milt Jackson. However, the "All-Star" sides Miles recorded with Milt Jackson in 1954 are indispensable jazz classics and, outside the Fantasy *Chronicle*, are available on two separate CDs—*Bag's Groove* (Prestige/OJC, 1954) and *Miles Davis and the Modern Jazz Giants* (Prestige/OJC, 1954/'56). In these sessions, Miles's mature style is in full voice, especially powerful on the blues "Bag's Groove" and his stunning statement of the melody on "The Man I Love."

Around this same time Miles recorded some sides with Blue Note that I think are equal to the very best Prestige sessions. (They are available on Blue Note as *Miles Davis Volume One* and *Volume Two* [1952–'54]). I particularly like a quartet session with pianist Horace Silver in which Miles stretches out his rhythmic conception while playing with great melodic invention. And Miles himself often referred to the sides here with J.J. Johnson as being among his own favorites from this earlier period.

Then, of course, are five albums made by the quintet, the group Miles formed after his triumph in Newport in 1955. This group, considered one of the most important of all post-bop units, included John Coltrane, Red Garland, Paul Chambers and Philly Joe Jones. I have always liked the first session, recorded in 1955, available as *The New Miles Davis Quintet* (Prestige/OJC), mainly as a glimpse of Coltrane's style early in its development, but it has some fine playing by Miles and it serves as a blueprint for much of the work Miles would produce with his small groups for the next few years.

Things get a bit complicated here as far as chronology. Miles signed with Columbia before his contract with Prestige was up and he recorded some sides with his quintet for an album, *'Round About Midnight*. To complete his contract with Prestige, Miles and the quintet had two marathon recording sessions during which they recorded enough material for four albums, *Workin'*, *Relaxin'*, *Cookin'*, and *Steamin'*, all equally good. But the Columbia album is probably the single best recording of this important group.

For Miles's second album for Columbia, he collaborated with Gil Evans for the first of three orchestral albums, *Miles Ahead*, another personal favorite. Evans's music is absolutely gorgeous; his magnificent command of a kaleidoscope of tonal colors is a perfect backdrop for Miles's flugelhorn playing, some of the warmest and most lyrical of his career. This album is a must, but be careful—the original CD consisted completely of outtakes. More recently, the master version has been released. However, all of this may be moot since Columbia is planning to put out a boxed set containing all of Miles's orchestral collaborations with Gil Evans, and withdrawing the individual CDs.

In 1957, Miles recorded his first film score, for the French director Louis Malle's first feature, *Escalator to the Scaffold* (Polygram, 1957). Miles and a group of French and American musicians improvised this score as they watched a rough cut of the film. Miles's playing is remarkable, some of the most heartrendingly emotional of his career. Definitely worth hearing.

In late '57 Coltrane, after several months with Thelonious Monk, rejoined Miles; the technically superb altoist Cannonbal Adderley was also in the group. This sextet, with various changes in personnel, is in my opinion the greatest in the history of modern jazz. Coltrane by now had developed his mature style and his playing with this group was consistently magnificent, often searching and expansive, but always powerful. The first album by this group is *Milestones* (1958, Columbia), and it is a must, if for no other reason than Miles's first modal piece, "Miles" (originally called "Milestones"). Miles's playing is achingly lyrical and Cannonball seems to eat up this new challenge. Interestingly, only Coltrane seems hesitantly unsure of this innovative harmonic structure. This is more than a little ironic because Coltrane would eventually become, inarguably, the greatest modal player in jazz history.

As a matter of fact, Trane's mastery of modes can be heard in the group's next studio album, the masterpiece *Kind of Blue* (Columbia, 1959). I have listened to, thought about, and written about this album so many times that it is difficult for me to find any new words to describe it. Quite simply, it is one of the most beautiful works of art of this century. I am certain this piece of music will still be listened to on the day the sun implodes. If for some reason you have never heard this album, you are very lucky, because you have a magnificent experience waiting for you. It is amazing how it continues to stir my soul every time I hear it, so many years after I first put it on my turntable.

Although my intent was only to list "official" Miles albums, I must mention *Miles Davis and John Coltrane in Stockholm* (Dragon, 1960). This was recorded on the last tour Coltrane would take as a member of Miles's band. Listening it is easy to tell why—Coltrane dominates the proceedings, taking lengthy, fiery solos brimming with adventurous ideas. It was clearly time for him to become a leader in his own right, although Miles desperately wanted him to stay with the band. Miles himself was playing at a peak during this time and the Wynton Kelly, Paul Chambers, and Jimmy Cobb rhythm section was one of the best in modern jazz history. This set is easy to find, although you may have to buy it as part of a four-CD set which includes a concert Miles gave a few months later with Sonny Stitt in the sax chair. Miles's own playing is stronger now, and Sonny himself plays consistently well, so this set is also worth getting.

Chronologically, the *Porgy and Bess* (Columbia) album, Miles's second orchestral collaboration with Gil Evans, precedes *Kind of Blue* since it was released in 1958. This is another gorgeous album, and one of Miles's own favorites. Like *Blue* it is indispensable.

The third Evans/Davis orchestral album, *Sketches of Spain*, was released in 1960. There have been those who have expressed negative opinions about this album, although this puzzles me. I have always found it stunning. In terms of dense tonal colors, it is probably Evans's greatest achievement. And Miles plays with overwhelming emotional intensity, even in those parts with little or no improvisation (such as the perform-ance of a movement from Joaquin Rodrigo's "Concierto de Aranjuez"). Miles told me that playing this music was probably the most demanding task he ever had as a player—he had to capture the voice and feeling of an alien culture. He succeeded magnificently.

You may want to get the 1961 studio album *Some-day My Prince Will Come* just to hear Coltrane's won-derful solo on the title tune as well as on the album's one modal tune, "Teo" (named, of course, for Miles's long-time record producer). Coltrane was no longer a member of Miles's group, so here he is just the "spe-cial guest." Miles also plays inventively throughout, al-though this record was more of a holding action than a move forward. However, it is of historic interest for capturing the last time Miles and Coltrane would play together.

The first glimpse of that move forward would be heard on the 1963 release *Seven Steps to Heaven*. Half of these six numbers are performed by an early version of the great sixties quintet, with George Coleman in the saxophone chair at this stage. Those tracks are in-teresting as a hint of great things to come, but the showpiece of this album is Miles's brooding, slow (es-pecially in contrast to the usual snappy tempo) version of "Basin Street Blues," which sounds like a deep, mel-ancholy meditation on Louis Armstrong, the long course of jazz, and the irony of lyrics which celebrate the jazz fantasy of a place where "white and dark" can truly meet on equal ground.

In 1964, Miles played a benefit concert at Carnegie Hall with his current quintet, again with Coleman playing tenor. It was originally packaged as two albums, one containing mainly ballads and the other the hard-driving tunes, most of them played at an incredibly fast tempo. Columbia has put out a two-CD set of this concert with the material programmed in the original order. By the way, ignore what I said about this version of "My Funny Valentine" in the body of this book. It is a masterpiece. Although it seems to be made up of fragmented sections, careful listening reveals that there is an organic cohesiveness to Miles's, and the rhythms section's, improvisations. The entire piece, which goes through several changes in tempo and meter, makes an impassioned statement that is felt in the heart and mind.

At the end of 1964, Wayne Shorter took George Coleman's place and now the great sixties quintet was in place. The band's first album, *ESP* (Columbia, 1965) is interesting in its hint of things to come and has some great moments. Due to Miles's illness, the group was idle for most of the rest of 1965. But late in the year, the group played the Plugged Nickel in Chicago. Two nights of that gig were recorded, seven sets altogether. Every note recorded by the group has been released by Columbia in an eight-CD boxed set (the music is also available on LPs from Mosaic, a small mail order company which puts together magnificent boxed sets of jazz). This set is pricey, but if you can afford it, it is well worth getting. One can clearly hear how adventurous this group was. Even on the same night, tunes that are played more than once are always completely different in every way. One astonishing example is when a version of the closing theme—usually just a brief fanfare to get the band off—turns into a lengthy duet by Miles and Shorter of twists, turns, dialogues, and swift struts into the stratosphere that simply take the breath away.

Most of the Plugged Nickel sets were still the same repertoire Miles had been using with his small groups for years. In the next studio album, the strangely titled *Miles Smiles*, Wayne Shorter emerged as the group's principal writer. Such classic Shorter pieces as "Footprints" and "Dolores" are on this album, as well as a modal ballad, "Circle," composed by Miles. The rhythm section is particularly thrilling, especially on Jimmy Heath's "Gingerbread Boy" and Eddie Harris's "Freedom Jazz Dance." Ron Carter and Tony Williams seem to have almost re-invented the jazz rhythm section by this time. And there is a definite group sound which, despite the energy of the rhythm section, is kind of post-bop surrealism, a trance-like world of strangely shifting angles, shapes, and colors.

In their next two albums, *Nefertiti* and *Sorcerer* (Columbia, both recorded in 1967), the group stake out this musical world of theirs. Both are examples of "the sound of surprise" in that the music is completely unpredictable. I think many listeners will be surprised at how free some of the pieces on these albums are (such as "Limbo" on *Sorcerer*). Incidentally, the last tune on *Sorcerer* is, for some reason, a brief version of "Nothing Like You," a sprightly ditty sung with a strange reedy voice by its composer, Bob Dorough, and recorded in 1962. It utterly destroys the hypnotic mood created by the entire rest of the album, like being slapped awake out of a fascinating dream.

The next quintet album, *Miles in the Sky* (Columbia, 1968), is of great historical importance: it is the first indication of Miles's inclination toward jazz/rock fusion. On one piece he uses a guitarist (George Benson) for the first time in his recording history, and "Country

Son" goes through several changes in mood, tempo, and meter—ranging from a sad ballad to a funk beat. But it was "Stuff," in which for the first time Herbie Hancock played electric piano and Ron Carter electric bass, that startled most Miles fans when this album was released. Played with a sort of funky cha-cha-cha beat, it was one of the early steps that eventually led to the "electric" seventies work.

The last quintet album, *Filles de Kilamanjaro* (Columbia, 1968), was a Miles masterpiece. The group was in transition, and Chick Corea and Dave Holland respectively replaced Hancock and Carter on some tracks. But the album as a whole has great cohesiveness. Also involved in this album, but given no official credit, was Gil Evans, who helped Miles with the arrangements. This is kind of a concept album, all of the tunes having a convincingly Gallic flavor. Rock and funk rhythms are alluded to throughout the album, but never made obvious. And the playing by all is superb. Evans's hand can be detected in the ingenious arrangements and the attempt to give the album its wholeness. Perhaps Miles and Evans were spurred by the Beatles' *Sergeant Pepper* "concept" album, for Miles greatly admired the Beatles. Actually, *Sergeant Pepper* might have been directly or indirectly influenced by the Davis/Evans classic *Miles Ahead* in which each tune segues cleverly right into the next without pause, a device used on *Pepper*.

In a Silent Way (Columbia, 1969) is the first full-fledged "electric" Miles Davis album, using three electric pianists and John McLaughlin's electric guitars (the Scottish McLaughlin is one of the pioneers in forging a guitar style blending elements of rock with jazz). But instead of rock thunder, both of the album's two lengthy pieces seem to be space-age lullabies. As adventurous as the album is—and it really does explore new sonic territory—ultimately it produces a trance-like lulling effect rather unlike anything else in jazz.

Silent Way now seems like a whispered introduction to the apocalyptic thunder of Miles's next album, *Bitches Brew*. It has been often contended that *Bitches Brew* sparked the Fusion era which dominated the Seventies. Of course, it was not the only cause. What is overlooked is that purely on its own terms this album is a masterpiece. Once again, Miles uses multiple electric keyboards and McLaughlin's guitar, as well as two bassists, one acoustic, one electric (an idea which should have been explored by other musicians), and several percussionists. It sounds like a recipe for chaos, but at its best it is music unlike anything ever heard yet convincing in its emotional reach. I have long thought that it should have been truncated to a single album, that there is too much repetition on this two-record set (and now two CD set). But "Pharoah's Dance" and "Spanish Key" are powerful pieces of music. "Miles Runs the Voodoo Down" starts nice and funky but eventually goes nowhere, which is the basic problem with the title piece also. But this was very experimental, unprecedented music. The fact that so much of it is cohesive and ripe with a new kind of jazz beauty is a tribute to Miles, the superb musicians involved, and Teo Macero's brilliant editing. In many ways *Bitches Brew* reflected Coltrane's influence. I do not believe that Miles would have made such a radical move if he hadn't been impressed by the sheer daring of Coltrane in traveling new musical routes despite the risk of losing much of his audience. Many aspects of *Bitches Brew* reflect Coltrane's latter-day music—group improvisation, the Afro-Latin polyrhythms, the free-floating pitch, etc. And most of all, of course, Trane's courage.

Miles contributed the music to a documentary about the great prize fighter Jack Johnson. I have not seen this seldom-shown film and I have no idea how this music, which is the closest Miles ever came to playing straight rock, could possibly fit in with the story of a boxer who gained fame in the early part of this century. But the album itself, *Jack Johnson* (Columbia 1970), is a lot of fun—perhaps not Miles's most profound music, but play it loud and rock on out.

Miles's next important statement was *On the Corner*. This album was lambasted by most critics and many fans when it was released, but in retrospect it has taken on the aura of a classic modern musical statement. Once again one can hear Coltrane's influence (Miles only had one picture of a musician other than himself on the walls of his New York home—Coltrane). But also here are new, important influences—Jimi Hendrix, James Brown, and Sly Stone. Miles combines Sly/Brown funk with Indian drones, sitars and tablas, multiple keyboards, and he plays trumpet with a wah-wah peddle, obviously echoing Hendrix's brilliant—and subtle—use of this device.

Some of Miles's important seventies electric albums are out of print, like *Get Up With It* and *Big Fun*, but Sony/Columbia has pledged to reissue everything in Miles's catalog. However, *Agartha* is available on a two-CD set (Columbia, 1975), and its companion double album—recorded at the same Japanese concert—*Panagea* is fairly easy to find as a Japanese import (Sony/Japanese Columbia 1975). Miles's working band now included two guitarists, Pete Cosey and Reggie Lucas, who created a blistering, loud, electric drone over which Miles played mostly with wah-wah. Actually, *Panagea* is the more exciting set of the two, especially the first half hour or so. This music has been especially influential on such avant-garde rock groups as Sonic Youth and the "downtown" composer/performer John Zorn. But it is not for those whose listening has not advanced beyond '*Round About Midnight*. These are the last albums Miles recorded before his 1975 "retirement."

The picking's in the post-"retirement" period are slim, as I indicated in the "Phoenix" chapter. You may want to check out *Man With the Horn* out of curiosity—and it does have its moments, like every Miles album (although beware those vocals). Probably the best album from this period, *Star People*, is, ironically, out of print, as is the live *We Want Miles*, which also has some fine playing. I have already warned you about the obnoxious skit that opens *You're Under Arrest* (Columbia). However, I have to admit that the rest of the album is quite enjoyable in spots, and is probably the most entertaining Miles album from this period.

Aura was Miles's last orchestral project (at least of a new orchestral composition) and it is probably the most musically interesting of all the post-"retirement" albums. Palle Mikkelborg's composition has some superb moments, and it is always interesting, although the influence of Gil Evans is present throughout most of this lengthy piece. And Miles's playing is at a peak. He is obviously revitalized by genuinely fresh and intelligent material.

Aura would be Miles's last Columbia recording—which means that we are now in the "Warner period." I am tempted to say that one can just as well ignore all the albums from Miles's final few years, since Miles only plays on these recordings; he is not involved, at least not officially, in any of the writing or arranging. I think the best of these is the soundtrack *Siesta* (Warner), although Marcus Miller's settings are kind of a synthesized, ersatz version of the Miles/Gil Evans classic *Sketches of Spain*. However, Miles plays with the type of intensity and conviction which had been mostly absent from his post-"retirement" music.

Amandla is really not too bad at all, with some fine Miles improvisation. If you are curious about what might have been Miles's direction if he had not died, listen to *Doo-Bop* and wonder if Miles would have continued experimenting with the marriage of hip-hop rhythms and jazz improvisation. But unless you are a masochist, program out the horrendous raps.

And you may want to check out *Miles and Quincy at Montreux* (Warner, 1991). As I indicated, these versions of the classic Miles/Evans collaborations are weak in every way compared to the originals, but as a document it is a poignant and moving experience.

Tracing Miles's career through these recordings serves as a kind of road map to where we, as a society and culture, have come from, and where we are going. For Miles was never really ahead of his time. He was constantly plugged into the Zeitgeist and because of his intuition, intelligence, and curiosity, was always able to steer us toward new territories of sound and feeling.

Index

Note: this index covers only pp. 1–237.

Index

Index

Index